D0282568

Age 50 marks the highpoint of a man and woman's life in these 1850 prints by Currier & Ives.

IN OUR PRIME

The Invention of Middle Age

Patricia Cohen

Scribner
New York London Toronto Sydney New Delhi

SCRIBNER
A Division of Simon & Schuster, Inc.
1230 Avenue of the Americas
New York, NY 10020

First Scribner hardcover edition January 2012

SCRIBNER and design are registered trademarks of The Gale Group, Inc., used under license by Simon & Schuster, Inc., the publisher of this work.

For information about special discounts for bulk purchases, please contact Simon & Schuster Special Sales at 1-866-506-1949 or business@simonandschuster.com.

The Simon & Schuster Speakers Bureau can bring authors to your live event. For more information or to book an event contact the Simon & Schuster Speakers Bureau at 1-866-248-3049 or visit our website at www.simonspeakers.com.

Designed by Carla Jayne Jones

Manufactured in the United States of America

1 3 5 7 9 10 8 6 4 2

Library of Congress Control Number: 2011038406

ISBN 978-1-4165-7289-3
ISBN 978-1-4165-7985-4 (ebook)

Photo credits: Frontispiece, page 3, page 192: Library of Congress, Washington, D.C. Page 15: Munson-Williams-Proctor Arts Institute, Museum of Art, Utica, NY, 55.107. Page 32: The *New York Times* Photo Archive. Page 60: Nikolas Muray. Page 80, page 242: *The New York Times*. Page 99: Robert Walker/*The New York Times*. Page 123: Courtesy of Bert Brim. Page 140: Waisman Brain Imaging Lab, University of Wisconsin, Madison, WI. Page 163: *Ladies' Home Journal*, May 1928, page 77. Page 180: New York Public Library Picture Collection, NY, Image ID: 807971. Page 211: Associated Press. Page 228: Ken Regan/Showtime

Lyrics from the song "Life Begins at Forty" are used by permission of JACK YELLEN MUSIC.

For Alexander,
who proved that middle age is the best age of all

A man in middle life still feels young, and age and death lie far ahead of him.
—Carl Jung (1921)

Contents

IN OUR PRIME

Part I

The Invention of Middle Age

1

The Prime Meridian

"The Four Seasons of Life: Middle Age—The Season of Strength," Currier & Ives, 1868

For the first time, middle-aged men and women are the largest, most influential, and richest segment in the country. Floating somewhere between 40 and 64, they constitute one-third of the population and control nearly seventy percent of its net worth. In booms and recessions, a trillion-dollar economy feeds and fuels their needs, whims, and desires. Better-educated and healthier than their predecessors, these early and late midlifers are happier, more productive, and more involved than any other age group. Women are part of the first generation to enter their 40s and 50s after the feminist movement, and they have options that their mothers and grandmothers could barely imagine. Life spans have increased as scientific advances have overcome many of the body's once-unavoidable limitations. Viagra has recharged the sex lives of middle-aged men. Beauty treatments like Botox and facial fillers can erase the stigmata of facial wrinkles. New surgical procedures and recuperative strategies for worn-out knees and creaky rotator cuffs allow aging bodies to ski moguls and surf twenty-footers.

A century ago, circumstances—from the disillusionment that followed World War I to the emergence of Hollywood and mass consumerism—conspired to create a cult of youth. "The hero of our 20th century" was the adolescent, the historian Philippe Ariès declared in his seminal book *Centuries of Childhood* (1963), celebrated for his "purity, physical strength, naturism, spontaneity and joie de vivre." Those circumstances have changed. Now, with an unprecedented number of Americans in midlife who can expect to live three, four, or five more decades, it seems the twenty-first century belongs to the middle-ager.

Yet if this is the best possible moment to be middle-aged, why then is this period of life still commonly greeted with resignation or regret, disappointment or evasion? No one is eager to show off the AARP membership card that arrives in the mail unbidden shortly before you turn fifty. Birthday congratulations are replaced with jokes about hearing loss, plunging libidos, and afternoon naps. Middle age is a punch line.

Hundreds of self-help manuals, spiritual handbooks, and memoirs promise to guide anxious readers through the middle decades. *Cooking with Hot Flashes, How to Survive Middle Age, In a Dark Wood: Personal Essays by Men on Middle Age* are among the titles that offer advice on sex, exercise, diet, looks, childbirth, elderly parents, menopause, midlife crises, divorce, remarriage, religion, and memory loss. Countless online blogs and print columns supply personal recollections, counsel, and relentless cheerleading. Facebook and Twitter are flooded with middle-agers' quotidian dramas.

Such anxieties and ministrations would have thoroughly baffled Americans living in the early 1800s because the concept of middle age did not exist; it had not been invented yet. Middle age may seem like a Universal Truth, a fundamental law of nature, like Earth's rotation around the sun or the force of gravity, but it is as much a man-made creation as polyester or the rules of chess.

The notion that the term "middle age" would be a source of identity, shaping the way we envision our inner lives, view our family and professional obligations, and locate ourselves in the community and culture, would have been as alien to our ancestors as iPads and airplanes. For ordinary men and women, middle age was not a topic that merited reflection or analysis. Scholars did not devote years to its study. Periodicals and books did not publish essays on the topic, nor did correspondents and diarists devote pages in their letters or journals to its qualities. Advice manuals did not refer to behavior, clothes, or activities that were appropriate for people in their middle years as opposed to any other time of life. There were no medicines, organizations, leisure activities, treatments, music, or empowerment gurus designated specifically for people in middle age. Prior to 1900, the Census Bureau did not even bother to ask for a date of birth. You were young, you were an adult, and then you were old.

Life stages are all manufactured. As Ariès showed when he traced the invention of childhood back to the sixteenth and seventeenth centuries, or C. S. Lewis when he dated the invention of romantic love to the Middle Ages, even the most familiar assumptions were not always a part of our mental map. Only over time did they become second nature and recede into the grain of everyday existence to become "just the way life is."

Of course, people have always fallen in love, just as there have always been children. But Lewis, in *The Allegory of Love* (1936), pointed out that the happily-ever-after story based on mutual respect, affection, and individual choice first arose in the West among medieval troubadours. In *Centuries of Childhood,* Ariès demonstrated that children were perceived as miniature adults until the Renaissance, when their status changed among the aristocracy. The idea finally trickled down to the rest of society in the late nineteenth century as evidenced by the push for child labor laws and universal schooling.

Similarly, Aristotle and Shakespeare refer to the "ages of man." Dante begins the *Inferno* "Midway in the journey of our life." But only in the last 150 years was middle age acknowledged as a discrete category of development with unique characteristics; only then was it subjected to bureaucratic dictates, scientific classification, political concerns, and business and marketing interests.

The choice to chop up the uninterrupted flow of years is just that—a choice. Whether age 13 signals the coming of adulthood as in the Jewish religion, whether 18 or 21 is mature enough to vote and drink, whether a minimum age of 35 is necessary to be president, whether 65 is the time to retire are choices made by a particular group at a particular moment for particular reasons. Currently, academics and policy makers are debating the existence of a new stage—"emerging adulthood." Americans between 20 and 34 are taking more time to finish their education, establish themselves in careers, marry, have children, and become financially independent. The road to adulthood has lengthened because of a shift from manufacturing to a globalized, technological, and service-based economy, the women's movement, and shifting attitudes about single parenthood and marriage. Other experts suggest that extended life spans mean people between 55 and 70 or 75 constitute a new stage—post–middle age, pre–old age—because of their ability to keep working and pursue personal or civic endeavors.

Whether or not these are genuinely new stages, they do illuminate just how contingent our notions of midlife really are. Middle age is a "cultural fiction," constructed differently around the globe, says Richard A. Shweder, a University of Chicago anthropologist. Outside America and Europe, middle age is often defined by one's position in the family. Hindu women in the Indian state of Orissa have a term—*prauda*—for the period when a married woman takes over the household, but not for middle age. In Samoa, where birthdays are seldom celebrated, there is no word for midlife; instead *tagata matua* is used to denote a person of maturity and good judgment.

I thought about our cultural fiction one sun-bleached afternoon while sitting on a beach with some friends, all of us past 40. As our children busied themselves building crab condominiums in the sand, we talked about the cycle of our lives, the opportunities and experiences we had compared with our parents and grandparents. According to the calendar, we were in middle age, but that was not at all the way we felt. For those of us born after World War II, the middle age we inherited did not fit quite right. We slipped our arms into the sleeves, but middle age pretty much hung there, heavy and oversized, like a bulky, drab woolen greatcoat. The oldest members of the baby boom generation have been trying to tailor midlife to suit them better, but it still feels like a hand-me-down. When my mother watched me play in the sand, she was in her 20s. By the time she reached middle age, I was finishing up graduate school and traveling. I married at 39, became a parent at 40, and still thought about what I wanted to do when I grew up. Some of my friends were on my mother's timetable, while I was checking out preschools and shopping for tricycles.

Considering how dramatically the experience of middle age had shifted in one generation, I wondered what it was like even further back. I wanted to examine how specific ideas about midlife were created and why one won out over another. When the average life expectancy was 40, did people think of 20 or 25 as middle age? Now that it is pushing past 80, has the traditional 40-year-old starting line moved forward? Before the twentieth century, did Americans view the middle years as a time of decline and retrenchment, a prelude to death? Did they lie about their age to make themselves seem younger? Were women embarrassed about creases around their mouths? Did men fret about the first gray hair? How is it that midlife is portrayed simultaneously as crisis-ridden and dully uneventful? Despite a freighter's worth of books written about midlife, hardly any explore its history in depth.

This book is a biography of the idea of middle age from its invention in the second half of the nineteenth century to its current place at the center of American society, where it wields enormous economic, psychological, social, and political power. This stage's advent has generated an unfamiliar landscape of possibilities, creating new conceptions of our selves, our business opportunities, and our avenues of social control.

The history of middle age is a companion to America's entry into the modern world. Its invention accompanied the country's astonishing metamorphosis into an urban, bureaucratic, and industrial society.

Middle age was a product of scientific rationalism, which assumed that every aspect of existence could be managed, categorized, and controlled. It was molded by the buoyant growth of mass consumerism, which extolled the young and new as a source of vitality, innovation, and renewal at the expense of the old and familiar. Advertisements, movies, and later television dressed, powdered, and repackaged middle age and then circulated the image through the miles of cable and constellation of satellites that connect the far corners of the country and globe.

Our attitudes toward middle age were shaped by the American individualist ethos and never-ending search for fulfillment. The exuberant self-help ideology that assumes people are self-directed and capable of positive transformation is the legacy of a merit-based democracy. The task of improving our midlife selves is an expression of a profound belief in what the literary critic Alfred Kazin labeled the "most revolutionary force in modern times": the "insistence on personal happiness." This impulse has led to profound creativity and satisfaction, but it has also been cleverly exploited by marketers, resulting in wasteful consumption and a warped image of aging.

Middle age is also a story we tell about ourselves. Colonial- and Revolutionary-era Americans saw the middle years as part of a spiritual journey, a pilgrim's progress that ended with an ascension to heaven. Early capitalists and social scientists set middle age in a Darwinian tale of survival where older workers were pushed out by more adaptable younger ones. Doctors, con men, and dreamers have written it into utopian fantasies, imagining a healthy, fit, and wrinkle-free aging process. Middle age has been cast in a series of roles: a measure of productivity, a threat to beauty and sexuality, a scientific conundrum, a marketing tool, a stage of psychological development, a social and political metaphor, a literary device. These interpretations or frames have affected how individuals have understood and experienced the middle decades and influenced the narratives we construct about our lives.

Our ideas about middle age are continually evolving, which is one reason it remains elusive, a changeling with no fixed entry or endpoint, clinging to youth and spilling over into old age. Forty has long been the traditional turning point in adulthood in the West, although there is no particular biological or sociological basis for it. Scholars believe the number's symbolic power dates back to biblical times (i.e., the flood lasted forty days and nights, as did Jesus's fast in the wilderness; the Israelites wandered in the desert for forty years). The New American Heritage dictionary defines middle age as "the period between youth and adulthood, generally 40 to 60." The Oxford English Dictionary cites 45 to 60, while Webster's and the U.S. Census Bureau peg middle age at 45 to 64. The nonprofit Pew Research Center uses 50 to 64 (dubbing it the "threshold generation") and classifies those between 30 and 49 in its "younger adult" category. Extensive surveys reveal that the definition shifts depending on a respondent's age, sex, class, and ethnicity. Those with more schooling tended to mark its onset later, as do those who are older; men thought it began earlier than women did. Males between 25 and 34 said middle age commences at 40 and ends at 56, for example, while females between 65 and 74 said it starts at 48 and lasts until 62. As life expectancy has increased (by more than three decades in the twentieth century), people have stretched the ribbon of middle age like a rubber band, extending it into their 70s. In 2009, Pew asked people between 50 and 64 when midlife ended. Most chose age 71. Middle age is a kind of never-never land, a place that you never want to enter or never want to leave.

The mammoth ongoing study of middle age currently funded by the federal government and called Midlife in the United States opted for comprehensiveness over specificity. Its originators considered the core of midlife to be between 40 and 60, with outer boundaries of 30 and 70. Yet outside of a petri dish, a category that encompasses a 30- or 40-year period and includes a single woman finishing up a graduate degree, working parents with school-aged children, and a retired widower with grandchildren is not very meaningful. We are like the tourists in a John Donohue cartoon: "You Are Here," a street-corner map instructs, with an "X" in the middle of a line labeled "birth" at one end and "death" at the other.

As Bernice Neugarten, a pioneer in the study of adult development, put it: "Life is restructured in terms of time left-to-live rather than time-since-birth." Midlife is a point of no return, that place in a journey where the beginning is further away than the end.

Middle age is much more than chronology, however. Biology may leave its mark with a delicate fan of lines around the eyes, but it is insufficient for understanding the way middle age plays out in our culture and our psyches. Historically, middle age has frequently been defined in terms of social relations or psychology. It arrives when children leave home, careers are settled, or parents are failing or dead. Alternately, it is considered a state of mind, when a person confronts his or her own mortality or pauses to assess what came before and what lies ahead.

To tell the story of middle age, I reached back into history and ahead to the latest research, visiting laboratories and scouring newly constructed digital archives. Frederick Winslow Taylor, founder of scientific management, who introduced efficiency, segmentation, and standardization into the workplace, the home, and theories about aging, is among the personalities, famous and obscure, who figure in the drama. I write about Serge Voronoff, the Russian surgeon who sparked near-riots in the twenties with his promise to return middle-aged men to vigor with grafts of monkey testicles, and about Bruce Barton, a founder of modern marketing who envisioned Jesus Christ as the first adman.

I begin in Madison, Wisconsin, where scientists are mapping the middle-aged brain, and travel to Las Vegas, where antiaging charlatans and visionaries who practice a new kind of middle age medicine gather annually to share the latest elixirs and technological advancements. I have interviewed neurologists and social scientists, television executives and writers, film directors and actors, advertisers, drug manufacturers, and many others to chronicle the varying forces that shape our current understanding of middle age.

I was frequently surprised by what I discovered. Living longer is *not* the primary reason middle age emerged in the latter half of the nineteenth century; much more important was that parents had fewer children. Women in midlife, so often the target of deprecatory aging jokes, initially benefited most from the invention of middle age because it created a new episode in their lives aside from the child-rearing years. And what delicious irony to discover that the decade when research into middle age began in earnest was the 1960s, the era of not trusting anyone over 30. The flood of studies that followed revealed that supposedly common fixtures of a middle-aged household such as the midlife crisis and empty nest syndrome are actually quite rare. Even now, amid the ceaseless discussion of middle age in the media, members of some poor and minority enclaves don't think of themselves as "middle-aged" or even use the term. It is a "missing category" from their lineup of life stages. In a place where employment is intermittent and grandmothers fill in for absent parents, middle age does not describe personal experience much more meaningfully than the term *prauda* or *tagata matua.*

Two themes run through the history of middle age. The first is the constant struggle over how it is defined and by whom. Whether the words "middle age" conjure up an influential, wealthy, and satisfied figure or a paunchy, sexless, and discouraged one depends on who is doing the conjuring: bureaucrats, doctors, philosophers, politicians, advertisers, novelists, or filmmakers. Each has an interest in relating his or her own version of middle age. Gray hair is unsightly if you manufacture hair dye, and male menopause is a genuine affliction if you produce pharmaceuticals; middle age extends to 70 if you worry about the solvency of Social Security and want to encourage people to work longer, or ends at 60 if you hope they'll retire and create opportunities for the next generation.

The second theme concerns the tension between self-help's ability to empower or manipulate us. The market has largely co-opted the vibrant tradition of personal improvement to draw its own version of the middle-aged face and body, to set midlife priorities and produce a sense of security or anxiety. The overt message of advertisements is that you, too, can have a middle age that is vital, innovative, sexy, and fun, but underneath lies the implicit threat that a failure to take advantage of proffered enhancements will leave you unhealthy, unwanted, unsexy, and unemployable.

Before the twentieth century, men and women were often seen as reaching the height of their power and influence in their 40s and 50s. When middle age grew into a subject of popular conversation after the Civil War, an orchestra of voices offered comments and assessments. Descriptions of middle age as the prime of life were as common as depictions of it as old-fashioned and stale.

By the 1920s, science and business had seized the discourse and defined middle age primarily as a biological phenomenon as opposed to a psychological or spiritual one. Factory work favored the young for their speed and stamina, while businesses created an array of products from smoothing creams to cereals that promised to help customers mimic an idealized youth. Midlife was narrowly measured in terms of productivity and youthful beauty. In this context, middle age became a powerful metaphor for decline—one that has remained with us.

In the fifties and sixties, psychologists "rediscovered" middle age and recast it as a psychological stage of human development. For the first time, social science researchers considered midlife to be a significant period in which positive change was possible, but they also burdened it with psychic maladies. Middle age was an unavoidable "passage," to use the term Gail Sheehy popularized in her 1974 blockbuster book. "A sense of stagnation, disequilibrium, and depression is predictable as we enter the passage to midlife," she wrote, when we are obsessed with our own death.

By the mid-1970s, a handful of researchers recognized that this definition, too, was wanting. The cultural revolutions that the sixties launched into orbit were settling into place, and the neat series of life stages carefully lined up like dominoes—childhood, adolescence, middle and old age—were toppled as women in great numbers entered or returned to college classrooms, joined the workforce, and delayed or rejected marriage and children. Divorce, single parenthood, cohabiting gay and straight adults, and frequent job shifts were all on the rise. As researchers attempted to redefine midlife to take account of these novel circumstances, they ended up transforming the way human development as a whole was studied. Stage theories were nudged aside by a more comprehensive perspective that emphasized development as a lifelong process continually shaped and pounded by physical, mental, historical, and economic changes.

The idea of middle age has shifted position in the popular imagination as baby boomers (born between 1946 and 1964) reached their 40s, 50s, and 60s and as Gen Xers (born between 1965 and 1980) followed close behind. The association of midlife with deterioration and torpor is still strong, but a growing countercultural story that emphasizes more positive affiliations is gaining momentum.

Today, we exist in a world of multiple middle ages. We each have a personal midpoint molded by individual experience, a generational midpoint determined by the historical era of our birth, and a huge cultural storeroom of off-the-rack middle ages offered by Hollywood and marketers. Varieties of middle age also depend on whether we graduated from high school or college, work as janitors or bankers, use the women's or men's room, and live in rural Texas or downtown Chicago.

Our ability to defy biological, social, and psychological clocks and construct a more enriched version of middle age has never been greater. Yet instead of re-creating middle age, this generation is trying to disown it. Americans haven't abandoned their youthful infatuations. The contemporary ideal of beauty continues to spurn mature voluptuousness, thickening waists, and wrinkles, and glorifies ice-cream-stick figures and whipped-butter complexions. Middle-aged men and women are applauded for their ability to simulate the attributes of those twenty to thirty years younger rather than for their experience and wisdom. A successful midlife has become equated with an imitation of youth.

There is a more capacious conception of middle age, one that contradicts itself and "contains multitudes," as Walt Whitman put it in "Song of Myself" when he was on the cusp of middle age, "in perfect health begin, / Hoping to cease not till death." This middle age recognizes the inevitable loss of youth and a foreshortened future, but it also celebrates a deeper well of experience and insight, and takes advantage of an expanded buffet of prospects. Middle age takes many forms. Men and women of a certain age push strollers, drop the kids off at college, embark on world tours, and take up pole dancing. They forsake basketball for golf, pack away the small sizes, fill prescriptions for Lipitor, try and fail and try again to give up fatty foods; they take care of their grandchildren, leave jobs, switch careers, get fired, marry for the first (or second or third) time, strike out on their own after a divorce, or avoid matrimony altogether. They are the anchor point for children, new graduates, and aging parents.

Think of the word "meridian" and its manifold meanings. It can refer to one of the many imaginary lines that circle the globe from north to south, dividing it in half, and it can denote the high point or peak of one's powers. Middle age is like a meridian: it was imagined into existence, it can create a legion of pathways, and it marks a time when we are in our prime.

2

Now and Then

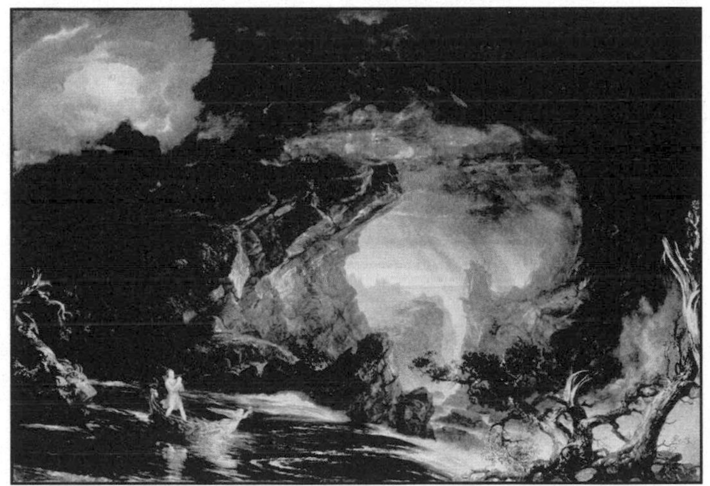

Thomas Cole's 1840 painting *Voyage of Life: Manhood*

Surprisingly little attention has been given to the middle years, which, for most individuals, constitute the longest segment of life.

—Midlife in the United States national study (2004)

If you want to get a sense of what middle age in the twenty-first century looks like, a good place to start is the Laboratory for Brain Imaging and Behavior at the University of Wisconsin–Madison, where Richard Davidson is conducting research into the middle-aged brain. The $10 million lab, which Davidson helped found and now directs, is in the Waisman Center at the western end of campus. On the day of my visit, groves of upturned brown dirt with cranes and plows stand about like muddied yellow dinosaurs. A maze of concrete barriers, orange cones, and netting divide the beige-and-aqua-colored center from the surrounding construction sites.

Outside it is hot and moist, but in the windowless room where I'm lying, waiting for my brain scan, it is cold enough for a blanket.

"Comfortable?"

The voice travels through layers of stuffing, as if I were the pea under the princess's sixteen mattresses. In my ears are two squashed yellow foam plugs, like mini marshmallows, covered by DJ-sized padded earphones. The lyrics "Ground Control to Major Tom" from David Bowie's song "Space Oddity" suddenly pop into my head as I lean back into a clear plastic pillow filled with tiny white balls the size of peppercorns. With the turn of a valve, Michael, the lab technician, has suctioned the air out of the pillow so that the plastic encases my skull like a bonnet. Two rectangular foam pads are pushed against the top of my scalp, a further bulwark against the slightest wiggle. Even a millimeter shift will distort the scans of my brain that are produced by the large beige functional magnetic resonance imaging (fMRI) machine I'm about to enter.

"Remember, don't move," Michael tells me.

Nikki Rute, the study coordinator for Davidson's research on the middle-aged brain, has already given me a practice run of the procedure in another room with a computer screen and a facsimile of the machine, a square contraption shaped like the mouth of a cave with a narrow tube through the center. The Potemkin apparatus is a way to familiarize the 331 subjects who are participating in Davidson's experiments with what will happen when they are in the real fMRI and are expected to lie motionless on their backs for two to three hours. Davidson plans to use the pictures he takes to investigate how the architecture and circuitry of the middle-aged brain affect emotional control. Some tests have shown that in younger adults the amygdala, the brain's emotional nut, located deep within the temporal lobe, is activated when exposed to both upsetting and uplifting images. Adults in their middle and upper decades, by contrast, seem to have the ability to screen out or tamp down negative emotions; their amygdalae light up when they see positive images but ignore the disturbing ones. Davidson wants to find out more about this filtering action.

Before I enter the real brain scanner, Michael swings over a bulky set of goggles similar to those eye doctors use to adjust prescriptions. The lenses are close enough to brush my eyelashes. Michael puts my right hand around the control box and I place my fingers lightly on top of the three buttons.

"Remember, there is no right or wrong answer. Rely on your first impressions," Nikki says. "Don't think too much."

Then I slide into the tunnel.

Nikki had warned me it would be loud. Even through my shrink-wrapped head, I can hear the relentless clanging, like the backhoes slowly pounding away at the construction site outside. Through the lenses, a parade of small headshots against a royal blue background appear. Anonymous Tom, Dick, and Harrys. Bald, curly-headed, mustachioed; 20-something, 40-something, 60-something men; oval- and moon-faced, blue-eyed and brown. No impish grins or curled lips, no furrowed brows or flared nostrils. They could have been posing for a driver's license. "Please evaluate how much you think you would like the person in the photo," the printed directions instruct. Under my right hand is the control box with buttons, which I use to register my sentiments on a scale directly beneath each photo from "very much dislike" all the way across to "very much like." The faces make no more of an impression than a passerby during the lunchtime rush. For nearly every one, I leave the cursor dead center—no one's face moves me one way or the other.

Next comes another series of photographs. Once again I use the button box, pressing my forefinger for negative, middle finger for neutral, and ring finger for positive. Every so often a man's headshot will appear again, but this time I am not supposed to press any buttons while it is displayed.

The photographs whiz by every couple of seconds: a group white-water rafting; a corpse buried in a pit; a woman stuffing her mouth with potato chips; a crashed car. Positive. Negative. Negative. Negative.

Another headshot appears, one of the expressionless men.

Inside the machine, a doughnut-shaped magnet produces an electromagnetic field that passes through my body, stimulating hydrogen atoms that give off radio signals. These signals are then collected by a special scanner and turned into images that Nikki and Michael can watch on a monitor in the other room. Though I don't press any buttons, they can see where the most neural activity is occurring—where the lights go on in my brain.

Measuring someone's emotional resilience is tricky. It's not as if you can scan a person's brain the moment she is getting fired or he is dumped by a girlfriend. For his midlife research, Davidson and his team had to devise an experiment to capture emotional responses. The series of photographs I was shown, some gruesome and sad, others uplifting and funny, were designed to do just that.

These images help to make up the International Affective Pictures System, or IAPS, a series of color slides that serve as a standard reference for measuring subtle shifts in emotion. Through the years, hundreds of volunteers have looked at and rated the images—cemeteries, starving children, serene sunsets, a coiled snake, a couple kissing, bunnies—on a scale from pleasant to unpleasant and calm to excited. The images that elicited the most uniform responses—whether positive, negative, or neutral—from a broad range of people were selected for the IAPS series.

You expect someone to respond negatively to pictures of hungry children, mutilated bodies, or wrecked homes. But what Davidson and his team were interested in was the duration of the negative reaction. Are you able to quickly shut off the spigot of bad feelings or do they drip into your view of other things, inciting a negative response to an image that you might otherwise view benignly? That is the purpose of the Tom-Dick-and-Harry headshots I was shown, those variously aged men with blank expressions. Let's say you are neutral, as I was, about these images. What happens when you see the same face repeatedly flashed right after looking at photographs of a cadaver buried in mud, a hypodermic needle stuck into a pile of feces, or a crashed car? Is there a hangover from the negative photographs that influences your judgment and causes you to rate those completely unremarkable faces more negatively than before?

What about the positive photographs? Do they also have a hangover effect? As Davidson and his team track the electrical activity in a subject's brain, they also examine the brain's anatomy and measure pulse rate, blood pressure, bone density, and cortisol levels, an indicator of stress. They want to find out if people who have the most difficulty containing their negative emotions also have the most ailments. Just as someone with high blood pressure can reduce the risk of heart disease with early treatment, Davidson wants to test whether learning to control stress can reduce the risk of hypertension, type 2 diabetes, atherosclerosis, and other stress-related maladies. He thinks the answer is yes. The more quickly someone can recover from a negative experience—whether witnessing an accident or getting bawled out by the boss—the better one's physical health will be.

After I watch a series of photographs, Michael asks how I'm doing. "Fine," I answer. He reminds me not to move, saying that the next scan takes seven minutes.

"Is there anything special I am supposed to think about?" No, he replies.

"Can I close my eyes?" Yes.

I wish I had thought to ask which part of my brain my silently humming "Ground Control to Major Tom" was causing to flash.

The Manhattan Project of Middle Age

Richard Davidson's experiments are part of the pathbreaking research now known as Midlife in the United States. The John D. and Catherine T. MacArthur Foundation agreed to finance the project in 1989 as the vanguard of postwar babies were reaching their middle years. Bill Clinton, the first boomer president, was planning his run for the White House, 40-something masters of the universe were settling into corner suites, and middle-aged protagonists like Murphy Brown and Frasier had carved out a home on the small screen when MacArthur gathered some of the best minds in the country to map the landscape of midlife.

Beneath the monumental enterprise is a simple notion that middle age is the pivot around which society is structured. "People in midlife raise the children and care for the elderly," Orville Gilbert Brim Jr., the project's founder and first director, explained, "and when they succeed, they carry the young and the old along with them."

Given the number of poets and philosophers, self-help authors and filmmakers who have devoted verse and song to the middle years, it may be surprising to learn that only a generation ago, middle age managed to escape systematic scientific study. As Brim declared in language that brings to mind the *Enterprise*'s cosmic mission on *Star Trek,* middle age "is the last uncharted territory in human development."

"No one knew what was going on in that world," said Brim, who prefers "Bert" to "Orville." Much of what we understood about middle age came indirectly from studies focused on children or the elderly, like a sideways reflection in a mirror. With a $9.4 million grant from MacArthur, Brim and his eleven colleagues agreed to throw out the whole tangle of assumptions that had grown up around this period—the expected dread or restlessness, the looming fear of death. "Millions of persons make decisions about their lives based on unsupported beliefs and imperfect knowledge . . . that are transmitted from one generation to the next as our cultural legacy of falsehood and myth about midlife," he reported. His team started with a clean slate to investigate "the who, what, when, where, and why of midlife events and the beliefs people hold about them."

They established what could be considered the Manhattan Project of middle age by gathering extensive information through large-scale surveys and in-depth interviews about what Americans in their middle years think, feel, and do every day. The researchers wanted to find out if—and how—one's personality, mental health, brainpower, stresses, and attitudes shift in midlife. What is the impact of education, income, intelligence, background, family structure, work, friends, religion, genetics, race, and sex? Why are some individuals more resilient than others? By looking at how middle-agers negotiate the challenges of midlife, they hoped to learn what caused people to flourish or fail in the middle years and beyond, and whether anything could be done to alter that process.

The breadth and depth of the project, dubbed MIDMAC, were unprecedented. Throughout most of the twentieth century, social scientists and medical researchers were guilty of defining the "average"

American as a middle-class white man. As for the relatively small niche of investigations devoted to midlife, nearly all of the significant ones involved men studying men. "Considering the major studies on adult development at midlife, it seems only men survive past the age of 40," a scholarly assessment from 1997 dryly observed. MacArthur recruited nearly 7,200 men and women between the ages of 25 and 74 so that middle-agers could be compared with those younger and older. In the mix were hundreds of twins and siblings to help researchers sort out biological and environmental differences.

What distinguished the MacArthur group's approach was its attempt to knit together various disciplines—psychology, anthropology, economics, biology, sociology, and more. "No single component of aging can be understood without reference to others," a report explained. A chemical in the brain may be the cause of someone's depression, which may in turn be the reason he withdraws from family and friends. A hard-charging, controlling type A personality may be more susceptible to coronary disease. Later on, a move to a nursing home, where she is cut off from familiar surroundings and a mix of age groups, may hasten physical and psychological deterioration.

The team also embraced a novel conceptual approach to assessing health and happiness in middle age. Traditionally, physicians and psychologists have defined success in terms of what was missing: health was a lack of illness and disease; a well-adjusted psyche meant an absence of depression and dysfunction. Middle age begins, one cultural critic declared, the moment you think of yourself as "Not-Young." MacArthur, by contrast, was interested not merely in what was missing but in what was present. Rather than define middle age by its deficits—the end of youth and fertility, decreased stamina and flexibility—MIDMAC investigated what ingredients contribute to feeling fulfilled and purposeful. Researchers wanted to know what a half-full glass contained as well as what had spilled out of it.

Carol Ryff, a member of the MacArthur network and the director of the Institute on Aging at the University of Wisconsin–Madison, developed a list of eighty-four questions to measure well-being and divided them into six broad categories: personal growth (having new experiences that challenge how you think about yourself); autonomy (having confidence in your opinions even if they are contrary to the general consensus); supportive social relationships; self-regard (liking most aspects of your personality); control of your life; and a sense of purpose. The questionnaire was meant to capture more than the fleeting pleasures of a few beers. It was designed to gauge whether an individual was also functioning at full capacity and flourishing. The ancient Greeks called it *eudaimonia,* and midlife researchers and positive psychologists have adopted the term to refer to the kind of profound satisfaction and meaning one derives from raising children, training for an Olympic event, completing a college degree, or helping your neighbors rebuild after a disaster. As Ryff said, "Sometimes things that really matter most are not conducive to short-term happiness." Dirty diapers, screaming tantrums, and sleepless nights are not particularly pleasurable on a day-to-day basis; nonetheless, most people consider children a source of deep happiness, of *eudaimonia.*

With this framework in place, the MacArthur team's first task was to create a comprehensive database on middle-aged Americans. Starting in 1994, thousands of subjects answered telephone interviews and filled out lengthy forms that asked:

> Are you sad, nervous, restless, fidgety, calm, satisfied, curious, optimistic, cheerful, creative, hardworking, softhearted, responsible, outspoken, active, careless, broad-minded, talkative, sophisticated, adventurous?
>
> Are you bothered by cold, heat, loud noise?
>
> Do you talk about your problems to a rabbi, priest, therapist, social worker, doctor? Attend meetings for alcoholics, addicts, people with eating disorders, widows, empty nesters, cancer sufferers?
>
> Do you have pain when you have sex; do you leak urine?
>
> Did you confide in your mother; did she love you; did she punish you; did she understand you; did she push, grab, or slap you; did your father? Did you stomp out of a room when angry or sulk?
>
> Do you feel obligated to serve on a jury, raise the child of a close friend who died, call your parents regularly, give money to

a needy friend, testify in court about an accident you witnessed, collect contributions for heart research, pay more in taxes so those worse off than you would be helped?

How much do you drink, smoke, eat, sleep, worry, tremble, get the chills, get hot flashes?

How often do you say hello to your neighbors; how often does your family get on your nerves?

Have you ever been born again; have you ever been catheterized; have you ever been on welfare?

How would you rate sex you have now; ten years ago; how do you think it will be in ten years?

Even as the surveys were being administered, the team updated its questionnaires. In the early 1990s, for example, the public discussions of menopause surrounding the publication of Gail Sheehy's *The Silent Passage* and Germaine Greer's *The Change: Women, Aging and Menopause* reminded researchers that they had neglected to address this universal event. All in all, respondents answered a hundred pages' worth of detailed questions, revealing their most intimate feelings, embarrassing behaviors, physical idiosyncrasies, and emotional tics. The nearly two thousand twins who participated received little packets instructing them to gently scrape the inside of their cheeks and mail back the results for DNA testing.

Almost 1,500 of the participants sat through additional telephone interviews eight nights in a row to enumerate the precise kinds of stresses they faced each day. Another group of 750 subjects answered detailed questions about turning points and crises in their lives as researchers scanned for hints that might forecast such events in advance. Other, smaller clusters sat through extended interviews to talk about social responsibility, their strategies for handling stress, and how they defined "the good life."

After MacArthur's funding ended, the federal government officially adopted the project and renamed it Midlife in the United States, or MIDUS, in 2002. The National Institutes of Health awarded $26 million to forty professors and scientists at sixteen universities to expand the research into the future, transforming it into a long-term, or longitudinal, study—the gold standard in science. The snapshot of middle age was turned into a motion picture. MIDUS, now headquartered at the University of Wisconsin–Madison, has collected what may be the most comprehensive data ever assembled in a national survey. Since then, organized professional interest in middle age has continued to spread: to neurology, where researchers are examining the brain's operation; to orthopedics, where clinical practitioners are developing new procedures to deal with a more active generation of middle-aged weekend athletes; to biology, where scientists are tracking the midlife roots of heart disease and dementia.

The results will be described in more detail in later chapters, but in the first two decades of MIDUS's existence, it has punctured some of the most stubborn myths about midlife in America. Theories about a midlife crisis and empty-nest syndrome were blown away like feathers in a windstorm, as were the imagined ranks of sweaty women raging against menopause and middle-aged husbands abandoning decades-long marriages for dewy young trophy wives. Midlife was a "watershed period" when people began to shift from taking care of family to becoming more active in community and public affairs. Stress reached a high point as worries about children, money, aging parents, and other responsibilities piled up. But as burdens grew so did confidence in one's own capabilities. People reported feeling more in charge of work, marriage, and finances as they entered the middle decades. That sense of control—that you can personally take steps to influence what happens in your life—is both a crucial source of happiness and a catalyst for taking action to stay healthier.

The latest research into the middle-aged brain is slowly revealing the intricate and enigmatic workings of the human mind and body. Along with other investigators, Richard Davidson has discovered that this three-pound handful of gray and white matter is much more adaptable in midlife than previously thought. Nerve cells do not die off in droves, and the ability to think more conceptually can actually improve with age. At the same time, middle-agers are much more experimental and open to novelty than previously imagined. Freud rejected patients "near or above the fifties" for psychoanalysis, claiming, "the elasticity of the mental processes . . . is as a rule lacking." But further study has revealed middle age to be a time of psychological complexity, when individuals become less neurotic and more open, reflective, and flexible.

Overall, the majority felt healthy, in control, and satisfied. They had left behind the tumultuous adolescent years, and had worked through the struggles and uncertainties of embarking on a career and family. They learned how to more skillfully handle crises and were better equipped to screen out petty stresses and disappointments and to manage the strain of juggling a job and family. When researchers asked people over 65 what age they would most like to return to, the majority bypassed their teens, 20s, and 30s in favor of their 40s.

"From many points of view, midlife permits many of us to feel on top of the world, in control of our lives, and well enough pleased with what we have accomplished to seek new outlets of both self-expression and giving back to society some of what we have earned—and learned," Alice S. Rossi, a member of the original MacArthur team and a former president of the American Sociological Association, concluded.

This description of middle age comes surprisingly close to matching the definition of *eudaimonia*. Corey Keyes, a sociologist at Emory and a MIDUS investigator, cites studies that show individuals who are flourishing or "functioning well," as he translates *eudaimonia,* have lower rates of disability, heart disease, and chronic physical illness compared with people who are merely "feeling good." They also have nearly half the rate of mental illness. In 2010, Carol Ryff and her colleagues found physical evidence: MIDUS participants who scored high in *eudaimonia* had lower levels of a protein called interleukin-6, which is associated with cardiovascular disease, osteoporosis, and Alzheimer's.

These clues and others are helping MIDUS deliver information about what can be done, in addition to the oft-repeated directives to exercise and diet, to prevent, delay, or reduce both physical and mental failings.

In 2011, MIDUS researchers, funded with more than $25 million from the National Institutes of Health, geared up for a third round, in which they will check back with their subjects. In the meantime, hundreds of experts with and without a formal connection to the project continue to use the exhaustive survey data, looking to capture middle age in cholesterol levels, white blood counts, and EEGs that dance across the page; in the number of hours each week that people work, exercise, have sex, run a vacuum, and help with their children's homework; in the pills they consume, the pounds they gain, and the vacations they take; whether they are black or white, straight, gay, or transgendered, rural or urban dwellers.

Before Middle Age

To get a glimpse of what the middle decades were like before they were genetically mapped and neurologically monitored, you can travel to the Munson-Williams-Proctor Arts Institute in Utica, New York, where the four enormous river and landscape paintings in Thomas Cole's landmark 1840 series, *The Voyage of Life,* hang. Cole, the influential founder of the Hudson River School of painting, depicted the familiar metaphor of life as a journey through different seas: Childhood, represented by a plump infant; Youth, by an androgynous-looking teenager; Manhood, by a strapping, bearded figure (illustration on page 15); and Old Age, a seated, white-haired man of 70 or more. These four broad categories, popularized in journals and schoolbooks in the eighteenth and nineteenth centuries, reflected the way men and women viewed themselves. The young have "vigor and firmness," an orator told the crowd at the 1825 groundbreaking for an Ohio canal, manhood is endowed with "strength and firmness," and old age "confers wisdom."

For early Americans, middle age did not seem worth discussing or formally labeling. "It appears, in fact, that they did not regard this interim period as distinctive at all," the historian John Demos writes. "Instead, the middle years represented for them simply the full flowering of human capacities. Someone in his thirties, forties, or fifties was a fully developed person—a norm against which childhood and youth, on one side, and old age, on the other, could be measured as deviations."

A man's landholdings and economic resources were at their greatest in midlife, and his position in political councils or the church was firmly assured. His wife ruled over her home, children, servants if she had them, and other family members, while overseeing any farm or retail business. Popular illustrations sold by Currier & Ives in the 1850s depicted life in decade increments "from the cradle to the grave" (as in the frontispiece). At the top of what could have been a five-tier wedding cake was the fiftieth year; on the layer just below sat the fortieth year on one side and the sixtieth on the other.

When most knowledge is handed down through word of mouth rather than widely available in print, seniority is an advantage and an aspiration, and the experienced eye and touch of the master craftsman are essential. In the seventeenth and eighteenth centuries, young people strove to look older to give an impression of credibility and authority. The fashion of the day favored powdered white wigs, beards, and tailoring that emphasized narrow, rounded shoulders, and broader hips and waists to project an appearance of maturity. The elderly's insight and experience were all the more valuable given how few there were—less than four percent of the population was over 65 in 1850—like a white Bengal tiger amid a streak of orange-and-blacks.

One might occasionally hear the term "middle age," but it had no significance beyond a mere chronological measure. As the historian Howard Chudacoff concludes in *How Old Are You?*, his study of aging, "Before the 20th century, middle age was seldom considered as a separate time of life." The word "midlife" first appeared in the dictionary in 1895, when Funk & Wagnalls defined it as "the part of life between youth and old age."

Aging in Cole's day was still conceived of primarily as a spiritual progression. In each of his detailed and naturalistic landscapes, an angel hovers above the traveler's boat on the River of Life, shining a light through blackened clouds during Manhood's rough sailing or closely guiding Old Age toward heaven, his eternal home. References to the various "ages of man" can be found in earlier texts, but were largely unknown by the general population. They were the theoretical constructs of Byzantine and medieval scholars who divided the life cycle according to grand abstractions. The stages have at various times numbered four (twenty-year segments) to correspond with the seasons, twelve for each of the astrological signs, and ten for the number of decades in a hundred. Texts from the Middle Ages, for instance, frequently counted seven ages to match the number of planets known at the time: infancy, childhood (till 14), adolescence (which could last till 30 or 35), youth (till 45), senectitude (halfway between youth and old age, when a "person is grave in his habits and bearing"), old age (till 70), and very old age ("when the old man is always coughing and spitting and dirtying"). The divisions served as a reminder of the link between man's destiny and the planets, not as a guide to daily life.

Prior to 1850, age was rarely used to measure status or grant entitlements, endowing someone with the right to drink, live independently, or drive a carriage. There were no legal standards for becoming an adult, no clear demarcation between a juvenile and a full-grown criminal. Age was not an essential ingredient of one's identity. Most Americans seemed either not to know or care very much about their precise age. Thomas Cole's eulogist cited the wrong year of his birth.

Such a mistake was not unusual in an era when birthdays were seldom celebrated with great fanfare. The term "happy birthday" did not appear with any frequency in English-language books until after the Civil War. Receiving a card to mark one's entrance into the world would have been as odd as being congratulated for growing out of a pair of shoes. The practice of sending cards began in the 1870s and 1880s, when Christmas card producers retrofit leftover holiday postcards with birthday greetings. Cards created exclusively for the occasion did not appear until the twentieth century.

For women, adulthood was one long, undifferentiated stretch of mothering with scarcely any leisure time. Mothers gave birth, then gave birth again, and again, and again. In 1800, the average woman had seven children and spent seventeen years either pregnant or breastfeeding, although without antiseptics, anesthesia, or antibiotics, there was barely a parent who escaped burying a child. Giving birth often left women severely weakened or disabled. A prolapsed uterus was treated by hanging the new mother upside down from a ladder in the hopes that gravity would push the womb back in. The image of the sickly middle-aged woman finds its way into Emily Dickinson's poem "I Cannot Live with You": "Like a cup / Discarded of the Housewife, / Quaint or broken; / A newer Sevres pleases, / Old ones crack." With so many births, a mother could end up changing her own child's and her first grandchild's diapers simultaneously. By the time all the children were grown, she was well into her sixth decade—or more likely dead.

Most men grew up on or near a farm and stayed there. Often they were married for several years before their fathers finally deeded them a parcel of land. With so few choices, the psychological questions that we now associate with a midlife crisis—Did I choose the right career path? Did I accomplish what I set out to do?—did not arise. And the soulful encounter with death that today marks the middle-aged man's awareness of his own mortality would have seemed oddly incongruous in a society where fifty percent of all deaths struck children 15 and younger.

Stark differences between generations did not exist. Families were large and spanned a wide range of ages. On the farm, everyone worked for as many years as possible. At about age 5, children were given daily chores. Most were expected to handle a full load by the time they entered their teens. Adults worked nearly eighty hours a week for as many years as they could. The one-room schoolhouse had no space for age-divided grades, while ad hoc schooling with time out for harvests severed any links between ability and age. Sunday church services, dances, revival meetings, and quilting bees engaged young and old. As for homes, they were small and crowded. A large family could live in a one-story log cabin with a clapboard floor and a loft for the children's bed. The kitchen, dining room, parlor, and bedroom might occupy a single room less than twenty-four feet long. There was no physical or psychic space to separate work from play, public from private, or young from old. No one had a room of her own.

Forming a group identity outside one's immediate locale requires a connection to the larger world, a kinship with others in the same position. But most early Americans' information about what existed beyond their front door was constricted. In 1850, eighty-five percent of the population lived in rural areas; cities were small, with less than half a million residents.

In these years, knowledge tended to stretch no farther than a neighbor's farm, or perhaps the nearest town. Distant communications were carried hand to hand. Once settled, few souls wandered far from home. Women outside cities who left written accounts of their lives frequently spoke of loneliness and hard work. "It was beautiful to look at, but lonely in the extreme. We were nearly a mile from the nearest neighbor," wrote Virginia Ivins Wilcox, who settled with her husband on a ranch outside Petaluma, California, in the 1850s. Mountain lions, coyotes, and rattlesnakes greeted her on all sides. To buy fresh vegetables, her husband had to drive his ox team fifteen miles. Mary Murdock Compton, one of the millions of Irish immigrants who flooded America in the mid-nineteenth century, led a similarly insulated existence. After marrying, in 1860 she moved with her husband to a cattle ranch by the Sacramento River. The nearest town, Chico, was nine miles away. The post office in Fall River Mills, visited only when supplies were needed, was a five-mile trek and the only source of news. Grizzlies and wildcats were much more common than human beings. "Mary often said that during the 11 years she lived there she was in Chico about twice," her daughter-in-law noted after recording Mary's oral history years later. "It was not really necessary to go into town often since much of what they needed they made or produced at home." Mary, like women throughout the mostly rural nation, "did all of her own housework, including cooking, baking, washing, ironing, mending, and making practically all the clothes that they wore." So did Mary Ann Hafen, who lived in Utah in the 1860s and, in addition, took on the backbreaking work of picking cotton to earn extra money.

Did these women think their lives were unusual? Did they identify more with middle-aged women who lived in cities hundreds of miles away or with the newly married wives or grandmothers nearby? Could they imagine their days freed up by factory-made clothing and store-bought food? Perhaps. But they were not bombarded by advertisements, articles, or films warning about deepening facial lines, or parading products and luxuries, homes and lifestyles different from their own. Indeed, they may not have owned mirrors, which didn't become a staple household item until factories manufactured them in great quantities later in the century.

To form a generational identity, middle-aged women and men need to share experiences and cultural touchstones. Today, a 50-something reader instantly gets the joke in Christopher Buckley's novel *Boomsday,* when the Association for Baby Boomer Advocates lobbies for giant flat-screen TV subsidies, a cosmetic surgery benefit, and a federal acid reflux initiative. The relative isolation that prevailed in most parts of the United States in Mary Compton's day undermined the creation of a common sensibility of middle age. That remote life is highlighted by her memory of a special trip the family made on the Fourth of July in 1870 to see the big parade in Chico. "Just as they neared the railroad crossing, they heard the locomotive whistle. They whipped up the horses and approached the crossing just in time to see the train steam into Chico. It was the first train the children had ever seen and the first passenger train to come to Chico."

What Mary Murdock Compton did not realize during that carriage ride to Chico was that in America's booming urban centers the idea of middle age had already begun to form amid the onrush of scientific, industrial, and commercial progress. Within another decade or two, middle age would be transforming the way adults like Mary thought about the world and their place in it.

3

The Tick of the Time Clock

Frederick W. Taylor, 1911

Taylor seems to have expressed . . . with almost visionary clarity the general spirit of the age.

—Cultural critic Hubert Zapf

The painter Thomas Cole felt tired and chilled after returning home from church one Sunday in February 1848. Three days later he died. He was 47.

At a memorial at the National Academy of Design, William Cullen

Bryant, the Romantic poet and editor of the *New-York Evening Post,* delivered the funeral oration. Death comes in childhood, youth, and old age, Bryant said, noting that Cole "passed into that next stage of existence" while "in the strength and activity of his faculties," and in "mid-strength of his intellect." Or, as Cole himself had labeled it in his *Voyage of Life* series, in Manhood. Bryant did not utter the words "middle age."

By the time Bryant died thirty years later, however, the term was popping up in everyday conversation to denote a distinct phase of life. "Thirty is the age of the gods—and the first gray hair informs you that you are at least ten or twelve years older than that," *The Ladies Repository* explained in 1861. "Apollo is never middle-aged, but you are." As the decades progressed, headlines like "The Privileges of Middle Age," "At Forty Year," and "The Middle-Aged Woman" became more common. The December 1874 issue of *Scribner's Monthly* offered some thoughtful seasonal advice under the heading "Holidays for Middle-Age." (In a mini-forerunner of *The Feminine Mystique,* every family was urged to give mother a winter vacation, so she was not driven insane by overwork and anxiety.) In 1881, the *New York Times* declared a man's "powers are at the highest point of development" in middle age. Later in the decade, *Harper's Bazar* initiated a regular column titled "Middle Age." In 1889, the magazine helpfully defined the term with more specificity for its readers: "those who have arrived at middle age—that is to say women who number anywhere from forty to sixty years."

References proliferated. In 1893, Henry James, just 50, titled his short story about a writer "The Middle Years." In 1898, Thomas Hardy included "Middle-Age Enthusiasms" in his collection *Wessex Poems.* Romantics who found James and Hardy a bit taxing after dinner could turn to tales of amour in *Middle-Aged Love Stories* (1903), a forerunner of Harlequin romances. That same year, *The Cosmopolitan Magazine* published an essay titled "The Woman of Fifty," which noted: "The woman who today is celebrated for distinctive charm and beauty, ripe views, disciplined intellect, cultivated and manifold gifts would, two score years ago, have been relegated to the heavy ranks of the dowagers and grandmothers—forced by the stern conventions of prevailing opinion to confront the bitter knowledge that, just as she had gained a mastery of the rules, she was expected to retire from the game."

Clearly, something happened between Bryant's funeral oration for Cole in 1848 and the regular appearance of columns devoted to middle age three decades later. A wisp with a barely discernible outline, middle age condensed into a sturdy stage of life that took up space in people's thoughts, discussions, and writings. Social change, of course, occurs gradually. Ideas spread in fits and starts, and cultural shifts occur in years, not months. Various currents of thought eventually converged in the second half of the nineteenth century and altered the stories people told about the ebb and flow of their lives. Between Cole's death and his own, Bryant had seen the development of the germ theory of disease, anesthetics, and vaccines; the invention of the internal combustion engine, electricity, the telephone, the phonograph, practical refrigerators and typewriters, elevators, a faster process for making steel, a dozen ingenious tools of measurement, including the radiometer (to gauge radiation), galvanometer (electricity), dynamometer (force), and the interferometer (distance); the spread of railroads and gas lighting, pocket watches, and the laying of the first transatlantic cable; the publication of Darwin's *On the Origin of Species,* the introduction of new novelistic techniques to mark the passage of time, the Census Bureau's categorization of residents in ten-year age groups, and the rapid falloff of the apprenticeship system. Bryant had witnessed the creation of a new industrialized, bureaucratic, and technological epoch.

Enter the Timekeeper

Frederick Winslow Taylor, known as "the father of scientific management," was a child of this new science-centered world. His obsessions and interests mirrored those of the rapidly changing era. In 1878, the year Bryant died, Taylor got a job at Midvale Steel Works, where he later commenced his pioneering time-and-motion studies. He believed that, through careful observation and experiment, he could discover the optimal way to perform every task in the workplace to maximize productivity. He broke down each job into tiny pieces, meticulously analyzing the sequence, tools, and motions in order to put them all back together in the most efficient form. From the mundane to the complex, every job was explained in a set of minutely detailed instruction cards that workers were supposed to follow assiduously. Describing his later experience at Bethlehem Steel in 1898 with the hapless workman Schmidt, Taylor wrote in *Principles of Scientific Management* about calculating the best way to load a four-by-four bar of pig iron weighing ninety-two pounds: "Schmidt started to work, and all day long, and at regular intervals, was told by the man who stood over him with a watch, 'Now pick up a pig and walk. Now sit down and rest. Now walk—now rest,' etc. He worked when he was told to work, and rested when he was told to rest, and at half-past five in the afternoon had his 47½ tons loaded on the car." Every motion and moment mattered.

Whether or not Taylor was a fraud who cooked his data and exaggerated his success, as some historians later claimed, there is no disputing his impact. Taylor's ideas about efficiency and standardization eventually served as a strut for mass production and a mass market as homebuilders, homemakers, libraries, schools, and hospitals incorporated his time-and-motion studies and scientific management theories into their designs and practices. *Principles,* published in 1911, influenced Henry Ford's assembly lines in Detroit. In 1913, Ford's workers took twelve and a half hours to assemble a car. By 1914, it took just over an hour and a half. The abundance and affluence that industrialized countries enjoyed in the last century were partly founded on the tremendous gains in productivity that Taylor's system extracted, enabling goods to be made faster and more cheaply. One management scholar judged that "the United States owes a large, if incalculable proportion of their immense productivity and high standard of living" to Taylor.

For a society that used roosters and sunsets to track the hours and kept a sloppy record of birth dates, Speedy Taylor, as he was known in the shop, preached that every second counted and demanded that every second be counted. His views resonated in an era when time and space seemed to shift and collapse as technological advances like the railroad, telegraph, and electric light altered the way people thought about and experienced the passing of the hours. Clocks began adorning walls in the 1830s; pocket watches became widely available in the 1860s. In the 1870s, phrases like "on time," "behind time," and "ahead of time" entered the English language. The first international conference to synchronize timekeeping took place in 1884, when Greenwich Mean Time was established as the standard and the globe was divided into time zones.

Between 1890 and 1920, Taylor's approach revolutionized the way Americans thought as much as the way they worked. He roped modern man to the clock and helped bring an exacting awareness of time into every nook of the culture. Laying out his ideas with the diligence he advocated in the factory, he wrote that "the same principles . . . can be applied with equal force to all social activities; to the management of our homes; the management of our farms; the management of the business of our tradesmen, large and small; of our churches, our philanthropic institutions, our universities, and our governmental departments."

Scientific management was to be the overseer of the entire range of human existence, including the very process of aging. Taylor's attention to time, his valuation of efficiency, his belief in science, and his insistence on classifying and standardizing created the conditions that led to the invention of middle age.

Just as Taylor instructed managers to "break down each task into its component parts," psychologists, educators, and doctors dissected a single life into separate phases: childhood, adolescence, middle age, old age.

Just as Taylor created a standardized set of step-by-step instructions for every job, the nascent class of experts established norms of behavior, dress, sexual practices, and attitudes that were deemed appropriate for each stage of life.

Just as Taylor valued a worker solely in terms of timed productivity, so was a human life, once conceived in spiritual and moral terms, reduced to its economic essentials. This method of accounting found age to be a handy yardstick for measuring a man's potential worth on the factory floor and in the office; it ultimately led to the view that the young were much more valuable to society than the middle-aged and elderly.

And behind it all was the steady tick of the clock, piped into workplaces, homes, and schools. That tick, which Taylor tried to harness with his stopwatch, helped awaken society to ever-finer gradations of age.

A Generational Identity Emerges

Taylor's childhood obsessions well positioned him to become the modern world's timekeeper. He was born in 1856 to a wealthy Quaker family, whose ancestors came to America before the Revolution and settled in Germantown, near Philadelphia. His parents were moderate abolitionists and suffrage supporters. He grew up during the Civil War, when local factories were producing bayonets and army uniforms, and local hospitals cared for wounded Union soldiers.

When Frederick turned twelve, the family traveled to Europe for the grand tour, and stayed for three years. During their sojourn, he meticulously copied the departure and arrival times of the horse-drawn carriages his family took in Norway. While hiking, he experimented to see which stride covered the most ground with the least effort. When the Taylors returned to Germantown, Fred made his friends wait as he spent an entire sunny morning measuring a playing field down to the last inch before agreeing to let the game commence.

In 1872, Taylor was sent off to Phillips Exeter Academy in New Hampshire. There he witnessed "the first piece of time study that I ever saw made by anyone." He was studying mathematics with the legendary George Wentworth, a great bull of a teacher who had a tidy side income from thirty-four mathematics textbooks he had written. Wentworth sat behind a large wooden desk, his watch kept out of sight on a ledge while his fifty or so students figured out a handful of math problems. Each boy was supposed to raise his hand and snap his fingers when he had worked out the solution. When about half the class had finished, Wentworth, in a slipshod suit and sporting a long beard, called out: "That's enough." After some months, it dawned on Taylor that Wentworth was timing how long it took the boys to work through the equations and geometric drawings. He used the results to calculate how much homework to assign.

If Taylor had gone on to Harvard and become a lawyer as he and his family had planned, he might not have been watching the clock eight years later. Complaints of bad eyesight and pistonlike headaches kept him from moving south to Cambridge, however, and at his parents' urging Taylor decided to become an engineer, an occupation that required less studying and eyestrain. He traded in his Exeter tie and jacket for overalls and a lunch pail and became an apprentice patternmaker in a large, dusty, and growling Philadelphia foundry. His next job was at Midvale Steel, where Taylor was soon made foreman and in 1881, like Wentworth, timed his boys. He was not simply counting how long it took a machinist or a patternmaker to complete a task but also calculating down to the hundredth of a minute every movement along the way.

Robert Kanigel, Taylor's biographer, compares Taylor's impact to that of Charles Darwin, Karl Marx, and Sigmund Freud, noting that "each brought a deeply analytical, 'scientific' cast of mind to an unruly, seemingly intractable problem."

Most of the nineteenth century's emerging class of experts and managers did not have such grand ambitions, but in trivial and consequential pursuits, psychologists, physicians, biologists, managers, and civil servants shared their deep faith in scientific methods and a belief that human society could be organized rationally and controlled. Everything in nature and thought, from a single human life to the atom, was subject to subdivision and classification. Even modernist artists were influenced by science and sought to break experience down into its most elemental parts.

As people migrated to urban centers, the unself-conscious mixing of generations that naturally occurred in rural homes, farms, schools, social halls, and churches was replaced by age-related groupings. Growing government bureaucracies like the army used age to help identify, organize, and track the population. Age became the basis for education, statistical compilations, and military enlistment. Channeling schoolchildren into different grades was first introduced in the 1850s and 1860s. By the 1880s, private middle-class organizations like the YMCA, the Boy Scouts, Campfire Girls, 4-H Clubs, and civic associations began to group members according to birth year. In 1900, the U.S. Census, which previously had grouped inhabitants in ten-year increments, added a question about one's date of birth for the first time.

In cities, an array of leisurely pursuits developed as factory work replaced dawn-to-dusk farming and electricity lit up the night. Amusement parks, dance halls, social clubs, and fraternities and sororities were places where members of a single generation mingled. Women's clubs became "schools for the middle-aged woman," wrote Margaret Sanger, the birth control activist, where 50-year-olds can find "friends who like her are in the middle way of life."

This separation simultaneously introduced a generational identity and reinforced it. The spread of public junior and senior high schools (which picked up speed after 1910), segregated teenagers and provided them with a unique shared experience. High school extended their education beyond the level most of their parents had achieved, and delayed their entry into the adult world of work. The more people identified with one particular stage of life, the deeper the divisions between the stages became.

The health-care professions started to formally recognize and classify these groupings, so that by the century's end, stages, as Howard Chudacoff concludes, "were being defined with near-clinical precision, and more definite norms were being assigned to each stage." The ages that Shakespeare and Dante had written about were no longer invoked merely as literary metaphors but declared to be verifiable scientific fact applicable to everyone. Physicians and psychologists drew up schedules of biological, social, and mental development that turned the first few years of a child's life into a set of monthly checkpoints: the expected age for the first step, the first word, the first bite of solid food; for toilet training, for school; and eventually, for knowing what happened to Bambi's mother. These measured and sequenced phases were the medical counterpart of Taylor's scientific management theories, with each moment in time corresponding to an appropriate behavior or task.

Doctors determined that the unique attributes and illnesses of childhood required specialized expertise, and in the 1880s created the field of pediatrics. In 1900, the Swedish writer and feminist Ellen Key published her influential book on education and parenting, *The Century of the Child,* noting that children had a nature singular and distinct from that of adults. Arguing that the aged should similarly be in a separate category, an article in the 1904 *American Journal of Nursing* stated: "We must adapt our practice to the age of the individual. You must not treat a young child as you would a grown person, nor must you treat an old person as you would one in the prime of life."

Five years later, the physician Ignatz Leo Nascher identified senescence, or old age, as "a distinct period of life, a physiological entity as much so as the period of a childhood," and coined the term "geriatrics" for this "new special branch of medicine."

Adolescence entered popular consciousness around the same period. The legendary psychologist G. Stanley Hall officially introduced the idea in 1905 in his massive tome *Adolescence: Its Psychology and Its Relations to Physiology, Anthropology, Sociology, Sex, Crime, Religion, and Education.* Hall defined the stage as running from ages 12 to 24—peaking between 14 and 16—and marked by a volatile mix of naïve optimism, burning sexuality, intense emotionalism, instability, self-absorption, and rashness. The adolescent's literary precursor can be found in Goethe's *Young Werther,* who exhibited the regenerative powers and romantic temperament that enamored Hall, Key, and others.

Hall was a towering figure in his field. He founded the *American Journal of Psychology* in 1887, became the first president of the American Psychological Association, presided over Clark University for more than thirty years, and hosted Freud's 1909 visit to the States. Deeply influenced by Darwin, he developed what he called "genetic psychology" and applied his ideas about the evolution of species to a single individual. Each person repeats or recapitulates the same developmental stages that the human species experienced as a whole, he argued. Babies corresponded to the presavage state, while adolescents manifested the characteristics of ancient and medieval societies, in which there is a "peculiar proneness to be either very good or very bad."

Middle age lacked a grand chronicler and advocate like Hall. But as childhood, adolescence, and old age were more precisely defined and corralled, middle age stood out in sharper relief. The idea of a separate midlife period swept through the culture, pulled along by age-graded institutions, industrialization, and urbanization, as well as drops in birth and mortality rates.

A look at early life expectancy charts can give the faulty impression that middle age was simply the result of longer life spans. After all, if death comes at 40 (the average life expectancy in 1800), there isn't much of a middle to enjoy. But that is just a tiny part of the story. Average life expectancy hadn't increased that much; it was only 47 in 1900. In any case, neither the 1800 nor the 1900 figures reflect how long people actually lived. The all-too-frequent death of babies and children is what kept *average* life expectancy statistics so low. Even in colonial times, most people who made it past age 15 had a good chance of living to 60. Knowing that the Bible allotted a life span of "three score and ten years," no one mistook 45 or 50 for old age.

More crucial to midlife's invention was the fact that women had fewer children. Discoveries like antiseptics and the microorganisms that caused cholera and diphtheria led to a plunge in childhood mortality and stanched the flood of women seriously disabled or killed in childbirth. Better diet and sanitation helped infants and children survive past adolescence, which contributed to the drop in birth rates. With fewer babies and more time and money, parents invested more in each child. Americans' growing sense of autonomy also encouraged women to consider children a personal choice rather than solely a matter of God's will or male authority, a view supported by the increasingly visible presence of feminists and birth control advocates, who counseled families on the logistics of vaginal jellies, douches, and withdrawal. "Always carry to bed a clean napkin," Dr. James Ashton advised affianced men. The invention of vulcanized rubber that Charles Goodyear turned into a tire dynasty added to the array of methods by cheaply producing reliable rubber condoms, which became popular in the 1870s.

By 1900, the typical mother had two or three children, less than half as many as her counterpart one hundred years earlier. On average, she was 53 when her last child left home, and she died at 71. Adulthood was no longer an unvarying, seamless whole filled with farmwork and child-rearing until death. Middle-aged women were able for the first time to turn to other pursuits, like fashion, shopping, working, and volunteering. There was life after children.

The New Normal

For all the public discussion of these new stages, the label "middle age," with its recently gathered retinue of associations, was initially meaningful to a relatively small segment of the population. As historians note, societies are governed by "laws of uneven development" that sabotage efforts to generalize. The number of urban residents did not inch past that of their rural neighbors until 1920, when they made up fifty-one percent of the country's 106 million people. Divisions were not as stark between parents and children in rural areas, where fathers maintained power over land and inheritance and claimed greater authority. The fashions and amusements of middle-aged women and the factory life of middle-aged men detailed in the press primarily referred to white city dwellers.

Age consciousness was most keenly felt in urban hubs, "the storm centers of civilization," where opinion makers lived and people were headed. The growing middle class—the white professionals, managers, and bureaucrats who administered the industrialized economy—formed a new tier beneath wealthy landowners and businessmen, and above unskilled laborers and subsistence farmers. Divisions between classes and between men and women hardened in the late 1870s and 1880s. Couples moved from the farm, where all work was shared, to the city, where men and women were separated into the domestic or the business realm. Dire economic conditions stoked class identities and resentments, further parting professionals and businessmen from manual laborers, whose numbers increased daily as shiploads of immigrants streamed into America's ports.

In 1900, fewer than a fifth of employed men, about four million, held white-collar jobs. At the top of this stratum were lawyers, scientists, clergymen, doctors, and managers; at the bottom were clerks, teachers, and governesses who did not earn as much money but shared the same values of hard work, moderation, responsibility, and prudence. Two-thirds of Americans still lived in rural areas, and half of the population was poor at any given time.

Later in the twentieth century, the middle class dominated and defined the United States, but even at this early stage, this relatively small group, along with the nation's wealthier class, controlled the levers of influence and power; their voices dominated the media. These cultural brokers helped fashion the images and explanations of America's disorienting hurly-burly. They command special attention because they steered the conversation and shaped perceptions of their own middle age, as well as those of the ethnically varied working classes they viewed as their inferiors.

The cable lines and periodicals that connected the Eastern part of the country with the West, and the North with the South, disseminated their tastes and prejudices. In 1890, there were nearly 200,000 miles of railway track, 250,000 miles of telephone wire, and 1,610 daily newspapers in print. By 1900, automobiles had entered the landscape. Residents from coast to coast could share photographs, cartoons, news, jokes, styles, and ideas through advertisements, novels, journals, newspapers, the Sears Roebuck & Co. and Montgomery Ward catalogs, and later, movies in a fraction of the time it used to take for information to travel. The public drew on this store of unfamiliar pictures, gestures, attitudes, and behaviors to construct a generational identity. In many parts of the country, the media's "Middle-Aged Man" (and Woman) came into being before the flesh-and-blood article.

Fashion manufacturers and editors were among the first to assign appropriate clothes to various age groups. In rural America in the early 1800s, a sweet 16 and a sedate 60-year-old could wear the same style without embarrassment. By the end of the century, expectations had altered as each age developed its own dress code. The *Los Angeles Times* in 1895 even offered fashion tips for "a little roly poly grandmamma," so that she need not "look wider than she is long." Mrs. Wilson Woodrow (married to James Wilson Woodrow, a cousin of the future president) sternly informed *The Cosmopolitan*'s readers in 1903, "Sweet simplicity at fifty is absurd." Middle-aged women should indulge in elaborate design and adornments, "the splendor of jewels, forbidden to the debutante, is her privilege." *Harper's Bazar* advised that 25 was the upper limit for simple clothing, and told perplexed 45-year-olds how to dress: "Fine clothes and jaunty and piquant fashions are in fact the property of middle life; not of old age, indeed, any more than of early youth."

Men's fashions also distinguished among generations, with the width of a brim or the placement of a crease as reliable a guide to age as the number of rings on a tree. "The New Styles That Are Designed for Young, Old and Middle-Aged Men" that appeared in the newspaper the *San Francisco Call* in 1904 explained: "There are straw hats for the young man, straw hats for the middle-aged man, straw hats for the old man and straw hats for the boy. Each age has its own particular and exclusive style more pronouncedly this year than ever before."

Etiquette manuals, reform pamphlets, academic lectures, government reports, medical conferences, journals, and advertisements laid out the appropriate age for everything from marriage to eating meat. They set the social clock, defining expectations for when someone should finish an education, live independently, or have children. These new norms informed middle-aged wives how to dress and how often to have sex (alas, for them, it tended to be never). James Foster Scott, a former obstetrician, wrote in his 1898 text *The Sexual Instinct* what he considered appropriate sexual activity for every stage of life, declaring that when "the individual is in the afternoon of life" he and she are "again sexless from a physical standpoint." He estimated that this turning point occurred in women between 42 and 50, and in men between 50 and 65. According to John Henry Kellogg, the food reformer and health spa founder (who helped perfect the humble cornflake with his brother, William Keith), men and women in different stages of life should not marry because older people didn't have the energy to withstand the youthful demands of sex. Meanwhile, the forerunners of Miss Manners were policing the social corridors. "The haste and impetuosity so becoming to 18 are immoral at 50," Celia Parker Woolley wrote in 1903. "It is neither pleasant nor edifying to see an aging man or woman aping the behavior of the young."

Failure to conform to these widely proclaimed standards risked placing one outside the new "normal," a word that passed into common use around mid-century, when it began to enjoy a steady rise in popularity. "Deviation," previously a neutral statistical term, took on a more negative connotation. Fitting in mattered. As assorted experts displaced religious authorities, being normal was emphasized more than being moral.

Taylor had plenty of acolytes eager to take a scientific approach and spread standardization and segmentation to other spheres of human endeavor. The Progressive Era reformers who flourished between 1890 and 1920 were his social and political counterparts, and they sought to put his ideas into practice. With a base in the growing urban middle class, activists like Theodore Roosevelt, Woodrow Wilson, and Margaret Sanger believed that through the application of scientific expertise and efficiency they could find solutions to society's ills. In the health field, Kellogg organized his popular wellness sanitarium in Battle Creek, Michigan, on a "rational and scientific basis under regular scientific management." Frank and Lillian Gilbreth, whose lives were later portrayed in the book and film *Cheaper by the Dozen,* were probably the best known of the scientific management gurus. Also in the domestic arena was Ellen Richards, a chemist and sanitary engineer who founded the discipline of home economics. She was similarly inspired by scientific management and its promise to eliminate "wasted motions." Science, Richards declared, compelled women to ask themselves, "Am I making the best use of my time?" Richards was counseled by her friend Melville Dewey, the meticulous founder of the library cataloging system and the president of the New York Efficiency Society. He economized the spelling of his own name to Melvil Dui.

After *Principles of Scientific Management* was published in 1911, Taylorization seemed to be everywhere. The following year, Christine Frederick, a magazine editor, consultant, and home economist, initiated a series of articles in *Ladies' Home Journal,* each preceded by Taylor's pig-iron story, instructing women on how to apply scientific principles to the drudgery of housekeeping. Wealthy women had maids; the poor, who often worked as servants, had less complex demands and appearances to keep up, Frederick wrote. "The problem, the real issue, confronts the *middle-class woman* of slight strength and still slighter means, and of whom society expects so much—the wives of ministers on small salary, wives of bank clerks, shoe salesmen, college professors, and young men in various businesses starting to make their way," she explained. "They are refined, educated women, many with a college or business training. They have one or more babies to care for, and limited finances to meet the situation." Frederick advised them to break each chore down into individual steps and then time each to find the most efficient way to peel a potato or iron a shirt. A few years later, she created a correspondence course titled "Household Engineering: Scientific Management in the Home." In 1913, *Life* magazine published a cartoon in which an efficiency expert breaks up a workplace embrace, admonishing the young man for employing "fifteen unnecessary motions in delivering that kiss."

There were opponents, fierce ones, in fact. To them, Taylor was a scourge, a soulless champion of the Machine Age, who valued efficiency above humanity. After *Principles* appeared, Samuel Gompers, president of the American Federation of Labor, wrote that Taylor's system makes "every man merely a cog or a nut or a pin in a big machine, fixed in the position of a hundredth or a thousandth part of the machine."

Taylor saw no conflict between efficiency and humanity, because he profoundly believed that his standardized system would rescue the workingman from the whims of exploitive managers and raise wages. With impartial science as the guide and arbiter, acrimony between labor and management would disappear. Progressives like Louis Brandeis, the future U.S. Supreme Court justice, championed scientific management because it promised "industrial utopia." For Taylor, there was no contradiction between the definition of "standard" as a model of excellence and the definition of "standard" as a commonplace, identical and unvarying. Conformity was a virtue. If you found the best, why change it? That's the way Babbitt, the middle-aged hero of Sinclair Lewis's 1922 novel, sees it. "Here's the specifications of the Standardized American Citizen!" Babbitt proudly declares. "Here's the new generation of Americans: fellows with hair on their chests and smiles in their eyes and adding-machines in their offices."

Taylorites shared the belief that a right way, "the one best way," and a wrong way also existed in the personal sphere. Forget Calvinism's predestination. Following the prescribed norms would enable each person to reach his optimum best self. Pauline Manford, the wealthy modern matron in Edith Wharton's 1927 novel *Twilight Sleep,* thinks science can help society's elite turn out babies "in series like Fords." She invoked scientific management in the fight against aging. "Nervousness, fatigue, brain-exhaustion . . . had her battle against them been vain? What was the use of all the months and years of patient Taylorized effort against the natural human fate: against anxiety, sorrow, old age—if their menace was to reappear whenever events slipped from her control?"

Poor Pauline. On the factory floor, Taylor—or the owner or manager—

was the one to set the pace. Workers could not be relied on to determine the most efficient method on their own. But outside the industrial arena, men and women were expected to vigilantly monitor their own activities and implement improvements. In the home, Taylorization was adopted by the self-help movement as a method of exerting individual autonomy and achieving happiness in an era of mass production. Christine Frederick explained the goals in *Ladies' Home Journal*: "The end aim of home efficiency is not a perfect system of work, or scientific scheduling, or ideal cleanliness and order; it is the personal happiness, health, and progress of the family in the home."

The unclouded faith in science and reason to improve human existence may look naïve from our perch in the twenty-first century, where we have a view of environmental devastation and efficient killing technologies. But there was an almost childlike awe in what these amazing new tools could achieve. John D. Rockefeller established the Laura Spelman Rockefeller Memorial Foundation in the early twenties with the express purpose of promoting "scientific" solutions to social problems. The belief was that war, poverty, and class conflict were, as the foundation put it in its final report, "irrationalities" that could eventually be remedied by reason and science. Scientific management was a way to tame "the natural human fate," as Wharton's Pauline would say.

The creation of rational standards was reassuring at a time of breakneck and puzzling transformation. Livelihoods, homes, and habits, previously passed from one generation to the next like family Bibles, disappeared. Men who grew up on farms lost sight of the world they knew after moving to cities for factory work. Women who entered the workplace, either out of necessity or desire, raised fears about the unraveling of family life and traditional values. Waves of exotic immigrants, ten million between 1860 and 1890, with strange habits and tongues crowded into the urban stew. If an inhabitant of 1890 were suddenly transported to his own home thirty years later, he would be dazed by its unfamiliar marvels: hot and cold running water, an indoor toilet, a toaster, a washing machine, a telephone, fresh fruit and vegetables in winter, cosmetics, a closet of differently styled clothes, a radio, and maybe even a driveway with a car in it. If he entered a grocery store or pharmacy in 1920, hundreds of new products, many for problems or maladies that he had never heard of—from halitosis (the obscure medical term for bad breath that Listerine made famous) to homotosis (the lack of attractive home furnishings)—would greet him like a roomful of strangers. On the same street he would find businesses that had not existed before—commercial Laundromats, beauty parlors, movie houses.

In this daunting environment, life stages offered a solid and logical framework for a society uncertain of what was coming from one day to the next. For someone who felt lost in the mammoth urban industrial machine, the advice on how to act and dress, when to marry or expect a promotion provided a detailed map. Here's what is expected, what is standard or normal, for someone like you.

Middle age satisfied a profound need; it offered at least a partial identity to people in the midst of a historical identity crisis. Physicians and psychologists like G. Stanley Hall were convinced that a series of distinct phases was biologically determined, as natural as teething. But as Voltaire said of God, if middle age didn't exist, we would have had to invent it.

4

The Renaissance of the Middle-Aged

The actress Lillie Langtry in middle age, 1900

The woman of today "is just beginning to live at 30 . . . and she absolutely refuses to consider herself old until she is 70."

—San Francisco Call (1910)

The single-minded focus on efficiency reveals how much thinking about the purpose and value of a human life had shifted by the end of the nineteenth century. Early Puritans were not unmindful of the need for economic production. In a 1701 sermon, the great American preacher Cotton Mather told his congregation that all Christians had two callings, "to service the Lord and to pursue useful employment." But the ultimate purpose of both was salvation. "Their main end must be, to, acknowledge the great God, and His glorious Christ." The accumulation of years brought one closer and closer to realizing that great project. On this spiritual journey, "every age has its joys and sorrows."

The spread of Taylorization laid the groundwork for viewing midlife as the gateway to decline. It converted age into a proxy for efficiency. The notion of "saving time," as if minutes were pennies in a bank, infiltrated everyday consciousness. An industrial worker was valued solely in terms of his output: how many loads of coal he could shovel in a minute, how many bricks he could lay in an hour. Neither seniority nor experience, judgment nor instinct mattered. Men who had seen their fathers till the land for as long as they could stand upright were themselves superfluous at 45 because they were not as quick or adaptable on the factory's rumbling floors. Middle-aged and older workers had more trouble keeping up with the physical demands dictated by Taylorism, even when it meant earning more money. If they couldn't produce, they were fired. If they gummed up the works, they were heavily fined. Scientific management stripped age of its other attributes and reduced it to a set of physical capabilities. Before the 1920s, among white-collar workers and women, midlife remained a period when talents and influence were recognized as reaching full flower. But among those who toiled in the guts of America's industrial machine, where profit margins were calculated to the last cent, being middle-aged became a distinct disadvantage. In the factory, the biological clock was forced to synchronize with the time clock.

Taylor's scientific management favored the young, but ironically, so did the backlash his clockwork efficiency provoked. Although industrialization brought many Americans great wealth, an assortment of radicals and traditionalists rejected the notion of technological salvation and feared industrialization was creating an insensate, alienating society, one that valued productivity above humanity. Hope came in the form of the next generation, unsullied and uncorrupted. G. Stanley Hall claimed youth symbolized purity and regenerative power; it was an "oracle" that "will never fail." In 1911, the same year Taylor published *Principles,* the 25-year-old Randolph Bourne, a musician, intellectual, and vehement antiwar activist, started writing the essays that would constitute *Youth and Life,* an early countercultural manifesto. Bourne, his face scarred from a botched delivery and his back hunched by childhood spinal tuberculosis, became a spokesman for his generation, whom he urged to rebel against Victorian convention. Bourne maintained that one's ideals were set by the age of 20. "It is a tarnished, travestied youth that is in the saddle in the person of middle age," he wrote. "Middle age has the prestige and the power," he added, "but too seldom the will to use it for the furtherance of its ideals." For different reasons, both supporters and critics of the newly mechanized age honored youth and devalued middle age.

Hall and Bourne were addressing a lettered audience. Their warnings about the failings of middle age among society's leaders, professionals, and artists were preceded by another champion of youth, however, the doctor and neurologist George Miller Beard.

The Fixed Period

Beard was much more interested in "brain-workers" than in the "muscle-workers" who fascinated Taylor. Resources and expertise were abundantly expended on the simple, straightforward diseases of the poor and working class, Beard noted in his 1880 treatise on nervous exhaustion. He decided to devote his expertise to "the miseries of the rich, the comfortable, and intelligent," which have remained "unstudied and unrelieved."

An engraving of Beard made at his 1862 graduation from Yale shows a handsome face with thin hair combed flat to cover a receding hairline, neatly trimmed muttonchops, and soulful eyes. He served as a medical aide during the Civil War and then attended medical school at Columbia. Mostly forgotten today, he acquired worldwide fame in his day for popularizing the term "neurasthenia" to refer to the nervous disorders, generally a mix of fatigue and depression, that afflicted "nearly every brain-working household" in the country's industrial centers. (The revered Harvard psychologist William James dubbed neurasthenia "acute Americanitis.")

Beard believed nervous breakdowns resulted from a dwindling of the electrical energy or "nervous force" that carried messages from the brain to the body. His favored treatment was electrotherapy, which he offered soon after he got his medical degree in 1866. A cathode attached to a large generator was placed under the patient's feet or rear while the doctor held a damp sponge in his hand to conduct the electrical current. A flip of the generator switch and a jolt of electricity was applied to the suffering organ: the chest for a weak heart, the womb for menopausal pain, the penis for impotence. Beard's vocal and enthusiastic endorsement of electrotherapy prompted one doctor to label him "the P. T. Barnum of medicine."

Middle-class Victorian women were known to suffer from nervous hysteria well before Beard came onto the scene. Their supposedly delicate constitutions were easily overstimulated by urban hustle and bustle, which led to anxiety, sleeplessness, erotic fantasies, nausea, headaches, and fainting spells. Appearing on the witness stand at the 1883 murder trial of a woman in New York, various experts testified to the plague of hysteria among women. "Women educated in convents and brought up where they do not come in contact with the world are especially subject to hysterical manifestations," noted the state's consulting medical examiner at asylums. Alice James, William and Henry's sister, suffered through such frequent bouts that she spent much of her time in bed and wrote often and longingly of her desire for death. Beard indicted "the mental activity of women" as a cause of neurasthenia, but he argued men were newly vulnerable because of the modern ills of "steam power, the periodical press, the telegraph," as well as rigid schedules, required punctuality, and omnipresent clocks. Neurasthenia was the male version of hysteria.

In 1881, just as Taylor was inaugurating his time-and-motion studies at Midvale, Beard published *American Nervousness,* a mix of clinical observation and philosophy intended for a popular audience. Included in the book is his study on the link between productivity and age. Whereas Taylor measured output in minutes and seconds, Beard used years.

The longevity study was part of Beard's attempt to rebut the popular notion that indoor intellectual activity was damaging to one's physical health. He investigated how long brain-workers lived, as well as when they produced their most significant accomplishments, compiling lists of "the greatest men in history"—Byron, Shakespeare, Mozart, Napoleon, Michelangelo, Christopher Wren—to "determine at what time of life men do their best work."

His conclusion was that "seventy percent of the work of the world is done before 45 and eighty percent before 50. . . . The best period of fifteen years is between 30 and 45." Creative work has an even earlier expiration date, with the best accomplished between 25 and 40. To illustrate the results, Beard drew a graph titled "The Relation of Age to Original Work," which showed a steep, Everest-like ascent to age 40, followed by an unbroken downward slope till death. In this off-center bell curve, the second half of life was an uninterrupted slide from the apex. Beard considered his findings to be evidence of a "law." "The year of maximum productiveness is thirty-nine," he declared. As if celebrating an anniversary, Beard assigned a material to each decade of life. The golden age was between 30 and 40; silver was between 40 and 50; iron between 50 and 60, and tin between 60 and 70. The years between 20 and 30 were the brazen or brass decade.

Beard was preoccupied with quality, not quantity. Men may do more work after age 40, but their most original and creative work was already behind them. "In loneliness, in poverty often as well as under discouragement, and in neglected or despised youth has been achieved all that has advanced, and all that is likely to advance mankind." Beard dismissed the notion that the elderly had any special wisdom: "When an old man utters great thoughts, it is not age, but youth that speaks through the lips of old age."

Beard's theory was proved correct at least as far as his own life was concerned. He caught pneumonia and died in 1883 at the age of 44.

This idea of a limited number of constructive years was satirized by Anthony Trollope in his 1882 novel *The Fixed Period,* in which the young founders of the island nation Britannula mandate that before turning 68, a man will happily agree to be euthanized to avoid the decrepitude and expense of old age. The problem arises only when one of the original supporters finally turns 67 and realizes he is not quite ready to accept the "honor" of being chloroformed after all.

Trollope's fixed period intrigued Sir William Osler, the most influential and revered physician of his era. After deciding to leave the medical faculty of Johns Hopkins in 1905 at the age of 56, Osler gave a speech declaring: "In the science and art of medicine there has not been an advance of the first rank which has not been started by young or comparatively young men. . . . [The] effective, moving, vitalizing work of the world is done between the ages of 25 and 40 years—these fifteen golden years of plenty." In comparison, "men above 40 years of age" are useless. As for those over 60, there would be an "incalculable benefit" in "commercial, political and professional life, if, as a matter of course, men stopped work at this age." Leave and make room for younger men, he advised.

Reports of Osler's joking references to a Trollope-style solution sparked outraged editorials and letters. Newspapers responded with tales of the vigor and productiveness of older people. In published replies, the doctor took pains to emphasize that his comments regarding euthanasia were facetious, but he remained steadfast in the belief that "the real work of life is done before the fortieth year."

On the issue of aging, the scientist's view meshed with that of the businessman. Since older people were seen as having less energy and capacity, they had to be moved along to make way for the younger and more fit, just as Darwin's evolutionary theories, first published in 1859, suggested happened naturally.

Census reports before 1900 reveal that a growing number of people started to hide their entry into middle age. In eighteenth-century America, the added value of maturity and experience frequently caused young men and women to pretend they were older. People tended to round *up* their age to the nearest five or ten years. By 1880, however, Americans were rounding *down*. More and more, people were reluctant to admit they had turned 40, 50, or 60 and repeatedly told census takers, who grouped individuals according to decade, that they were 39, 49, or 59.

In reality, the view of midlife generally depended on one's class, ethnicity, and sex. Laborers most frequently tried to mask their true age in order to keep a job or get a new one. A 1904 article in the *New York Times* entitled "Youth Crowding Out Even Middle Age" noted that the "best customers for hair dyes are sometimes the working men," especially in the machinery and building trades, "where there is constant muscular exercise and where men age quickly." Henry C. Hunter, secretary of the New York Metal Trades Association, said, "When mechanics become middle-aged, they have to take less remunerative positions." Boilermakers, deaf after a few years from the noise, were let go because they were unable to hear directions as well. "There is no disguising the fact that a man of 40 is not worth as much as a man between 20 and 30," an official from the bricklayers union lamented.

The burdens of manual labor and poverty were what prematurely aged men and women. As the *Times* noted in its story: "There are plenty of gray-haired railroad Presidents and gray-haired men in other high positions, where years of experience are looked upon as a valuable adjunct to brains, but gray hair is a fatal obstacle to a mechanic in search of employment." Men like Osler may have talked about the need for an influx of younger "brain-workers," but few of them were actually pushed out. Men solidly in middle age dominated office suites and the professions, gaining respect with the years. Osler, after resigning from Johns Hopkins, accepted the Regius Professorship of Medicine at Oxford University, considered the most prestigious appointment in his field, a post he kept until his death in 1919 at age 70. Oliver Wendell Holmes, who disdained contemporaries who failed to produce a major work by 40, served on the Supreme Court for thirty years before finally retiring in 1932 at age 90.

Magazines and newspapers with large numbers of middle-class subscribers like *Ladies' Home Journal,* the *Saturday Evening Post, The Cosmopolitan,* and *American* reaffirmed that power accrued to those in their middle years. In a revealing study of fiction in 1890s periodicals, the sociologist Martin U. Martel concluded: "For both men and women, the middle-age period is the time of greatest independence, respect, esteem, prestige and social involvement . . . a time of active involvement in the affairs of the young." Out-of-touch parents and mocking teenagers were absent. "Middle-age is a central phase of life."

Newspapers reflected similarly positive attitudes. In 1905, the same year Osler gave his speech, the *Gainesville Daily Sun* declared that middle age "would seem actually to have stepped backward and marched alongside of youth. There is a jauntiness, a buoyancy, an elasticity, about the middle age of today at which our fathers would have shaken their heads as unseemly."

A Woman's Middle Age

The invention of middle age turned out to have a wonderfully liberating effect on privileged and professional women, initially filling their middle years with unaccustomed promise.

Women had started to carve out a more distinct identity in the public sphere after the Civil War. Those who became active as the fighting raged—raising money, nursing soldiers, and wrapping bandages—later channeled their efforts into urban reform. They were generally not radicals or social activists but, rather, traditionalists who saw womanly virtue as a counterweight to the corrupt and selfish world of men. These midlife matrons discovered that their new social roles brought them unexpected personal fulfillment. They formed temperance societies, settlement houses, and cultural clubs, reformed fallen women and young urban gang members, and worked to assimilate the swarms of strange (and, in their eyes, somewhat distasteful) immigrants. A number of these reformers became professional teachers, educators, nurses, social workers, journalists, and community and labor organizers. As the middle class was expanding, the availability of factory-made goods eliminated the endless cycle of sewing, planting, washing, canning, and soap-, candle-, and butter-making. Untethered to the house, the demands of subsistence living, and unending childcare, more and more women discovered a new phenomenon: free time. They busied themselves with good works and demonstrated their productivity in a different venue. "The needs of the world are endless and the middle-aged woman has usually more leisure to devote to them than has a woman of a younger period," an 1889 column on middle age in *Harper's Bazar* declared. "Who shall placate the querulous inmates of that somewhat forlorn hostelry the Old Ladies' Home. . . . Who shall so compassionately guide the orphan and look after neglected childhood and carry on the manifold work of churches and clubs as the woman not yet elderly, but still not young." The female activists and innovators that we remember today, including Elizabeth Cady Stanton, Mary Baker Eddy, Jane Addams, and M. Carey Thomas, hit their prime in their 40s or 50s. Indeed, middle-aged women remained the mainstay of reform efforts and clubs like the League of Women Voters well into the 1960s.

Whether they worked in a factory or an office, some women brought home money and a dollop of economic power, possibly for the first time, in their middle years. (In 1900, about a fifth of the female population worked, accounting for eighteen percent of the labor force; about half of those worked as maids or servants.) As the writer Gertrude Atherton reminded readers in an 1891 newspaper article: "Money is a controlling force in married life. . . . When a woman finds that she too can make it, her self-respect becomes colossal and quite swamps the little she has left for man." Magazines recounted stories of middle-aged mothers pursuing lifelong dreams. A 45-year-old who had always wanted to be a physician was finally going to medical school. Another went into business despite the protestations of her family and friends. Martin Martel, the sociologist who analyzed 1890 magazine fiction, noted, "The standing of the middle-aged woman in many ways is higher than that of the man." She is expected to be "a reservoir of emotional strength and fortitude . . . the possessor of a complex body of knowledge and skills brought to fruition over many years of experience."

Between 1890 and 1920, the years encapsulating the Progressive Era, a feminist wave helped promote what was popularly referred to at the time as a "Renaissance of the Middle Aged." Those thirty years "seemed to be the Eldorado for the middle-aged woman, both in social and business life," a letter writer to the *New York Times* noted. "For her mere sex, she was shown just as much consideration as the young girl, no work was refused to her on account of her years, nor did her sex or age bar her from taking an active interest in politics, science, social work, and business long before women obtained the right to vote."

One reason was that suffragettes, split over tactics since 1869, reconciled in 1890 and created a formidable women's rights movement. Feminist successes expanded opportunities for middle-aged women at a time when their male counterparts saw their economic options shrink, a scenario that was replayed in the twentieth century. The frail Victorian girl, prone to bouts of fainting, became vigorous and authoritative in her middle years. The "New Woman," a term that Henry James initially popularized, strode onto the urban scene in the 1880s and 1890s. This modern creature, a product of bourgeois affluence, was likely to attend college, wanted to compete with men on equal terms, and was willing to postpone, or even forgo, marriage. In 1906, a British writer observed in the *New York Times* that "old maids" no longer existed: "The majority of New York's spinsters past 30 are bachelor women." Newspapers outside large cosmopolitan areas also observed the phenomenon. The *Gainesville Daily Sun* informed its readers in 1905 that "the lament of many a matchmaking mamma is that the most dreaded rivals of her darling are not to be found so much among the girls of her own age as among women who not many years ago would have been relegated to the ranks of hopeless old maidenhood. The fact is that the middle-aged lady of today is much younger in manner and tastes." Whether or not mammas were thrown into a panic worthy of Jane Austen's Mrs. Bennett, among women who attended the newly endowed women's colleges and then pursued professional careers, the average age of marriage did rise.

In middle age, these women wielded social power as well. "Today the most influential factors in social life are the women of fifty and over," Mrs. Wilson Woodrow informed *The Cosmopolitan*'s readers. "The professional woman of 50" was "at the very zenith of her powers." Vital middle-agers also proved the fallacy of so-called experts who warned women in midlife against sexual activity. Edith Wharton, after suffering through a sexless marriage for more than twenty-eight years, discovered the ecstasies of sex at 45 with her friend, the mustachioed cad Morton Fullerton. "I have drunk of the wine of life at last," she wrote in her 1907 journal. "I have known the thing best worth knowing. I have been warmed through and through and will never grow cold again."

Menopause, which was often considered the end of a woman's utility in men's eyes, was celebrated by Anna Garlin Spencer in *Women's Share in Social Culture* (1913). She pronounced menopause the beginning of a "second youth," when "nature gives a fresh start and a fresh balance of power."

Successive generations of New Women helped feminism find a more stable foothold before they won the right to vote in 1920. In the years immediately before and after World War I, women managed to push their way into business, medicine, college classrooms, sports fields, and politics in numbers that were not reached again until the second feminist wave in the 1970s.

In the midst of these exhilarating gains, other social, cultural, and political forces were conspiring to cast the middle years in an unflattering light. The brief renaissance of the middle-aged would soon draw to a close.

5

The Middle-Aged Body

Bernarr Macfadden, publisher of
Physical Culture magazine, in the 1920s

My skin's tattooed with hours and days and decades,
head to foot.
—Mary Meriam, "The Romance of Middle Age"

The building up of one's physical assets should be recognized
as an imperative duty.
—Bernarr Macfadden, *Vitality Supreme* (1915)

George Beard and William Osler championed the mental vigor of younger men compared with those in middle age. Most scientists, health advocates, and members of the public in the second half of the nineteenth century were much more concerned with physical vitality. Their preoccupation was spurred by leaps in knowledge about how the body functioned. Science rather than religion had become the primary frame through which people interpreted their world. Attention shifted from the afterlife to this life, from spiritual transcendence to the material wonders of the here and now. Great minds were unlocking the mysteries of electricity, the evolution of species, the elements of the periodic table, and the movement of atoms. Louis Pasteur and Robert Koch's formulation of the germ theory of disease in the 1880s cranked up an already vigorous fixation on hygiene.

Taking responsibility for the care of one's body substituted for the unchallenged control that God and king once exercised over their subjects. Health reformers spoke of "physical capital"—a finite store of vital energy—that had to be wisely cared for and invested. In 1899, the bodybuilder and publishing entrepreneur Bernarr Macfadden put out the first issue of his magazine *Physical Culture,* the era's term for physical health and fitness. Macfadden (who reputedly changed his first name from Bernard to Bernarr because "it sounded like a lion's roar") built a huge empire that included exercise equipment, sanitariums, restaurants, and several books and periodicals. In 1903, he founded the Coney Island Polar Bear Club, whose members became famous for taking a dip in the freezing Atlantic in wintertime. During one of *Physical Culture*'s frequent contests, Macfadden discovered Charles Atlas, who later made a name for himself with a mail-order bodybuilding course that offered hope to ninety-seven-pound weaklings. Macfadden instructed his many followers that success depended on "developing the physical organism to the highest possible standard, and maintaining it there." Physical fitness could work hand in hand with Taylorism. He was convinced that his regimen of exercise, hydrotherapy, and "scientific feeding," a combination of diet and fasting, would enable American workers to become more efficient. Even Randolph Bourne, whose body was deformed by disease, glorified youth as much for its physical vigor as its untainted principle.

It was the "showery springtime of life," Bourne wrote in *Youth and Life,* distinguished by a "great, rich rush and flood of energy."

Physical culture was pursued with almost religious devotion. Worried that portrayals of Jesus Christ had lacked sufficient manliness, Christians presented a form of "Muscular Christianity" that was practiced in the growing number of YMCAs. Theodore Roosevelt, convinced that his own childhood maladies were cured by vigorous outdoor activity, extolled the virtues of the hearty physical life. Physical education and team sports were instituted at the girls' schools and women's colleges that were established at the end of the nineteenth century. The use of the word "hygiene" in English-language books, which began a steady rise after 1850, shot up exponentially around 1900. That year the British biologist William Bateson coined the word "genetics" to describe the physical material of heredity, the start of a phenomenal series of breakthroughs. Two years later, the British physiologist Ernest Starling discovered secretin, subsequently giving this and similar substances a name: hormones.

Science had transformed the body, which once represented a basket of cosmic forces and moral standards, into a collection of tissues and organs that signaled health or decay, normality or deviance. John Henry Kellogg wrote that he founded his Battle Creek sanitarium, visited by thousands of middle-class and wealthy patrons each year, in order to employ every aspect of modern medical science to determine "deviations from the normal standard of health." (Macfadden also ran a sanitarium in Battle Creek from 1907 to 1909, later renaming it the Macfadden Healthatorium and relocating it to Chicago.) A healthy body was seen as an emblem of a rational, individualized self. Many scientists at the time held that the state of the body determined mental health, just as earlier reformers assumed it reflected moral fitness. In women, the ovaries were believed to control personality. Troublesome changes in the female disposition were frequently treated by removing the offending organs. Cesare Lombroso, the Italian doctor who founded the field of criminology in the 1880s, linked the shape and size of the face and head to mental capacity and cultural differences. In his schema, some people were "born criminals"; they were throwbacks from an earlier stage of Darwinian evolution. Lombroso, whose views were particularly influential in the

United States among Progressive intellectuals and politicians, warned that physical "degeneration" presaged the social and cultural decline of Western civilization. Biology was destiny. Such views gained wider currency in the early 1900s after more of the mechanics of genetics were uncovered.

But defining age strictly in terms of biology carries an inherent bias toward the young. Inevitably, a purely physical inventory of middle age—stiffer muscles, dimmer eyesight, slower reflexes—will reveal deficiencies in comparison with youth so that the advancing years parallel a regression from health to deterioration. In this context, the very process of aging was seen as abnormal. Some scientists hypothesized that aging was not a natural condition at all but a disease caused by a virus. Elie Metchnikoff, who won the Nobel Prize in Physiology or Medicine in 1908 for his work in immunology, theorized the cause was toxic bacteria that was produced in the bowel and spread through the body. Other doctors attributed aging to a failing of the thyroid gland.

The emphasis on physicality trapped middle age in a destructive cycle. A focus on biology reinforced a negative view of middle age, which in turn drove attention to the body's decay.

The Sensual Life

A keen awareness of the body was further heightened by the spread of sensual comforts in everyday life. In this wealthier, democratic age, the middle class as well as blue bloods could enjoy indoor plumbing, silken fabrics, plumped-up comforters, and woven rugs. As America was transformed from a producer-oriented society that encouraged thrift and savings to an affluent consumer-centered society, more and more citizens were able to appreciate physical amenities. The flush of spending and display caused the "conspicuous consumption" that the economist Thorstein Veblen famously skewered. If the nineteenth century was like a sturdy wooden chair, the beginning of the twentieth was a plush red velvet cushion.

In the early 1900s, businesses catered to this newfound appreciation of comfort, physical hygiene, and looks by offering hundreds of new cosmetics and toiletries to ensure everything from a luminous complexion to a spic-and-span bowel. "All, with hardly an exception, pay far more attention to health and body-keeping than ever before and many evolve an almost fetishistic faith in the efficacy of some item of food or regimen to which they ascribe peculiar virtue," G. Stanley Hall remarked.

The flood of advertising and movies also put the physicality of the body on display as never before in magazines, Sunday newspapers, and theaters. America had turned into what the poet and author Vachel Lindsay, famous in his day for traveling throughout the country to give dramatic recitations, called "a hieroglyphic civilization." The flood of shared images helped mold expectations about how people should look.

Movies further modified accustomed ways of seeing. Images that streamed out of Hollywood in the first decade of the twentieth century imprinted ideals of youthful beauty on enthusiastic audiences. D. W. Griffith invented the close-up, zooming in on a lineless and wide-eyed face. By the early teens, millions of Americans were taking in a picture show every week. Certainly the tilt toward youth is part of the industry's founding story. Those in front of and behind the camera in the early days were barely past adolescence themselves. America's sweetheart, Mary Pickford, appeared in films at 16, as did Clara Bow, the original "It Girl," who ended up a has-been by 28. Rudolph Valentino was dead by age 31.

Pioneering filmmakers did not initially assume that actors would become obsessive objects of fans' desires; before 1910, most movies hid the names of players and creators. As modern advertising evolved in the twenties, studios used it to create and market movie stars. The large and lucrative industry that developed around fan magazines further forged the connection between beauty and youth. Actors gained a second profession as celebrities, creating models of glamour that were reinforced at every Saturday matinee. Concocting backgrounds for its budding stars, the studios encouraged readers to identify with their tales of ugly ducklings turned into swans. Advertisers offered readers the opportunity to buy products that promised to effect a similar transformation. "Is Your Skin Younger or Older Than You Are?" asked a 1923 ad in *Pictorial Review* for Pond's Cold Cream and Pond's Vanishing Cream. "Actresses tax their skin to the utmost. Yet they are noted for their beautiful complexions because they have learned to give their skin regularly the two things it needs to keep it in the fresh, supple condition that wards off age." Four young starlets were enlisted to offer their endorsements.

Films reinforced expectations about what styles, behaviors, and gestures were appropriate for a teenager or a middle-aged woman. In darkened movie houses, silent pictures communicated a screen character's personality and role through clothing and movements.

In such a visual culture, it was possible to create widely disseminated templates of beauty and style that people from San Francisco to Atlanta could view and imitate. Gibson Girl drawings, created by Charles Dana Gibson at the end of the nineteenth and beginning of the twentieth centuries, may have provided the first common national image of feminine beauty in America. Unlike the more voluptuous female forms prevalent in the latter half of the nineteenth century, Gibson Girls had tiny, cinched waists and youthful features. In 1930, McClelland Barclay's mass-produced illustrations of young and athletic girls were adopted as an emblem of the Fisher Company brand, which produced automobile hulls. The Fisher Body Girl, modeled on the artist's 19-year-old bride, presented another idealized, youthful image to which women could aspire.

Greater numbers of advertisements carried the message that physical beauty, even more than chronology, was the definitive barometer of aging. "When it came to age, how old you look is more important than how old you actually are," a 1923 ad for Boncilla face powder declared. "If you are fifty and your face is clean and fresh, and your facial contour firm and youthful—you are young. If you are twenty—and your skin is dull and lifeless, and the outline of your face is drooping—you are old."

Camera Vision

Awareness of one's own appearance grew with the invention of photography. Americans were so unaccustomed to regularly seeing themselves that when portrait photographs first became popular in the 1840s, subjects sometimes rejected the finished product, refusing to believe the image on paper was theirs. On occasion, customers even picked up the wrong photograph, mistaking someone else's face for their own. Affordable portraits, like inexpensive mirrors before them, encouraged a new level of narcissism about one's face and physique. Marketing campaigns and, later, movies fueled the indulgence. Individuals viewed themselves through a "double gaze," imagining how they appeared in the eyes of someone else.

This heightened degree of self-consciousness, of watching your own self, is something the newspaper columnist Heywood C. Broun observed of the novelist F. Scott Fitzgerald in 1920: "He sees himself constantly not as a human being, but as a man in a novel or in a play. Every move is a picture and there is a camera man behind each tree."

As photographs and film images permeated everyday life, Americans developed what the fashion historian Anne Hollander calls "camera vision"—the way we see images that are captured by a camera. As she explains in *Seeing Through Clothes,* by the 1920s chic was no longer defined by graphic artists and portrait painters whose painstaking pen and brushwork was meant to be appreciated through prolonged examination but by the instant image captured through the camera's lens. This split-second glance in turn influenced standards of fashion and beauty.

At the turn of the century, for example, middle-aged women embodied stylishness. They dressed to present an S shape: hair piled high under a hat, and a bustle resting on the rear to emphasize the "mature bust and hips." Buxom actresses like Lillian Russell and Lillie Langtry offered models of beauty with thicker waists and seasoned features. Young ladies adorned with layers of silk, muslin, and crinoline hid the true shape of their bodies and mimicked the style of the middle-aged. "Until this century, and until the movies, the ideal well-dressed woman had been the Lady, a cultivated personage whose mature style and charms had been carefully developed over time, with the support of the social position and income of her father and her husband," Hollander writes. Compared with these formidable middle-aged ladies, young girls had "only a raw awkward charm and no style at all and their lives no scope. They lacked training, experience and fully developed bodies; elegance was not at all suitable to them."

Mrs. Woodrow explained the allure of a mature woman to *The Cosmopolitan*'s readers: "The woman of fifty, who is beautiful, is the woman who lives in the world's life, in its finer issues and ideals, its hopes and dreams. . . . In a word, she has not been afraid to live." *Harper's Bazar* noted in 1912 that middle-aged women "express a degree of elegance, dignity and charm in her mode of dressing which a younger person striving after bizarre and smart effects cannot hope to attain." Then, the supermodel body would have looked a lot more like Helen Mirren's than Naomi Campbell's.

By 1925, the 20-year-old Clara Bow represented the new look, sexy and self-sufficient, rather than mature and experienced. Abstract graphic design incorporating simplified shapes mirrored the preference for sleek body outlines popularized in films. "Since that time," Hollander notes, "women have had to be slender."

Fashion photographers of the 1920s, like Edward Steichen at Condé Nast, helped transform the slenderized figure into a glamorous ideal. Unlike turn-of-the-century reform-minded photographers who captured grainy, pockmarked reality, Steichen created a flawless paragon of feminine beauty. For the first time, young girls rather than middle-aged women embodied elegance. A 1927 ad for Ivory Soap in *Photoplay* claimed "youth 'de-bunked' clothes and living." Beneath an illustration of two women, one in a long gown with a bustle, the other in a short slim dress, was the text: "Youth demanded simple clothes instead of these fussy, elaborate styles of the 1900s. Clothes more expressive of youth's own slim natural grace. . . . Youth has taken the artificiality out of American taste."

In Edith Wharton's *Twilight Sleep,* the middle-aged Dexter Manford notices the altered female form as he flirts with an acquaintance his age. Wharton herself was more like the "rich armful" that Manford remembered: "how splendid he had thought plump rosy women in his youth, before money and fashion imposed their artificial standards." By comparison, the young and wanton Lita, with whom he is nonetheless fascinated to the point of ruin, is a "stripped skeleton."

Rejuvenation Therapies

The heady wave of breakthroughs, from the internal combustion engine to the telegraph and airplane, reinforced Progressives' belief that all human behavior and social ills could be managed with help from technology and scientific rationality. Amazing creations that their grandparents would have considered fanciful had materialized—machines that lifted occupants to the heavens; devices that permitted conversations across the country as if across a parlor; potions that could cure previously fatal fevers. Science was magical. Thomas Edison was described as a "wizard" who could transform night into day.

In this atmosphere, the idea that science could restore the body to its youthful form did not seem so far-fetched. Revolutionary-era physicians like the founding father Benjamin Rush believed that certain organs and functions underwent "renovation." One of the early experimenters in rejuvenation was the 72-year-old French physician Charles Édouard Brown-Séquard, who in 1889 reported that he had injected himself with a mixture of testicular blood and semen extracts from dogs and guinea pigs, and had regained the energy of youth. His work was predicated on the widely held assumption that the weakening effects of old age were the result of a depletion of sperm.

Ernest Starling's discovery of human hormones in 1902 spurred a flood of experimentation into these wondrous chemical messengers that moved through the bloodstream and regulated growth, sexual development, physical shape, and more. Hormones looked like they might hold the key to stopping or reversing aging. "There seemed to be a more general agreement that a man is as old, not as his heart and arteries as was once thought, but as his endocrine glands," G. Stanley Hall concluded after surveying the leading medical authorities.

Fevered talk of "an elixir of youth" was further fueled in 1912 by the French surgeon Alexis Carrel, who announced he managed to keep a sliver of chicken-heart tissue alive in a culture. Headlines promised that the immortal chicken heart would defeat aging, among other miracles, but it was no more successful than the various kinds of rejuvenation treatments that followed it.

In 1918, Leo L. Stanley, a doctor at San Quentin prison, attracted attention after he transplanted the testicles of an executed man into a senile 60-year-old inmate. He subsequently claimed to have successfully implanted both human and animal testicles in 643 inmates, most of whom were feeble or mentally disabled, all with outstanding results—at least in his view. He also experimented with injecting inmates with a serum made from animal testicles, which, he reported, cured everything from senility to acne. His successes, however, never materialized outside the prison's walls.

One of the more publicity-minded surgeons who promised to restore youth by transplanting organs was Serge Voronoff, a Russian who lived in Paris. During a visit to the United States in 1920, he demonstrated his technique of grafting the testicles of young animals onto old ones. His reported success prompted a frenzy of attention and he received thousands of requests for lectures, demonstrations, and interviews. Later that year, he transplanted monkey testicles into men who had lost their sexual drive, and by 1922 claimed to have performed five hundred operations on men.

Many doctors scoffed at his boasts of restoring sexual vigor, eliminating senility and hair loss, and prolonging life. In October 1922, the French Academy of Medicine refused to allow Voronoff to deliver a paper on his gland grafts. But the public was enthralled and showed up in force the following day when he spoke at another venue about his work. There was a "near riot" the *Chicago Daily Tribune* recounted. "Hundreds of persons, almost half of whom were young girls and women, almost fought to enter the experimental laboratory of the College of France where the Russian savant had waiting some rejuvenated men, some rejuvenated rams, moving pictures, and a mass of fascinating detail. One woman became so thrilled with Dr. Voronoff's description of 'virile impulses' that she jumped up and shouted, 'When are you going to do something like that for us women?' 'You ladies will never need anything like that. It is only old men who need it,' Dr. Voronoff said smilingly."

As evidence, he presented one 74-year-old patient, who said the operation restored his health and hair, filled out his wrinkles, and reversed early signs of senility. The French press threw its support behind Voronoff and chastised "official scientists who [are] always retrograde owing to their dead weight of age and honors." Popular sentiment may have accounted for the academy's decision to permit one of Voronoff's pupils, a Paris physician named Francis Heckel, to deliver a paper in January 1923 about the twenty-seven operations he had performed grafting monkey testicles onto human beings. "Dr. Heckel said that a majority of those applying for grafting—there were many hundreds daily—were men of fifty or sixty years who gave as a reason that they wished to complete some life work they had undertaken or see some particular enterprise through, which had not yet been crowned with success," the *New York Times* reported. Later that year, the French Academy finally permitted Voronoff to perform two operations grafting chimpanzee glands onto human testicles. "Dr. Voronoff's triumph was complete last night when two of the best known surgeons in Paris defended the scientific worth of the gland operations," the *Chicago Daily Tribune* announced.

The accolades turned business-minded followers to Africa as investors excitedly talked about cornering the market on chimpanzees. In 1925, Voronoff commenced raising chimpanzees on a farm in the Congo to provide testes for his famed procedures.

The doctor's scientific acclaim was short-lived. Voronoff's accounts of the number of operations he performed kept changing, as did the duration of their success. Effects could dissipate in four to six months, he admitted. By 1926, an article in the *Journal of the American Medical Association* declared Voronoff's transplants to be useless and possibly harmful. His tales of miraculous rejuvenations continued to fascinate the public, though, influencing the popular imagination far beyond the actual number of surgeries or successes. Voronoff kept at it, telling an interviewer in 1939 that in the twenty years that followed his first animal-to-human transplant, he had performed two thousand gland grafts.

Commerce and science happily collaborated, as both respected scientists and basement dodgers promoted and sold rejuvenation therapies. Men were by far the most frequent patients and lab subjects. World War I's heedless slaughter of young men generated fears about the descent of the white race. Building up the "male principle" or "seminal liquor" might offer a means of restoring the vitality of absent youth. Both racial and class worries continued to surround surgical and hormonal efforts to regain the look and vigor of youth. In his 1920 tract, *Life,* Voronoff, referring to his own gland transplants, asked: "Does any scientific discovery of the ages exceed this in its importance to the individual and the race?"

There are no convincing estimates of how many people signed up for some kind of rejuvenation treatment, serious or faked. Celebrated physicians with impressive credentials performed the procedures on Park Avenue clients, but there were many more urban and small-town quacks who opened storefront rejuvenation clinics that lured in bankers, merchants, laborers, and farmers worried about their looks, their energy, their sexual appetite, or their jobs. Some physicians offered to graft testes from goats and rams onto men; other charlatans simply filled vials with colored water and injected the substances into a patient's arm or buttocks. If the snake-oil salesmen ran out of patients or, more likely, were run out of town, they simply set up shop elsewhere. Medical diploma mills and fraud made it easy for people to pass themselves off as qualified doctors. The procedures clearly did not work, but that did not dampen the public's fascination with rejuvenation, which crossed both class and gender lines. As David and Sheila Rothman relate in their book *The Pursuit of Perfection,* "Doctors were facing unhappy patients, old men complaining of reduced sex drive, impaired mental performance, fatigue and malaise. Rather than just standing there, the doctors were doing something."

Gertrude Atherton's bestselling novel *Black Oxen,* published in 1923, captures the widespread fear of midlife's physical waning and the promise of science to cure it. The book tells the story of the stunning and mysterious Countess Zattiany, whose sudden appearance in New York provokes whispers because of her uncanny resemblance to a fashionable society figure who sailed for Europe thirty years earlier. Zattiany, it turns out, is actually the 58-year-old Mary Ogden, restored to her youth and vigor through scientific rejuvenation treatments discovered in Vienna. The book's title comes from the 1912 play *The Countess Cathleen* by William Butler Yeats: "The years like great black oxen tread the world, and God, the herdsman goads them on behind, and I am broken by their passing feet."

Atherton—an arresting beauty with a tumble of blond hair, a triangular nose, and a smooth neck that she liked to display with off-the-shoulder dresses—was obsessed with maintaining her looks. At 19, she stole a suitor whom her 37-year-old mother hoped to marry, George H. P. Atherton, a charming 24-year-old wastrel. Years later, she described the incident as "the old story of youth calling to youth against the declining charms of middle-age." After eleven years of George's failing businesses, frequent moves, and gambling losses, Gertrude was relieved when he traveled to Chile to seek a fortune in 1877. A few weeks later, he was dead after hemorrhaging from a kidney stone and returned home doubled over in a barrel of rum. Freed from the confines of a conventional marriage, Atherton became a journalist and an author. Of the sixty books she wrote, *Black Oxen* was her most famous. Her friend, the novelist and critic Carl Van Vechten, called it "a book for flappers to laugh at, for middle-aged women to weep over, and for really aged ladies to be thankful for."

A year after its publication, Hollywood turned the book into a film, with Clara Bow as the sweet-faced young seductress and the stunning silent-film star Corinne Griffith as the middle-aged European countess. Atherton's tale is fictional, but it was inspired by her own experience with youth-enhancing techniques developed by the most celebrated hormone researcher of the day, Eugen Steinach, at his exclusive spa. Like Brown-Séquard before him, Steinach believed that a dissipation of sperm was responsible for the body's overall decline as men aged. His solution was to perform a vasectomy. By sealing off the passageway through which sperm traveled from the testes, he believed he could build up the concentration of male hormone and "reactivate the entire endocrine system and organism." Fertility was the trade-off for male potency. (Yeats subjected himself to a Steinach rejuvenation treatment in a British clinic in 1934.) To stimulate more hormone production in women, Steinach repeatedly exposed their ovaries to X-rays. On Central Park West, the procedures were offered by Harry Benjamin, a German endocrinologist who regularly traveled to Vienna to study with Steinach. Benjamin, who lived to 101, was ultimately best known for coining the word "transsexualism" to refer to patients who were convinced their bodies had betrayed their true nature. Introduced by the sex researcher Alfred Kinsey to a young man who insisted he was a woman, Benjamin later performed the first sex-change operation in America. In the 1950s, he counseled the British writer Jan Morris about a sex-change operation, saying: "If we cannot alter the conviction to fit the body, should we not, in certain circumstances, alter the body to fit the conviction." Although the context is different, that same advice applies to rejuvenation efforts undertaken by those in midlife. Altering the body to create an identity or fulfill a desire is commonplace today, but this notion took root in the twenties with rejuvenation treatments and plastic surgery.

Benjamin believed in the efficacy of Steinach's practice of giving men vasectomies to concentrate their hormones and zapping women's ovaries with X-rays to stimulate them. One patient said his eyesight improved, another claimed his bald head grew a thick thatch of hair. The same year *Black Oxen* appeared, Freud went under Steinach's knife in the hope it would stave off his painful oral cancer and reinvigorate him.

Some of Steinach's critics suggested the effects were all psychological, that he had simply freed his patients from society's view that aging was inevitably linked with decline. But Benjamin remained enthusiastic. After examining a handful of Steinach's patients, in 1921 Benjamin wrote up an assessment of the Viennese physician's procedures for the Academy of Medicine that was reported in the *New York Times*: "Dr. Benjamin was of the opinion that the Steinach discovery was one of the most scientifically founded." As soon as Atherton read it, she sought out the doctor. While the treatments, long discredited, make for cringe-worthy reading today, Atherton was a gloriously satisfied customer, claiming that the eight treatments over a period of three weeks gave her renewed energy as well as smoother skin. She became an ardent fan of Dr. Benjamin's, and her book was read not only as a juicy romance in gilded New York but also as a promotional tract for the method.

"Poor Dr. Benjamin! I nearly ruined him," she wrote in her autobiography. "Women besieged him, imploring him to give them the treatment free of charge or at a minimum price. It was the first time they had seen a ray of light in a future menaced with utter fatigue and the clutching of young hands at the jobs that were wearing them out." Not that Atherton blamed them. "We live in an age of scientific marvels," she declared, "and those who do not take advantage of them are fools and deserve the worst that malignant Nature can inflict upon them." For decades afterward, Atherton continued to get letters from middle-aged housewives and working women desperate to be let in on this supposed cure.

A decade after Atherton published *Black Oxen,* C. P. Snow presented a much darker vision of rejuvenation in his anonymously published 1933 novel *New Lives for Old.* Here, two scientists discover how to synthesize a rejuvenating hormone called collophage. Initially hailed as a miracle drug, it ends up sowing bitter social tensions in Britain between those who can afford treatment and those who can't, between older workers who refuse to retire and younger ones unable to get jobs, between mothers and daughters who vie for the same young men. The mania for collophage results in an underground market that causes malpractice and death. Finally, the poor riot and overthrow the government.

As negative views of midlife spread in the twenties, rejuvenation was frequently seen as a means of preserving the upper classes from the deleterious effects of aging. Steinach believed his treatments were a boon for the "intellectual class." Benjamin shared his bias, reporting happily in 1925 that among his patients "the intelligent class predominates by far"—doctors, writers, businessmen, professors, and lawyers. They were also, not coincidentally, the ones who could afford such elective treatments.

The Promise of Hormones

The major glands in the body were identified in the early decades of the twentieth century, and by the 1930s, advances in organic chemistry enabled scientists to synthesize inexpensive versions of the sex hormones. Hormone therapy could claim impressive accomplishments, curing or treating debilitating diseases like cretinism and diabetes. To some practitioners, hormones held limitless potential to solve nearly every physiological, psychological, and behavioral malady—or, rather, what they considered to be maladies, including aging. Hormones secreted by the reproductive organs in men and women were thought to cause physical and mental decline, including hair loss, senility, decreasing libido, nervous exhaustion, and more. A hormonal imbalance was widely believed to cause homosexuality, and many psychologists blamed hormones for psychosis. Male endocrinologists and those in related fields defined what was "normal" and "deviant" in terms of glandular functions.

The most extravagant claims proved false, but in the coming decades hormone supplements would form the spine of a colossal antiaging industry built around middle-aged men and women.

Plastic Surgery

Rejuvenation aimed to restore the physical condition of youth, while the rudimentary field of plastic surgery attempted to simulate its appearance. If middle age was defined by the body, then perhaps modifying the body could keep middle age at bay.

Few people underwent plastic surgery in these early years, but its adoption by physicians illustrates important themes that relate to perceptions of midlife: a fundamental expansion of the medical profession's very purpose, from preventing illness to promoting happiness, and the conviction that happiness can be attained through physical improvement.

Remolding a person's features for aesthetic purposes, which began in the late nineteenth century, initially elicited mixed feelings that revealed underlying anxieties about class and race. Elites were already disturbed by how burgeoning consumerism permitted people to mask their social origins by buying the outward trappings of a higher caste. Surgeons who performed nose jobs were welcomed for facilitating personal transformation and contentment, yet they were also considered suspect for enabling people to "pass" as something other than what they were—a syphilitic with a disfigured nose as a healthy man, a black trying to pass as white, or a Jew pretending to be a Christian. Reviewing the history of plastic surgery in *Making the Body Beautiful,* the cultural critic Sander Gilman connects its growth to assumptions that race and physical appearance were outward signs of intelligence and worth, a Dorian Gray's–eye view of the world. After Darwin, the nineteenth-century criminologists Cesare Lombroso and Alphonse Bertillon, and the psychologist Frances Galton (Darwin's cousin and the founder of the new "science of eugenics") created classification systems to identify immigrants, criminals, and the insane according to their facial features. Lombroso, who treated crime as a disease with a biological component, described murderers as having straight aquiline noses "like the beak of a bird of prey"; rapists were identifiable by their "bushy eyebrows"; and counterfeiters by their small eyes and large noses. Later Alexis Carrel, who gained fame with his immortal chicken heart, became a staunch eugenicist and admirer of Hitler. He wanted to extend life as a way of protecting the white race against its inferiors.

Industrial consumer society's preoccupation with physical appearance did not necessarily lead to unsavory philosophies, but it was at odds with the values of character and self-discipline widely promoted for much of the nineteenth century. School lessons and Sunday sermons praised self-sacrifice. Inner virtue was said to be valued above outer beauty (whether people acted on their principles is another question). In Nathaniel Hawthorne's 1846 story "The Birth-Mark," a scientist's desire to rid his wife of a reddish birthmark on her cheek ends in her death. In Louisa May Alcott's *Little Women* (1868), Amy is chastised for being overly concerned with the shape of her nose; such vanity is seen as a moral defect.

Fabulously popular success manuals emphasized this familiar old-fashioned morality and tied it to flourishing in life. "Keep in mind the great truth that you are forming a character for eternity," Harvey Newcomb wrote in *How to Be a Lady: A Book for Girls* (1850), which contained useful hints on the development of character. William Mathews, an English professor at the University of Chicago, reminded men to be true to thine own selves in his 1872 tract *Getting on in the World; or, Hints on Success in Life*. "Blow some kind of a trumpet, or at least a penny whistle to draw the world's eye on you; but be sure that you are what you pretend to be, before you blow . . ." or "woe be unto you!" Orison Swett Marden, an unflagging motivational author, published *Character: The Grandest Thing in the World* in 1899. Wanting to improve one's character was "the highest ideal," he wrote, and ultimately the foundation for a happy and successful life. "True worth is in being, not seeming," he reminds readers, "inner character eventually out-shines the most seductive outward physical beauty."

As society reordered its priorities and values after the turn of the century, so did self-help manuals. By 1909, the very same Orison Swett Marden declared in a new book: "You cannot estimate the influence of your personal appearance upon your future. . . . It does not matter how much merit or ability an applicant for a position possesses, he cannot afford to be careless of his personal appearance." By 1921, Marden had further fine-tuned his advice, telling women to use their beauty as a way of attracting and holding attention and friends. Hundreds of self-help books and articles offered similar advice, emphasizing that one's appearance and a good first impression were stepping-stones to personal success.

Freud had exposed the split between an individual's inner psyche and external consciousness at the same time industrialization was separating private from public life by shifting work from inside the home to the factory. Regardless of whether people had read the great Viennese doctor, they had firsthand experience operating in different worlds. There was the self when you were safe at home with family and the self you presented to the harsher world.

Later social scientists like Erving Goffman, David Riesman, and Christopher Lasch expanded on the division between the private and public selves in a modern market system. Goffman talked about the "outer mask" that people offered others to win plaudits. Riesman's outer-directed personalities, products of an affluent consumer-oriented society, took their cues from friends and the mass media. Success was gauged not by internal standards of conduct or achievement but by how adept one was at passing, at physically adapting and fitting in.

That is why in the early years of the twentieth century, altering features because they were linked with racial and ethnic inferiority—like a Semitic nose, dark skin, or kinky hair—was considered a legitimate reason to apply the crude techniques of plastic surgery and other chemical treatments. Individual transformation was seen to depend less on social or political change than on biology.

The Pursuit of Happiness

The first plastic surgery specifically undertaken to reverse signs of aging was performed by the German physician Eugen Holländer in 1901 at the request of a Polish female aristocrat who desired a rhytidectomy, or "face-lift." In 1906, Charles Conrad Miller developed a procedure to remove baggy eyelids. "Signs of maturity in women must go," he contended. More innovations followed.

Attempts to treat severely maimed soldiers who returned from the Great War spurred technical developments in plastic surgery and widened interest in the procedures. While reconstructive surgeons initially took pains to distinguish themselves from aesthetic or beauty surgeons, discontent with aspects of one's appearance soon became an equally acceptable reason for the technique. Twentieth-century medicine adopted a new goal apart from its mission to combat disease: curing unhappiness. Over time, healthy individuals who were dissatisfied with a nose, chin, wrinkles, weight, or breasts could expect to be offered a full menu of treatments, from hormones to surgery, as if they were sick.

This sort of self-improvement was linked to a particular view of humanity that spread throughout the nineteenth century: that individuals had control over their own lives. The sense of being in command was a relatively new experience. In the colonial era, most people adhered to the Calvinist precept that salvation was predetermined. In the divine cosmos, humanity was no better than a wretched worm, wholly dependent on God's grace. Jonathan Edwards, the New England preacher who became a leader during the First Great Awakening's religious revival, told his fearful congregation in 1741 that "the God that holds you over the pit of hell, much as one holds a spider, or some loathsome insect over the fire, abhors you, . . . and yet it is nothing but his hand that holds you from falling into the fire every moment." Piety was an individual's only option. The limits of a person's spiritual control paralleled the limits of his economic control. A farmer's son might follow in his father's footsteps or be apprenticed to a blacksmith or wheelwright. But a clear path leading from high school and college to a rich offering of different careers, lifestyles, and opportunities—in a word, choice—did not exist.

The fall-off in Calvinism in the first decades of the nineteenth century and the rise of evangelical Protestantism, with its emphasis on human effort, gave individuals a greater sense of mastery over their own spiritual fates at the same time political and economic progress was giving them more power over their material lives. The spirit of Protestant evangelism that underlay capitalism's advance also propelled the development of self-help. What makes aesthetic surgery a "truly modern phenomenon," Sander Gilman argues, is that it depends on a "cultural presupposition that you have the inalienable right to alter, reshape, control, augment or diminish your body, assuming you turn to surgeons whose expertise you can buy." And the right to improve your life (by altering your body if that is what you wish) is guaranteed by the Declaration of Independence as part of the inalienable right to pursue happiness.

The pursuit of happiness was also part of Freud's legacy. He reinforced the link between individuality and self-improvement when he turned the patient's gaze toward inward exploration. What is psychoanalysis if not a form of self-help, a person's intense and extended attempt to address his problems and failures through a deep examination of his unique experiences and feelings? The analyst serves as the mostly silent facilitator.

Happiness was the goal Christine Frederick cited in her *Ladies' Home Journal* columns when she urged women to institute Taylor's scientific management in the home. And happiness was a reason to undergo plastic surgery. In 1924, the *New York Daily Mirror* ran a "Homely Girl Contest," in which the contestant who best explained how ugliness marred her existence would win a surgical makeover. Many surgeons considered the new techniques a form of psychotherapy for women. In 1929, the beauty surgeon Adalbert G. Bettman wrote that aesthetic surgery would improve "patients' mental well-being," and foster "their pursuit of happiness."

There would always be people heralding the virtues of middle age, but the competition between positive and negative views of midlife became increasingly one-sided by the twenties. The emphasis on physiology—in the workplace, the culture, and the research lab—put middle age at a disadvantage compared with youth. Self-improvement through physical alteration promised greater happiness, a process that consumer capitalism adopted as its own. With its ingenious techniques for selling to a mass public, the burgeoning marketplace was able to exploit the fascination with the body. The market was modern, and being modern meant being young. A cult of youth seized the popular imagination after World War I and has kept a grip on it ever since.

6

Middle Age Enters the Modern Age

Bruce Barton, the father of modern advertising

The large national advertisers fix the surface of his life, fix what he believed to be his individuality. These standard advertised wares—toothpastes, socks, tires, cameras, instantaneous hot-water heaters—were his symbols and proofs of excellence; at first the signs, then the substitutes, for joy and passion and wisdom.

—Sinclair Lewis, *Babbitt* (1923)

An unexpected champion of middle age appeared in the twenties. G. Stanley Hall, after a career of rhapsodizing about the glories of youth, in retirement became interested in rescuing life after 40 from a growing malaise.

Hall collected his thoughts in *Senescence: The Last Half of Life,* a book he published in 1922, two years after he stepped down as president of Clark University and two years before his death. He was 78, and maintained his familiar neat long beard, though his sturdy face had thinned and his eyes had sunk a bit into their sockets. He poured his reflections and fears about old age and death into the 522-page text, roaming from discussions of aging's physiological features to meditations on Western civilization. Old age was the intended subject, but since Hall's target audience comprised "intelligent people passing or past middle life," the period gets extended treatment.

Hall scorned the proliferation of fervid efforts to ward off aging. Labeling midlife "the dangerous age"—a term used at the time to describe the madness that supposedly afflicted women going through menopause—he warned that after 40 men exhausted themselves by trying to seem younger, "remain necessary, and circumvent the looming possibilities of displacement."

Hall acknowledged that these fears were well-grounded. The trends that had worried 40- and 50-something laborers early in the new century etched deep, disfiguring scars into the lives of the working class. By the twenties, machinery was replacing as many as two hundred thousand workers each year, bringing a new term, "technological unemployment," into circulation. A few years later, Robert and Helen Merrell Lynd reported in their classic study *Middletown*—in reality, the recently industrialized town of Muncie, Indiana—that men of the working class "reach their prime in their twenties, and begin to fail in their late forties."

In 1923, the Lynds and a corps of younger surveyors settled for eighteen months in this town of about thirty-eight thousand in order to capture what was happening in "average, midsize cities" in the middle of the country. Funded by the Rockefeller Foundation, Lynd and his team noted the anxiety and discouragement among factory employees and their wives over what one plant superintendent called "the age deadline" for men. "I'd say that by 45 they are through." Middle age meant a dead end. "I think there's less opportunity for older men in industry now than there used to be," the head of a leading machine shop said. "The principal change I've seen in the plant here has been the speeding up of machines and the eliminating of the human factor by machinery. . . . [In] general we find that when a man reaches 50 he is slipping down in production."

The personnel manager of another machine shop agreed: "Only about 25 percent of our workers are over 40. Speed and specialization tend to bring us younger men." For those over 40, sweeping floors was one of the few jobs available. The wife of a patternmaker, the job that Frederick Taylor himself once held, said of her husband, "He is 40 and in about ten years now will be on the shelf. A patternmaker really isn't much wanted after 45. They always put in the young men."

More surprising was that anxiety over an age deadline had extended to the white-collar world. In Muncie, such employees made up about a third of the town's workforce and those on the lower rungs of this class felt the pressure. Retail salespeople and clerical workers were learning that middle age could be viewed as a potential liability. "Even in the professions such as teaching and the ministry, the demand for youth is making itself felt more than a generation ago," the Lynds noted. For young men in the business class, "they reach their prime in their thirties."

Periodicals more broadly echoed the plaint. An *American* magazine article warned that after 50, men "go to pieces." Another article noted it was common to think "a man has reached the point of greatest efficiency at around 45, is at death's door at 50 and at 60 has cheated the undertaker." Advertising, the industry that was helping to set the nation's tastes and standards, was considered a young's man game in which those under 35 were most likely to excel. It was widely believed, said Stanley Burnshaw, a copywriter for the Biow Agency in the late 1920s, that a copywriter or layout man lasted no more than ten years before being "thrown on the ashheap."

Evidence of the waning appeal of middle age in comparison with youth was displayed on Broadway as well as in the Midwest. Elmer Rice's 1923 play *The Adding Machine* revolves around the 45-year-old Mr. Zero, who is fired after twenty-five years on the job and, in a rage, murders his boss.

In *Senescence,* Hall noted that men can be seized by a "meridional mental fever" or "middle age crisis," but the death they fixated on was their own. "Certain temperaments make a desperate, now-or-never effort to realize their extravagant expectations and are thus led to excesses of many kinds; while others capitulate to fate, lose heart, and perhaps even lose the will to live," he wrote. This fever, which can strike anytime in the 30s or 40s, is clearly the precursor of what we have come to know as the midlife crisis. Men who were struck often put furious energy into trying to appear young. In Hall's view, passing as youthful was self-defeating. Such deception wasted vital energy and interfered with the "normal" development of a meaningful old age.

The venerable psychologist turned the telescope around and defined middle age from the perspective of old age: "At forty old age is in its infancy; the fifties are its boyhood, the sixties its youth, and at seventy it attains its majority." Women embark on the same journey earlier, he said, but end it later. In his tract, Hall divided a human life into five fifteen-year segments. He labeled the middle segment, which spans 30 through 45, as midlife. But what we consider middle age today is the onset of what Hall called "senescence." He staked out his opposition to the neurologist George Miller Beard, who believed man's most productive years were fixed between 30 and 45. In contrast, Hall wrote, "Modern man was not meant to do his best work before 40." The intricate problems of the modern world required maturity, wisdom, and experience. Those could be provided only by a "superman," said Hall, referencing the German philosopher Friedrich Nietzsche. In Nietzsche's cosmology, Christianity had saddled humankind with a spurious set of precepts that hamstrung its potential. What was needed was a new savior, a "superman" to serve as a flesh-and-blood replacement for God, establish a new set of values appropriate to contemporary life, and lead humanity to greatness. Hall predicted: "The coming superman will begin, not end, his real activity with the advent of the fourth decade."

Hall argued that the human race "within the past few years had passed its prime," and "those higher powers of man that culminate late" are civilization's best hope for salvation. By the time *Senescence* was published, though, public attitudes toward the virtues of life's latter half had hardened. Four gangrenous years spent fighting the Great War tore down confidence in mature judgment. Writing from the front, the 22-year-old John Dos Passos (who later wrote a touching eulogy for his friend Randolph Bourne after his 1918 death from influenza) insisted that joy, desire, and hope rested with youth and not with "the swaggering old fogies in frock-coats." Young men like Dos Passos, who were sent into battle, were profoundly disenchanted with the middle-aged civilian and military leaders who had entangled them in the bloody enterprise. By the 1920s, youth had been all but sanctified as the savior of a corrupt and moribund European civilization that an older generation had dragged into years of ruinous war.

F. Scott Fitzgerald's fantastically popular debut novel *This Side of Paradise,* published in 1920, captured the sentiments of the young postwar generation. Taking its title from a poem by Rupert Brooke, the British golden boy whose death came to symbolize the war's grotesque bloodiness and waste, *This Side of Paradise* depicted the disillusionment of the younger generation in the person of Amory Blaine, a wealthy Princeton undergraduate. "Young students try to believe in older authors," Amory says, "constituents try to believe in their Congressmen, countries try to believe in their statesmen, but they *can't*."

In 1924, the critic Edmund Wilson poked fun at his friend Fitzgerald and the heady pronouncements of youthful superiority in an imagined interview in which Fitzgerald proudly claims to be the man "who has made America Younger-generation conscious."

Fitzgerald was one of the scores of artists, writers, architects, and filmmakers who fit under the multicolored coat of modernism, the far-flung cultural movement that hit its stride in the early twentieth century. Modernism reversed the baleful eighteenth-century connotation of words like "modern," "novelty," and "innovation." "Make It New!" Ezra Pound instructed his fellow artists. The historian Peter Gay explains: "The one thing that all modernists had indisputably in common was the conviction that the untried is markedly superior to the familiar, the rare to the ordinary, the experimental to the routine." And by extension, the new over the old and youth over experience.

Novelists of all stripes gave textured life to the idea of middle-age decline. Even though conditions for most Americans in the twenties were improving in substantial ways, writers, including Theodore Dreiser, Willa Cather, and T. S. Eliot, created a narrative arc of middle age failure and disappointment that helped establish a set of expectations about how people responded to their middle decades.

Jesus Would Have Been an Adman

No group was more adept at extolling the virtues of youth and progress than advertisers. They "proudly proclaimed themselves missionaries of modernity," the historian Roland Marchand writes in his classic study *Advertising and the American Dream.* "Constantly and unabashedly, they championed . . . the modern against the old-fashioned."

Bruce Barton was the most famous adman of his era. Born in 1886, he grew up in Oak Park, Illinois, the Chicago suburb where Ernest Hemingway was born twelve years later. The Barton family's trajectory reflects that of America itself. Barton's great-great-grandfather came over as a soldier in the British army during the Revolutionary War and, whether through principle or prescience, switched sides and settled in New Jersey after Britain's defeat. By the time Bruce was born, the Bartons had moved farther west. His father, William, a traveling preacher based in Robbins, Tennessee, rode a white horse to visit the mountain churches in his circuit. He had larger ambitions, though, and eventually became the minister of a prominent Congregational church in Oak Park.

In Bruce's childhood, retailers and their customers lived in the same locale. There were no chains or franchises, no easy method of informing consumers at the other end of the country about a product, and no cheap, efficient way to transport goods to distant customers. By the time Barton co-founded an advertising agency in 1919, assembly lines were churning out shiploads of different products, railroad tracks crisscrossed the nation, a new highway system etched lines in the country's plains, and publications reached from one coast to the other. Mass consumer capitalism took off with the force of a steam engine. Whether you brushed your teeth in Philadelphia or scrubbed a sink in San Francisco, the same brands of toothpaste and cleansers were in reach. And the same movie magazines and weekly journals that showed off the latest hat styles or warned of a common fashion faux pas decorated newsstands in Baltimore and Chicago. Sinclair Lewis captures just how quickly Taylorized mass production standardized materials, tastes, and expectations in his portrait of Floral Heights, George Babbitt's hometown:

> Two out of three parlors . . . had before the fireplace a davenport, a mahogany table real or imitation, and a piano-lamp or a reading-lamp with a shade of yellow or rose silk. . . . Eight out of every nine Floral Heights houses had a cabinet phonograph. . . . Nineteen out of every twenty houses in Floral Heights had either a hunting-print, a Madame Feit la Toilette print, a colored photograph of a New England house, a photograph of a Rocky Mountain, or all four.

Creating a mass market—selling an identical item to as many people as possible—was a singularly American innovation. Sales on this scale required a quantum leap in the status and power of marketing. Large companies started spending enormous sums on advertising and public relations to stimulate consumer buying. In 1900, approximately $542 million was spent on advertising in the United States, a figure that grew to more than $1.1 billion in 1910 and more than $2.9 billion in 1920.

Advertising's job was to ensure that the economic pump remained a perpetual motion machine by convincing the public to consume. Large-scale factories could spit out acres of goods, but what use was it if there were not enough buyers for them all? Purchasing a car that was, as Henry Ford boasted of the Model A, "so strong and so well made that no one ought ever to have to buy a second one," would soon put Ford out of business. Companies that produced a single product that lasted a lifetime would ultimately find themselves in the position of the Shakers, the fast-disappearing New England sect with a devout belief in celibacy. Planned obsolescence was a firm's way of avoiding extinction. In thousands of small communities across America, citizens raised with a traditional Protestant ethic of hard work and self-denial were enjoined to become consumers and fulfill their desires with the same urgency with which they were once entreated to save their souls. The Lynds witnessed this process in Muncie.

"The American citizen's first importance to his country is . . . that of consumer," a local newspaper editorialized in 1924. "Consumption is a new necessity."

Throughout the twenties, businesses conditioned the public to expect a change in style, extending a regular fashion cycle from clothes to cars, telephones and home decor. When American Telephone and Telegraph first coordinated the regional Bell systems into a national network in 1900, the telephone was marketed as a business or household necessity. Nearly three decades later, AT&T realized the campaign had been too successful: once an affluent family had one phone, why purchase a second? Company executives switched their sales pitch to portray the telephone as a convenience and a luxury, and extolled the glories of putting phones in every room, including the bathroom. Towel manufacturers used color and patterns to transform this utilitarian item into an object of design and luxury. They came up with the idea of color-coordinated ensembles that had to be regularly updated and urged people to bathe more than once a day, using a different towel set each time.

Bruce Barton captured the significance of advertising's mission to stoke consumption in a wildly popular 1925 book, *The Man Nobody Knows,* in which he envisioned Jesus Christ as a modern business executive (and a hardy outdoorsman with "muscles hard as iron," in keeping with the era's emphasis on physical culture). Jesus "picked up twelve men from the bottom ranks of a business and forged them into an organization that conquered the world," Barton explained in his thin parable. He described Jesus as a master of advertising who preached in the ancient world's markets; he would understand that in the present day, newspapers and magazines are "a bazaar, filled with products of the world's work. Clothes and clocks and candlesticks; soup and soap and cigarettes; lingerie and limousines—the best of all of them are there, proclaimed by their makers in persuasive tones."

"He would be a national advertiser today, I am sure, as he was the great advertiser of his own day," Barton declared of mankind's savior. Carpentry might be all right for first-century Rome, but for 1920s America advertising was akin to a divine calling. Some critics disdained the book as unsophisticated, but the public loved it.

The reverence was understandable. Consumer capitalism created unimaginable growth and stability in America, which suffered through severe downturns and financial panics in the nineteenth century. It brought affluence, dignity, and cohesiveness, easing social tensions by giving working people a legitimate means of attaining a comfortable and secure life. Social mobility was achievable in a way it had never been in an agricultural society. More than a cadre of greedy business elites were interested in maintaining the economic engine; a wide political consensus developed around the idea that government should promote economic growth as a way of taming the devastating bank panics and slumps that had periodically plagued the nation during the past hundred years.

Consumption, Barton argued, would enrich the nation as well as the individual by helping a man to help himself. Salvation and perfection, once attained by aligning personal will with cosmic forces, was instead achieved by aligning personal will with the market and technology.

Barton's long face and curled pompadour was a familiar sight on the lecture circuit. In "Creed of the Advertising Man," a speech he frequently delivered on advertising's role in capitalism, he said: "Advertising is the spark plug on the cylinder of mass production, and essential to the continuance of the democratic process. Advertising sustains a system that has made us leaders of the free world: The American Way of Life." President Calvin Coolidge offered a similar message to the "Creed." In a 1926 address to the American Association of Advertising Agencies, Coolidge told his audience that they were "molding the human mind." Upon them had been thrust "part of the great work of the regeneration and redemption of mankind." Namely, turning citizens into consumers.

Aging in a consumption-minded world, however, is fraught. Consumer capitalism, after all, is more than an economic system; it is a way of understanding the world. It is supported by a framework of values which maintains that at the very core of human experience is a desire for what is new, an urge to push beyond familiar habits, conditions, and activities. Marx and Engels memorably captured capitalism's restless nature in *The Communist Manifesto*: "All fixed, fast-frozen relations, with their train of ancient and venerable prejudices and opinions, are swept away, all new-formed ones become antiquated before they can ossify. All that is solid melts into air."

Individual ads for creams and elixirs may cynically decry middle age by promising to ward off midlife wrinkles, but the system's preference for youth is much more elemental. Capitalism links aging with decline because the ethos of the market demands it. New is better. What is old loses value over time, whether music, fashion, appliances, or experience. Such judgments do not stop at the store's doorway but inevitably seep into the sphere of human relations, demeaning age. Advertising and mass industry did more than reflect youth's growing appeal. They turned what was new, and young, into a moral virtue, an economic necessity, and an essential ingredient of personal success.

The conviction that endless consumption was a necessary component of a stable democracy intensified in the ensuing decades. Throughout the 1930s, policy makers and businessmen believed it was the solution to the misery wrought by the Depression. After World War II, mass consumption was elevated to a global ideology, the creator and protector of America's freedoms and the linchpin of American supremacy during the Cold War. In this new "consumer's republic," shopping was more than an indulgence; it was an obligation and an act of patriotism. That same theme has carried through to the present century. President George W. Bush, in his brief address to the nation after the 2001 attacks on the World Trade Center, declared, "The American economy will be open for business," as a rebuke to the terrorists. A month later, New York mayor Rudolph W. Giuliani said at a news conference that "freedom to shop is one of the fundamental liberties, what terrorists want to deprive us of."

The Inferiority Complex

In obvious and subtle ways, advertisements in the twenties disparaged midlife and reinforced the link between youth and progress. Then as now, young people were assumed to be on the cutting edge, the essence of modernity, and so their actions and styles were celebrated in ads. "It's the younger crowd that sets the standard," a 1927 ad for Fatima cigarettes declared. "Go to the younger crowd if you want the right word on what to wear or drive or smoke." A survey of 167 advertisements in popular magazines that same year found "the ever-increasing trend toward dramatization and appealing to youth." Helen Woodward, a consumer advocate and author, recalled a lecture she delivered to the staff of a large cosmetics firm during her days as an advertising copywriter in the early twenties: "Remember that what we are selling is not beauty—it is youth . . . above all things, it is going to be young, young, young!" In 1928, Paul Nystrom, a marketing professor at Columbia University, commented: "The tendency for people of all ages is to dress in the manner of youth, to act as young people do, to think as young people do, and to make believe, so far as may be possible, that they are young people."

Roland Marchand summed up the impression given by the era's ads: "An observer from another century might well conclude, from studying advertisements alone, that men and women of the 1920s and 1930s lost the power of locomotion and upright stance after the age of 55."

Many businesses forthrightly denigrated the middle decades, knowing that consumers in their 30s, 40s, and 50s who worried about aging were more likely to buy products to slow its effects. From cornflakes to beauty creams to laundry detergents, the goal of looking youthful, or escaping the burden of midlife and old age, was the inspiration.

Advertisers reiterated the message preached by self-help authors like Orison Swett Marden that one's physical appearance could mean the difference between success and failure. In 1927, the term "inferiority complex" began to circulate. It was coined by the influential psychologist Alfred Adler, a onetime disciple of Freud's, to refer to a crippling lack of self-worth. William Esty, an account representative at the advertising giant J. Walter Thompson, noted in 1930 that the inferiority complex was "a valuable thing in advertising." Could it be, he wondered, "that this standardized age has made people feel inferior?"

Advertising was both a cause and beneficiary. Activate insecurities about middle age and you create a lifelong customer. As soon as one imperfection is eliminated or repaired, another inevitably pops up to take its place.

During the twenties, more and more advertisers shifted their message from a product's qualities to consumers' dreams and anxieties. Unspoken or half-formed fears about becoming outdated or devalued in an industrial society were articulated and confirmed in advertisements. The Laundry Owners Association inflamed women's disquiet that husbands, now enmeshed in the sophisticated world of modern business and away from home all day, would grow tired of their aging spouses. The 1924 ad promised that with the free time generated by sending out laundry, a wife could make herself more attractive to her husband by setting on a course of self-improvement to keep her "young-minded, fresh and radiant."

A 1920s ad for Gillette blue blades provided the perfect visualization of these anxieties: a worried man with noticeable stubble is surrounded by a half dozen accusing eyes. The copy read: "I was never so embarrassed in my life!" An ad for Williams Shaving Cream warned: "Critical eyes are sizing you up right now." Alfred Adler's term even showed up in the advertising copy for Lux soap: "No Woman need have an Inferiority Complex."

Divide to Conquer

Ads reinforced the same sort of age-related separations and classifications that were instituted in schools, civic organizations, factories, and governmental institutions. Christine Frederick, the columnist, marketing consultant, and Taylor disciple, was a forerunner of the sophisticated strategists who advocated market segmentation in the 1960s. In the teens and twenties, she advised businesses to divide consumers into three age-related groups: young, middle-aged, and old. She then further sliced the youth category into nine parts. Focus on the youngest tier, she suggested, because middle-aged women are too set in their ways to alter their buying habits.

The J. Walter Thompson agency organized consumers into different social and generational groupings. An internal newsletter circulated in 1924 reminded account executives that female customers fell into different categories: housewives, young girls and flappers, businesswomen, and the newest type, the "club woman," the middle-aged member of social and volunteer organizations.

Pollsters soon joined the cadres of experts who arranged the population into classifiable categories. George Gallup and Elmo Roper described their work as scientific and used statistics to split the population into subgroups based on education, class, age, and more. Their characterizations of consumers were distilled from national survey responses and treated like drops of rose absolute reduced from thousands of petals. Replacing God and Nature, the "typical American"—as filtered through the pollster's art—was considered a norm to which people aspired. Members of the public wanted to know what the "typical" middle-aged American was eating, wearing, and driving so that they could eat, wear, and drive it as well.

By the thirties, the very acceptance of surveys was considered to be a marker of youth and modernity. It was "difficult for many oldsters to adjust their thinking to this new instrument," Gallup remarked, but "few persons under the age of forty (mentally or chronologically) fail to see the value of polls." As for those over 40? Well, they are middle age.

Noël Coward captured how substantially attitudes toward middle age had shifted in his hit 1924 play *The Vortex*. The plot involves a middle-aged socialite who fancies younger men and her cocaine-addicted son Nicky (originally played by the 24-year-old Coward). Nicky and his fiancée, Bunty, comment on the reversal in attitudes toward aging:

> *Bunty: You're getting older*
> *Nicky: God, yes, isn't it foul?*
> *Bunty: Hell, my dear.*
> *Nicky: It's funny how mother's generation always longed to be old when they were young, and we strain every nerve to keep young.*

By consistently using the body as the frame of reference in which to discuss middle age, capitalists, scientists, filmmakers, writers, and admen reinforced the idea that youth was an object of desire and middle age an object of scorn. "In Europe, a woman at forty is just getting to the age where important men take a serious interest in her. But here, she's a grandmother," wails Fran, the youth-obsessed 41-year-old wife in Sinclair Lewis's 1929 novel *Dodsworth*.

Amid the nightmarish realities of the Depression, anxieties about middle age deepened. In 1932, a letter writer to the *New York Times* evoked the "despair and utter hopelessness of many middle aged" who visit the city's Department of Public Welfare because they had "passed the forty-year deadline." These men and women are "thrust upon the industrial scrapheap," he lamented, echoing the worries expressed by laborers in Muncie nearly a decade earlier. "This question 'After forty—what?' is without doubt America's greatest problem."

Walter Pitkin, a journalism professor at Columbia, defended midlife using an argument similar to one G. Stanley Hall had made in *Senescence* to a much smaller readership a decade earlier. In his 1932 bestselling book *Life Begins at 40,* Pitkin blamed the Depression on the premature advancement of young and inexperienced men in business: "How little even our brightest college graduates know about anything in their late twenties and thirties! . . . And this, I feel sure, is one of the chief reasons for our shocking economic collapse. . . . Study the inside records of some of the most tragic bankruptcies and ruined fortunes; you will find a startling number of men under forty at the helm of the derelicts." The complexities of the modern world require the experience and judgment of the middle-aged. "At forty, in brief, most men have not yet arrived and have not yet found themselves fully. The ablest are just coming into power and self-understanding. But even for them, the peak of achievement is still more than seven years away."

His arguments did little to ease the discrimination against the middle-aged that continued through the decade. In 1939, the Social Science Research Council put both the middle-aged and physically handicapped in the category of "hard to place" workers, warning that they would remain on permanent relief unless the government employment service did more to find them jobs. Four months after the report appeared, President Roosevelt gave a nationwide address against "an unfounded prejudice based on age alone," which was preventing men above 40 from participating in the nation's economic recovery. Mentioning World War I veterans in particular—whose average age was 46—Roosevelt declared April 30 Employment Sunday and the kickoff to Employment Week to highlight the importance of hiring these workers. The unusual proclamation, which the *New York Times* displayed on the front page, acknowledged widespread discrimination against those in midlife: "It is particularly important that those men and women who have reached the age where their family responsibilities are at the peak receive their fair share of the new jobs and are at least allowed to compete for those openings on the basis of their actual qualifications, freed from the handicap of an unfounded prejudice against age alone." He noted that a panel of labor and industry leaders had conducted a study and concluded that there was no justification for the bias against workers over 40.

The president appealed to employers, social agencies, labor organizations, and the public to give "special consideration to this problem of the middle-aged worker." Ministers did their part by extolling the virtues of middle age from the pulpit. "It is glorious to be middle-aged," the Reverend Elmore M. McKee told his congregation at St. George's Episcopal Church in Manhattan on a winter Sunday in 1939, because "we are in a position to consolidate gain and even to make gains out of all losses and mistakes of the first forty years."

Fears of middle-aged superfluity nonetheless continued after World War II, when younger GIs returned home and entered the competition for jobs. "How Old Is Old?" *Business Week* asked in 1945, referring to a surplus of aging workers. Resuscitating the rhetoric of the 1930s, Conard Miller Gilbert issued a call to arms in 1948 titled *We Over Forty: America's Human Scrap Pile*. "Now is the time to fight. . . . There are millions, yes, millions of men and women past forty who are seeking employment and who are barred on account of their age. These folks are the tragic figures of this era," he wrote. "The purpose of this book is to arouse the interest of every man and woman over forty so that they will join with their fellows in a nationwide movement to aid in the fight to earn an honest living."

Again, a federal commission reported that bias against these workers was not based on any diminution in work quality, but the perception that middle-aged workers were not as valuable stuck. Fictional portrayals of the middle-aged reflected the negative sentiments. Arthur Miller's *Death of a Salesman* premiered on Broadway in 1949 and presented an aching portrait of Willy Loman, a man who in midlife discovers he is no longer of any consequence in mid-century America.

How much the nation's attitudes toward middle age shifted since its emergence is starkly illustrated by Martin Martel's comparison of magazine fiction published in 1890 and in 1955. After carefully analyzing the differing narratives, the sociologist discovered that nineteenth-century stories regularly portrayed "mature middle age" as the prime of life, whereas the later ones clearly depicted young adulthood as the best.

"Age changes its meaning," Martel observed, "from the connotations of 'experience,' 'wisdom' and 'seasoning' to those of 'past the prime,' partly 'out of it,' and perhaps to some degree of being 'not with it.'" For men, "the change applies most of all to work roles where age progressively becomes a negative factor in open-competition with youth," he wrote. For women, "age becomes associated with loss of glamour and function."

The obsession with the physiological aspects of midlife never waned, a constant reminder of the middle-aged body's deterioration, but in the fifties a fresh interest in midlife developed in a wholly different sphere. A small group of researchers provided a new lens through which to view middle age: as a stage of psychological development.

Part II

Middle Age Is Rediscovered

7

The Sixties and Seventies: The Era of Middle Age

Erik Erikson, 1969

We cannot live the afternoon of life according to the program of life's morning, for what was great in the morning will be little at evening, and what in the morning was true will at evening have become a lie.

—Carl Jung (1933)

"Middle age is certainly the least understood phase of the life cycle, and in terms of its opportunities, the most misunderstood," Thomas Desmond lamented in a 1956 *New York Times Magazine* article. Desmond, a New York State senator and the chairman of the state's Joint Legislative Committee on Problems of the Aging, called for more study of this neglected and maligned period of life. "Americans slump into middle age grudgingly, sadly, and with a tinge of fear. As a result of this immature reaction to maturity we carelessly fritter away what should be truly the 'prime of life.'"

A pinched view of the middle years had reigned since the twenties. In popular culture, middle-aged characters were pathetic: figures of ridicule, like the overwrought husband in *The Seven Year Itch* (1955), who is tempted to cheat by Marilyn Monroe's vent-blown white skirt; or figures of pity, like the 50-year-old silent-screen star Norma Desmond desperately hanging on to her youth in *Sunset Boulevard* (1950). Biologists were interested in middle age only in regard to how it affected the functioning of the body's hormones, glands, tissues, and organs. As for psychologists, when it came to explaining human development, most took Sigmund Freud's lead and assumed that the first years of life were all that mattered. In Freud's view, individual personality—that complex blend of affinities, fears, quirks, and humor—was largely set by age five. Those who got stuck in one of the early psychological and sexually related stages that Freud outlined were fated to be burdened with it as adults. Smoking, drinking, overeating, or nail-biting? Must be due to an oral fixation traced to infancy. Social institutions, religion, and historical circumstances were disregarded. Most psychologists did not consider the midlife period worth sustained examination. Freud thought middle-aged patients were poor candidates for psychoanalysis because they lacked the necessary "elasticity of the mental processes" and were "no longer educable," as he wrote in 1905. It is not surprising an air of stagnation surrounded middle age; stasis was essentially built into the definition.

There were dissenters. In his eighth decade G. Stanley Hall, who had hosted Freud during his visit to the United States, argued in his 1922 opus that "senescence, like adolescence, has its own feelings, thoughts, and wills, as well as its own physiology, and their regimen is important, as well as that of the body." Doctors had explored the "physiological and pathological aspects" of aging; Hall insisted the "subjective and psychological" perspective was similarly significant.

As Hall was reevaluating the second half of life, one of Freud's closest disciples, Carl Jung, also started to question the narrow focus on childhood. In 1913, his bitter falling-out with Freud sent him into a disorienting spiral of confusion and doubt. At 38, he embarked on a four-year period of intense self-examination that ultimately led him to form his own comprehensive psychological theory. "I felt something great was happening to me," he wrote.

Psychological Types was published in 1921, when Jung was 46 and "the unbearable age" of youth had turned into "the period of maturity," as he later put it. The book contained the beginning of a coherent theory of middle age renewal. Reflecting back, Jung saw how misguided it was to think that an individual's personality was wholly and permanently formed during childhood. "The middle period of life is a time of enormous psychological importance," he wrote in 1933. Jung believed a person could retrieve characteristics that had been repressed, bring them to the surface, and successfully integrate them into his personality. The more mature man has had "his consciousness . . . widened by the experience of life." He was ready to search for meaning and purpose. In this sense, Jung's vision of midlife had more in common with the Calvinist view of aging as a spiritual journey than with the biological preoccupations of his contemporaries.

Neither Jung's nor Hall's ideas on middle age were expanded on or popularized at the time, and for decades the notion of psychological progress beyond childhood remained alien. Bernice L. Neugarten, a groundbreaking researcher of middle age, remembered that students in her graduate course on aging in the early 1950s "were amazed at the idea that one developed throughout life. Children developed, they thought, but not adults. The same views were held by most psychologists and by the public. It was generally assumed that you reached a plateau simply called adulthood and you lived on that plateau until you went over the cliff at age sixty-five." In 1951, when she was assigned to teach the first college-level course on aging at the University of Chicago's Committee on

Human Development, Neugarten was unable to find published material to put on the syllabus. "There were no psychology or other social science books on the topic that I can recall," she said, because everyone assumed development occurred only in childhood. "No one earlier had seemed to be thinking about development in adulthood—no one except Erik Erikson."

Erik Erikson's Revolution

Though Erikson was born in Germany, in his outlook and optimism he was a consummate American. He arrived in the United States with his wife, Joan, in 1933 after Hitler came to power. Speaking only a few words of English, the 31-year-old émigré nonetheless found America's eager embrace of progress energizing, and it influenced his visionary theories about how individual identity is formed. In this rapidly changing nation, the possibility of self-invention in adulthood did not seem strange. Erikson himself took advantage of the opportunity. He did not know his biological father and as a child took his stepfather's surname, Homburger. He decided to rechristen himself Erik H. Erikson when he signed his naturalization papers, taking advantage of what he called "the freedom in America to become your own adult." At 37, he created himself anew.

Erikson considered himself a devoted Freudian. He trained at the Psychoanalytic Institute in Vienna and had been psychoanalyzed by Freud's daughter, Anna. But his differences with the master were ultimately what turned him into one of the postwar era's most creative and influential figures. Erikson began to see development as a lifelong process. He also parted company with Freud's single-minded focus on the inner psyche and sexuality. Identity was the result of one's place in history and culture and one's shifting relationships with others, Erikson maintained. Parents not only affected a child's development; they were, in turn, enormously affected by their children.

Erikson felt the force of that idea in his own life. In 1944, Joan gave birth to their fourth child, Neil, who had Down syndrome. Shocked and bewildered, Erikson immediately institutionalized Neil while his 41-year-old wife was recovering from the difficult birth. Two close friends, the celebrated anthropologist Margaret Mead and the Jungian analyst Joseph

Wheelwright, both agreed that Neil should be sent away even before his mother had a chance to hold him. In fairness, little was known about Down at the time, not even that it was caused by an extra chromosome, and the prevailing medical opinion was that professionals were best equipped to handle such children. Though plagued by guilt and doubt, Joan did not push to reverse the decision after she got better. The couple told their three other children that their newborn brother had died, although there was no funeral or burial. The children were instructed not to mention the subject or ask questions. Many of the family's close friends first learned of Neil's existence when Lawrence J. Friedman published his biography of Erikson in 1999.

Erikson, who had been exposed to Jung's thinking on adult development through Wheelwright, had worked on a theory about the life cycle before World War II. After Neil's birth, he decided to return to the topic. Both Friedman and Erikson's daughter, Sue Erikson Bloland, believe that Neil's handicap and banishment were behind the couple's renewed compulsion to put together a picture of healthy "normal" development from childhood through adulthood, something their own son would not experience. Friedman describes their work "as a path away from the crisis of family dysfunction rooted in Neil's birth."

Although Joan had a master's degree in sociology and a deep interest in child development, she viewed her own role primarily as devoted helpmate to her brilliant and charismatic husband. Joan, born in Canada, had always assisted Erik with his written English, co-authoring or editing his books. This time, she took the lead in urging Erik to look more carefully at their own family's development, and collaborated much more closely with him as he worked on his ideas about life as a series of stages. Erik created the theoretical framework, but the two shared most of the work. "My life cycle theory" was "really ours," he said decades later.

Like her husband, Joan was skeptical of psychoanalysis's preoccupation with sex. She credited Shakespeare with a much deeper understanding of human nature and the interplay of social forces by citing Jaques's famous speech on the seven stages of man in the second act of *As You Like It*. The couple read the passage aloud to each other:

At first the infant, mewling, and puking in the nurse's arms:
Then the whining school-boy with his . . . shining morning face . . .
Then the lover, sighing like furnace . . .
Then, a soldier . . . quick in quarrel . . .
Then, the justice . . . in fair round belly . . .
The sixth age shifts into the lean and slipper'd pantaloon . . .
Last scene of all . . . is second childishness and mere oblivion.

They began to use Jaques's characterizations as a frame for their own ideas about development, incorporating experiences from case studies that had not previously fit into child-centered theories. In Shakespeare's verse, the schoolboy followed the infant, but in constructing their model, the couple inserted a stage in between that focused on play, when the toddler overcame feelings of doubt and developed autonomy.

Joan Erikson remembered the moment when she was first struck by the idea of middle age as a separate stage. She was driving with her husband in 1950 from their home in the Berkeley hills to the train station in south San Francisco. Erikson had been invited to deliver a paper at a White House conference, and he was scheduled to give a preliminary version to a group of psychologists in Los Angeles. They were delighted with their discovery of a stage (the toddler) that Shakespeare himself had missed. "We felt amused and very wise," she wrote. But then, "sitting with the life cycle chart on my lap while Erik drove, I began to feel uneasy. Shakespeare had seven stages, as did we, and he had omitted an important one. Had we too left one out? In a shocking moment of clarity, I saw what was wrong: 'We' were missing," Joan recalled, referring to Erik and herself, who had both turned 48 that year. The last two stages of the couple's schema were Intimacy, when individuals entered into a long-term relationship, followed by Old Age. "We surely needed another stage between the sixth and seventh," she said. Middle age was absent from their chart. (Shakespeare's ages did not neatly match the Eriksons' progression.) Erikson called the new addition the "generative" stage and generally referred to it simply as "adulthood." As he summarized in a lecture he gave in 1973: "In youth you find out what you care to do and who you care to be—even in changing roles. In young adulthood you learn whom you care to be with—at work and in private life, not only exchanging intimacies, but sharing intimacy. In adulthood, however, you learn to know what and whom you can take care of."

In the Eriksons' typology, called "The Eight Stages of Man," each psychological stage is characterized by a normal "crisis"—a conflict between two opposing personality traits—that could be resolved in a positive or negative way. Infants are torn between trust and mistrust; young lovers between intimacy and isolation. The psychological struggle of their newly discovered adult stage pitted "generativity," the "concern in establishing and guiding the next generation," against self-absorption and stagnation. A successful resolution meant, in Joan Erikson's words, wanting to "pass on to the next generation what you've contributed to life." This benevolent stage includes activities like raising children, creating a work of art, or mentoring an assistant on the job. Erik Erikson explained: "A person does best at this time to put aside thoughts of death and balance its certainty with the only happiness that is lasting, to increase, by whatever is yours to give, the goodwill and higher order in your sector of the world."

Erikson's conception of middle age seemed to owe more to philosophy than psychology. Nearly a century earlier, John Stuart Mill wrote in his autobiography that those who are truly happy "have their minds fixed on some object other than their own happiness; on the happiness of others or the improvement of mankind, even on some art or pursuit, followed not as a means, but as itself an ideal end."

A shortened version of the White House essay appeared as the seventh chapter in *Childhood and Society,* published in 1950. "Human personality in principle, develops according to pre-determined steps," Erikson wrote, and society encourages and reinforces the orderly unfolding of those steps. (The Eriksons added a ninth stage, wisdom, in 1988, when they were both in their late eighties.) Decades earlier, a rational system of classification informed Taylor's theory of scientific management and physicians' schedules of biological development. The Eriksons borrowed the idea of a prescribed sequence of stages from doctors and applied it to the process of psychological development.

Their depiction of middle age was skeletal, no more than two pages in the initial printing of *Childhood and Society,* but it was sufficient to build on. Erikson presented the first comprehensive model of how a person grew throughout the "life cycle," and he included middle age as a discrete and meaningful period. He profoundly shaped the emerging field of child development and laid the groundwork for a new field of adult development. Texts about aging and human behavior frequently date the "discovery" of middle age to this postwar period.

Assumptions that sentenced those in middle age to a steady, inexorable slump were upended by Erikson's theory. Midlife was not a period of malaise and rigidity but a work in progress, a phase as momentous in character-building as adolescence. Indeed, middle age, when one generation nurtured and mentored the next, could be seen as the period in which the most important work of an individual and a society was done.

In Erikson's welcoming model, generativity was not confined to a rarefied group of enlightened individuals like Gandhi or Abraham Lincoln. With effort and self-conscious examination, anyone could work toward a more meaningful life.

Erikson's book *Childhood and Society* created a stir. It spurred psychologists to revise theories about personality development and adaptation, and prompted sociologists to rethink assumptions about social change and influence. In 1961, Margaret Mead nominated it in the *American Scholar* as the most important book of the last twenty-five years. As significant in popularizing his ideas was Erikson's publisher W. W. Norton, which in 1963 issued a revised paperback edition specially discounted for colleges that helped to spread his thinking on campuses. *Childhood and Society* became required reading in many courses, exposing a large cadre of students to his ideas.

"Eriksonian became almost a household term on many campuses," Erikson's biographer Richard Friedman notes, and eventually turned him into a "culture hero." Erikson's writings about identity and nonconformity struck a chord. His daughter, Sue, remembers eating at a restaurant when a nervous waitress came over to ask for her father's autograph; she had read *Childhood and Society* in her college psychology course and recognized his shock of wavy white hair and Wedgwood blue eyes.

Of all the movements, fads, and enthusiasms that blew across campuses in the 1960s, perhaps the most surprising was the so-called discovery of middle age. Adult development, a topic largely confined to a small group of scholars at a handful of universities in the fifties, spread during a decade that was punch-drunk on the power and promise of youth. As student activists stood atop police cars to demand free speech at Berkeley or brandished guns outside the student union at Cornell, inside college libraries and labs, established and aspiring social scientists began, for the first time, to examine the second half of life, initiating research and constructing theories. New doctoral candidates, ever in search of virgin territory to study, found human development to be a vast untrodden field. In universities, middle age and other periods of adulthood shared a feature with new academic areas like Black Studies and Women's Studies. Just as race and gender concentrations were created to make up for the neglect of those groups in existing departments like English, History, and Political Science, adult development arose to correct the child-centered focus in psychology. Reading through the avalanche of articles, studies, and papers published in the sixties, seventies, and eighties, one can detect the incredulity of graduate students and researchers as they announce with astonishment that "no one before has examined" divorce, marriage, contentment, and a slew of other events and emotions that occupy middle age.

Ideas about adults' capacity for change also matched the spirit of the age. Deeply rooted beliefs and institutions were being yanked from their moorings and heaved into once inconceivable formations. Race relations, sexual mores, women's roles, gay rights—all testified to the possibility that human beings were capable of deep, even disorienting transformations.

In 1956, Thomas Desmond hoped that "a new discipline of 'mediatrics' [might] blossom forth to care for middle-aged folks . . . just as pediatrics had emerged to center attention on the care of children." His title never gained traction, but a decade later, the idea had.

The Second Wave

Bernice Neugarten was one of the first of the psychologists interested in adult development to focus specifically on middle age and, like a scholarly Pied Piper, she inspired legions of followers with her pathbreaking work. Born in 1916 in the small town of Norfolk, Nebraska, Neugarten stuck out like a sunflower among weeds. She took her first college course before turning 13 and finished a master's degree at 21. Unable to find a job as a high school teacher because she looked so young, Neugarten was glad to accept a graduate assistantship at the University of Chicago's new Committee on Childhood Development. She went on to earn her PhD in 1943. She then did something Erikson and many subsequent, mostly male, theorists had never considered: she took a break from her career for eight years to raise a family, undertake some part-time research, and volunteer in her community.

Only by happenstance did Neugarten later turn her gaze to adult development. After returning to the university in 1951, she was asked to teach a class on aging (and discovered the lack of any texts aside from Erikson's). The Committee on Childhood Development, renamed the Committee on Human Development, was expanding its focus under the leadership of Robert J. Havighurst, an education specialist who had worked with Erikson before World War II. Havighurst, too, was studying the aging process, and Neugarten ended up working with him on a new project, the Kansas City Study of Adult Life, the first community-based research to focus on middle and old age. For ten years, between 1954 and 1964, they and their colleagues followed more than two thousand men and women over 40.

The study provided Neugarten with something that her esteemed and honored predecessors lacked: data. Hall, Jung, and Erikson expounded on human nature, the meaning of existence, and the confrontation with death with enormous insight and creativity, but little actual evidence.

Neugarten used Erikson's theoretical framework, but her research provided a richer and more nuanced understanding of how people experienced their middle years. The presumption that individuals evolved over time was borne out. "Many people talk about how they grew up in new ways even after they were forty or sixty," Neugarten discovered. "No one says, 'I am the same person I was ten years ago.'"

And despite the culture's ever-deepening love affair with youth, the adults she studied did not feel overshadowed or sidelined by younger people. Americans might embrace hippies' studied scruffiness, salute the young's righteous activism, or recoil at their outrageousness, but they recognized that the middle-aged remained the "norm-bearers and decision-makers; and they live in a society which, while it may be oriented towards youth, it is controlled by the middle age."

Neugarten thought *Time* magazine was right—even if its conclusion was "less laboriously derived and more colorfully stated"—to feature middle agers on the cover of its July 29, 1966, issue and call them "The Command Generation." Listing White House occupants, Cabinet members, Nobel Prize winners, hundreds of corporate CEOs, as well as leaders in education, religion, science, industry, and communications, *Time* placed those in the 40- to 60-year age group at the center of influence. They are "the ruling class," the magazine declared, "that one-fifth of the nation between the ages of 40 and 60 (42,800,000) who occupy the seats of power, foot the bills, and make the decisions that profoundly affect how the other four-fifths live. . . . Even the revolt of the teen-aged is subsidized by middle-agers."

In 1967, Neugarten wrote up her findings from Kansas City and other studies and later included them in *Middle Age and Aging* (1968), a classic collection she edited that served as the discipline's first textbook for the growing number of universities and colleges that were instituting courses in this subject. (Martin Martel's comparison of the way middle age was depicted in magazine fiction in 1890 and 1955 was one of the selections.)

Because of her on-the-ground research, Neugarten recognized early on the degree to which women were transfiguring views of middle age. In 1966, the same year that Betty Friedan co-founded the National Organization for Women, more than half of women between 45 and 54 were in the labor force. (After age 20, women's participation dropped steadily as they stopped work to marry and raise children. It reached a low among 30-year-old women when forty percent had jobs, before rising again.) For women new to the working world, earning a paycheck meant they saw themselves as "economic adults" for the first time in their middle years (much as Gertrude Atherton had predicted). This development, Neugarten maintained, contributed to "the broad redefinitions of age groups" in America. "Most of the women interviewed feel that the most conspicuous characteristic of middle age is the sense of increased freedom," Neugarten reported in 1967. "Not only is there increased time and energy now available for the self, but also a satisfying change in self-concept." As one typical woman responded: "I discovered these last few years that I was old enough to admit to myself the things I could do well and to start doing them. I didn't think like this before. . . . It's a great new feeling."

Neugarten examined how society's expectations about the age at which someone should marry, have a child, find a job, or retire exerted significant pressure on individuals regardless of class or ethnicity. Deviating from this "social clock" could be discomforting, but it could also pry open opportunities. Neugarten's hopscotching around the expected progression of school, marriage, children, and career in the 1940s was extremely rare. By the seventies, though, notions of a smooth, predictable series of life stages were thrown topsy-turvy by feminism, a changing economy, growing divorce rates, and older mothers. The number of middle-aged women who landed their first jobs or returned to work after taking time off to raise children grew, as did their status both outside and inside the family. By the end of the decade, for the first time, a clear majority of women approved of wives working (even if their husbands did not). Many women went back to school and then into the workforce. In a 1982 study, thirty-seven percent of women who got a graduate degree were older than 40.

The aftershocks of such changes upended a boatload of assumptions about age-appropriate behavior. Middle age did not necessarily mean one was finished with child-rearing, settled in an occupation, or set in one's ways. Erikson's notion that generativity marked a new stage of nurturing did not sufficiently account for the fact that women had already spent most of their lives caring for the next generation at home and in school, and had channeled those energies into volunteer work after their children grew up.

The feminist movement, despite its primary attention to younger women, helped to widen the possibilities for women in midlife just as Progressive Era–feminism had in the late nineteenth and early twentieth centuries during the "Renaissance of the Middle Aged." In *The Coming of Age* (first published in English in 1972), Simone de Beauvoir dissected the way societies infuse different ages with meaning. Aging is both a biological and a psychological phenomenon, but the significance of any particular stage of life "is imposed upon him by the society to which he belongs," she wrote. "Every society creates its own values: and it is in the social context that the word *decline* takes on an exact meaning."

If middle-aged women were devalued, it was because society constricted their options. Embarking on a new path as an entrepreneur or oceanographer, an artist or a drummer, a passionate lover or global traveler was not a part of most middle-aged women's mental universe. Primarily typecast as mothers and housewives, in society's view they became functionally unnecessary after menopause and after their children had grown up.

The women's movement helped to transform middle age into a period of undiscovered possibility. As one woman wrote in a 1973 column in the *New York Times*: "It is pure gold to realize your life is opening up. You have freedom from and freedom to—just when you thought it was all but over."

The Midlife Crisis

While the women's movement gave middle-aged women a novel feeling of expanding opportunity and liberation, men's middle years seemed increasingly enveloped in gloom thanks to the appearance of a catchy meme that appeared in 1965: the midlife crisis. Of the many theories about adult development that arose in Erikson's wake, few have been more influential. This allegedly omnipresent affliction has remained a touchstone, a powerful presence in our imaginations if not our lives.

The phrase was coined by Elliott Jaques, a Canadian psychoanalyst and management consultant who studied with the child psychoanalyst Melanie Klein in London and later consulted for the Church of England and the U.S. Army. Unlike Erikson, who proposed a comprehensive model of lifelong development, Jaques concentrated on what he believed was a seminal turning point. He assembled a supposedly random sample of 310 renowned painters, composers, poets, writers, and sculptors—including Shakespeare, Goya, Bach, Gauguin, Purcell, and Dante—and then analyzed their art to assess at what age they created their greatest work. Jaques was investigating the same question that the neurologist

George Miller Beard had puzzled over a century earlier and he employed virtually the same flawed method. Jaques's project, nevertheless, differed from Beard's "Relation of Age to Original Work" graph in crucial ways. While Beard measured value in terms of productivity, a reflection of the era's industrial orientation, Jaques explored the psyche. The purely material evaluation of middle age was replaced by more intangible measures. To Jaques, the midlife crisis was wholly a psychological phenomenon. The cause was a new awareness of "one's own death, one's own real and actual mortality."

Jaques's conclusion that the midlife passage led to an artist's most impressive achievements squarely contradicted Beard's insistence that artists produced their greatest work before age 40. "Death and the Midlife Crisis," the enormously influential article he published in 1965 in the *International Journal of Psychoanalysis,* argued that a significant transformation occurs in their late 30s. There was a decisive change "in the quality of their work," the result of a midlife crisis, ranging from the mild and less troubled to the severe and dramatic. Despite the word "crisis," Jaques was in reality offering a counternarrative to the common story of slump that accompanied middle age. His theory was consistent with the classical view that connected aging to wisdom. He argued that men, recognizing the limits of time, could either be thrown into despair and artistic impotence or break through to deeper self-awareness and expressiveness. During the midlife crisis, he wrote, "tragic and philosophical content" emerged, "which then moves on to serenity in the creativity of mature adulthood, in contrast to a more characteristically lyrical and descriptive content [in] the work of early adulthood." The difference, say, between Beethoven's first symphony, written at age 29, and the ninth, composed in his late 40s and early 50s. Profound genius was midlife's territory.

Jaques's paper contained other familiar elements. G. Stanley Hall, too, had presented his "middle age crisis" in psychological terms. "The passage from late youth to middle age has many of the same traits as growing old," he wrote in *Senescence.* "We suddenly realize, perhaps in a flash, that life is no longer all before us. When youth begins to die it fights and struggles. The panic is not so much that we cannot do handsprings, but we have to compromise with our youthful hopes . . . . We lose the sense of superfluous time and must hurry."

To Hall, the midlife crisis could be triggered by an event. Nietzsche's, he said, began in August 1876, when he was 32, after a performance of Wagner's *The Ring of the Niebelung*. His disappointment in the score led him to think Wagner was not his long-awaited superman, an event that Hall believed prompted his descent into madness. In extreme cases, the midlife crisis could even lead to death.

Jung had also asserted that the transition in middle age was frequently triggered by a traumatically stormy period. The "severest shock" jolted one into wholly realizing one's self, but the end result was insight. In Jung's view, the full, authentic self could emerge only when traits that had been neglected or suppressed were integrated into the whole. A man might need to express the feminine elements of his personality, for example, or a shy woman might need to work on her more extroverted qualities. In midlife, people had to transcend their youthful preoccupations with beauty or lust and develop mature purpose and insight.

Resistance to aging was normal, but acceptance led to a breakthrough. As Jung wrote in "The Soul and Death" (1934): "Ordinarily we cling to our past and remain stuck in the illusion of youthfulness. Being old is highly unpopular. Nobody seems to consider that not being able to grow old is precisely as absurd as not being able to outgrow child-sized shoes. A still infantile man of 30 is surely to be deplored, but a youthful septuagenarian—isn't that delightful? And yet both are perverse, lacking in style, psychological monstrosities." Jung's description of this perverse arrested development are sounded in Aldous Huxley's dystopian *Brave New World* (1932) when "all the physiological stigmata of old age have been abolished," so that "characters remain constant throughout a whole lifetime" and "at 60 our powers and tastes are what they were at 17," with "no time off from pleasure," and no leisure to think.

People who successfully balanced their opposing traits sailed smoothly through middle age, Jung promised. Similarly, Erikson posited that the midlife clash between caring and self-absorption could be successfully resolved. Indeed, the very experience of a crisis, in the long run, was preferable to going through the period of identity formation without a ruffle. Jaques, too, assumed a traumatic transition. Poorly adjusted individuals, he maintained, overreacted to the midlife crisis with manic attempts to appear young, hypochondria, promiscuity, or a sudden religious conversion, the same kinds of responses Hall had warned about forty years earlier.

Jaques's term has been used as shorthand for disappointment and defeat, but that is a mistake. Like Jung, his conception of the midlife crisis did not assume a period of unending deterioration; rather, the crisis was the gateway to "wisdom, fortitude and courage, deeper capacity for love and affection and human insight, and hopefulness and enjoyment." A successful resolution resulted in artistic invention and a kind of spiritual transcendence. "There is no longer a need for obsessional attempts at perfection, because inevitable imperfection is no longer felt as bitter persecuting failure," Jaques wrote. "Out of this mature resignation comes the serenity in the work of genius, true serenity, serenity which transcends imperfection by accepting it." In Jaques's schema, the midlife crisis had a happy ending.

The positive spin on middle age was significant. Still, Jaques's theory was based on a series of dubious assumptions, such as midlife began at 35 and anyone not settled with nearly grown children by that age was suffering from a serious adjustment problem. He also insisted that the fear of death was the switch that set the whole machinery of the midlife crisis in motion, an assumption that has been proved false.

Women were shut out of the cathedral of the midlife crisis, just as they had been given the back hand by psychoanalysis. Freud had a particularly negative view of women over 40 and believed menopause triggered in them an Oedipal complex that focused on their sons-in-law. After menopause, women's characters altered, he wrote, and they become "quarrelsome, vexatious, overbearing, petty, stingy, typically sadistic and developed anal-erotic traits that they did not previously possess." Psychoanalytic interpretations assumed fertility was the essence of female identity and portrayed menopause as a "partial death," in the words of Freud's Austrian-American colleague Helene Deutsch, because it marked the end of a woman's "key life function as childbearer." Erikson adopted the Freudian assumption that women suffered from penis envy, and he often portrayed middle-aged mothers as neurotic. Jaques insisted female transitions were obscured by menopause. During the 1960s, female junctures were still primarily defined by biology: alterations in the face and body, the onset of menopause, or a shift in a woman's reproductive and maternal roles. Women escaped the midlife crisis for most of the twentieth century not so much because they were considered particularly well adjusted but because they were not deemed worthy of it.

Jaques's work engendered a mini-industry of research and writing about the midlife crisis. Two of the most influential were the psychologists Daniel Levinson and Roger Gould, who published their theories in the 1970s. Levinson, a student of Erikson's, undertook a ten-year study of forty men—hourly industrial workers, business executives, university biologists, and novelists—between the ages of 35 and 45. He concluded that throughout life men go through a series of regular and predictable periods of stability and transition (a term that, he later said, he preferred over "crisis").

Transition points are critical in determining a man's behavior, emotions, and attitudes, Levinson argued in his 1978 book *The Seasons of a Man's Life*. He defined middle age as occurring between 40 and 65, with a midlife transition between 40 and 45. Like Jaques, Levinson felt that the "experience of one's mortality is at the core of the midlife crisis." And like Hall, Levinson believed that at 40 a man has to "deal with the disparity between what he is and what he dreamed of becoming." He noted, however, that the most dramatic of the crises was not in midlife but around age 30, during "early adulthood."

Gould, a psychiatrist at the University of California–Los Angeles, was one of the few to include women in his studies. He pinpointed the midlife crisis a bit earlier, between 35 and 45, arguing it struck adults as they compared their own achievements with the tick of the social clock.

The midlife crisis gained a stable foothold in the popular culture of the seventies in a way that previous versions, like Hall's "middle age crisis," never did. One reason was that the midlife crisis had a powerful publicist. Gail Sheehy put middle age and its attendant crises at the center of the national conversation with her 1974 blockbuster book *Passages*. Sheehy adopted Erikson's central insight about the adult life cycle that people move across time from one transition to another. She then built on this framework of life as a series of stages with predictable turning points, borrowing ideas from Levinson and Gould, and including women in her narrative. She labeled the years between 35 and 45 the "Deadline Decade," when "most of us will have a full-out authenticity crisis." Her own midlife crisis was accompanied by "thoughts of aging and imminent death."

Sheehy, too, saw light on the other side. After a difficult transition, people can emerge into middle age stabilized, empowered, and content, she said, if they allow themselves to be "shaken into self-examination"; in other words, to effect their own transformation. Self-improvement was once again identified as the route to midlife happiness, just as advertisers and beauty surgeons had been saying for decades, but this time it involved the psyche instead of the physical body. Indeed, the intense preoccupation with personal fulfillment prompted the writer Tom Wolfe to label the 1970s the Me Decade: "Changing one's personality—remaking, remodeling, elevating, and polishing one's very *self* . . . and observing, studying, and doting on it. (Me!)" became an integral part of the midlife experience.

Sheehy created a sensation, but in the popular retelling that followed, important details, like the fact that such periodic transitions were normal or that crises were triumphantly resolved, were lost or minimized. The miserable crisis, like a toddler throwing a tantrum, received all the attention.

The vaunted discovery of a grim midlife segue seemed to go hand in hand with the increased political and social awakening of college students. Sheehy's book appeared after the United States had ignominiously pulled its troops out of Saigon, Nixon had resigned in disgrace, and the country experienced the worst economic downturn since the Depression, triggered in part by an Arab oil embargo as well as corrosive inflation. For men already in their middle years, vague intimations of sliding cultural primacy that came in the wake of the sixties' youth culture were supplemented by the sudden prospect of being pushed out of their jobs. Their unquestioned reign as head of the household was simultaneously threatened by women's demands for equality and liberation. In 1973, an article by the popular psychologist Eda LeShan, author of *The Wonderful Crisis of Middle Age,* noted: "Men seem to have been hit harder than women by the burdens of middle age. . . . [He is] uneasy if not terrified about his job and its future, the destruction of the twin myths of male superiority and sexual longevity have had devastating effects." Similar views were expressed in television documentaries titled *Male Menopause* and *Middle Age Blues,* which detailed men's vague feelings of obsolescence.

In the Long Run

In terms of researching middle age, the 1970s turned out to be a boom time. The behavioral sciences were growing up. New studies and ideas about adult development came together, each nudging the other forward. "It was a very exciting time," the psychiatrist George Vaillant recalled.

Fledgling attempts to study groups of children and teenagers that had been initiated years earlier were entering their fourth or fifth decade. Gawky 11-, 12-, and 13-year-olds who had lived in Berkeley in the 1920s; toughened Irish and Italian boys who spent the 1940s in Boston's inner city; and polished, highly ranked students from Harvard's class of 1941 had all grown into middle-aged adults. Such long-term, or longitudinal, studies provide a unique type of information; they allow you to see how someone evolves over time—whether a shy child is also a shy adult or whether intelligence scores shift. The very existence of these novel data sets attracted fresh recruits to study middle age, and prompted researchers to launch a new wave of longitudinal studies. Just as "the Child is Father to the Man," so was child development the father of adult development.

One of the early surveys was started in 1921 by Lewis Terman, the inventor of the Stanford-Binet IQ test, who recruited roughly 1,500 gifted children from California (later called "Termites") for an investigation of intelligence. The Berkeley Guidance Study followed 248 infants born in 1928 and 1929, most of them white and middle class, while in 1931 the Oakland Growth Study monitored 167 fifth and sixth graders. On the East Coast, the Grant Foundation began tracking 268 top sophomores at Harvard in 1939. The alumni have remained mostly anonymous except for a couple of outed participants, like John F. Kennedy and the former

Washington Post editor Ben Bradlee. George Vaillant later took over the alumni study as well as another project dating back to 1939 that included 456 inner-city Boston schoolboys.

Throughout the decades, these researchers and their successors followed the original participants, checking in with them at regular intervals through interviews, health assessments, and personality inventories. They monitored the men's physical and emotional well-being, their accomplishments and regrets, their personality traits and habits, and eventually their deaths. The longest-running studies included three generations: the subjects, their parents, and later their own children.

Vaillant declared that the Boston and Harvard men produced the first clinical data that confirmed Erikson's theories about lifelong personality development. He pointed out that annoying adolescent tropes, from acting out to sulky passive aggressiveness, had evolved into mature coping mechanisms like altruism or sublimation. "Such transformation becomes visible only through the vantage point of the prospective study of lifetimes," Vaillant said. "Once such studies are available, the evidence that defenses could continue to mature into late midlife seemed clear."

The ability to adapt, Vaillant declared, "is not the product of social class; it is not a product of I.Q.; and it is not a product of years of education. It has nothing to do with the color of our skin or our mother's schooling. Rather, the ingenuity of defenses is as democratic as our sex lives and our ability to play pool. And it has everything to do with increasing age." Over the course of someone's life, there are pendulum swings in outlook and behavior. Temperament may be more fixed, but character and personality are more flexible. As an adolescent, you might be reluctant to contradict your friends, while as an adult you are comfortable speaking your mind. "Our self-assurance, our tendency to criticize our children, our satisfaction with our lot, are highly inconsistent between ages 30 and 70."

Vaillant also concluded that the Harvard data undermined the fabled midlife crisis. Divorce, unemployment, and depression happen throughout adulthood with roughly equal frequency, he noted. "If such events occur during the dangerous, exciting ripening of the forties, we can pause and say 'Ah-ha! The midlife crisis, the dirty forties, menopausal depression!' but that is to miss the point. Progression in the life cycle necessitates growth and change; but crisis is the exception, not the rule." Looking back, Vaillant's Harvard men "regarded the period from 35 to 49 as the happiest in their lives and the seemingly calmer period from 21 to 35 as the unhappiest." The young men who had resorted to what he labeled immature emotional reactions to anxiety (like losing oneself in fantasy) had, by midlife, replaced those with mature defenses like creativity, humor, and altruism. In Vaillant's view, 20- and 30-somethings who anticipate middle age with dread and anxiety are like a 9-year-old boy who finds kissing gross, only to later discover the wonder and excitement of sex as he turns into an adolescent.

On the other side of the country, Glen Elder, a newly minted sociologist, considered the long-term studies that had been under the care of the University of California–Berkeley: the 1931 Oakland study, which revolved around the sample of fifth graders born in 1920–21, and the Berkeley study, which originated with a couple of hundred infants born in 1928–29.

When Elder looked at the older children, he was surprised by how many were able to flourish despite having grown up during the Depression's economic catastrophe. How, he wondered, were these Oakland children able to turn their lives around? Trained as a sociologist, Elder was inclined to look for social as well as psychological explanations. The particular historical circumstances had to be critical, he thought, perhaps even more so than the sequence of life stages that Erikson and others had proposed. In his now classic 1974 book *Children of the Great Depression: Social Change in Life Experience,* Elder argued that individual turning points occur at different ages in response to what is happening in the larger world. A teenager during the hungry years of the Depression might have less in common with a teenager raised in the affluent sixties and more in common with a 50-year-old who grew up during hard times. "Lives are lived in specific historical times and places, and studies of them necessarily call attention to changing cultures, populations, and institutional contexts," Elder wrote. The Oakland children who were young teenagers during the Depression fared much better than one might expect. They were able to understand what was happening and contribute to the household. The military rescued many from poverty and afterward marriage steadied them. This group "experienced the prosperous postwar years and many took advantage of educational benefits from the G.I. Bill," Elder explained.

Elder later contrasted the Oakland subjects with the younger Berkeley participants, who had spent their earliest, most vulnerable years in the darkest days of the Depression and their adolescence in empty households when fathers were fighting in World War II and mothers were frequently drawn into the workplace. The Berkeley children "hit both the Depression and war years at 'an untimely point' in their lives, and they followed a path of life-long disadvantage into the later years."

These long-term studies were a gold mine, but they had flaws. For starters, their creators did not necessarily assume they would continue for decades. Louis Terman, for instance, was thinking about bright children when he designed the questions, not middle-agers. Funding was scarce, limiting the extent of the surveys. Research methodologies and statistical computations were also not as advanced as they are today. The participants may not have accurately represented the population or been randomly selected. Similarly, Vaillant's findings were enlightening, but the experiences of privileged Harvard men could hardly be expected to apply to all Americans.

Elder realized some of these problems as early as 1962, when he worked as a part-time researcher at UC Berkeley figuring out how to code responses from study subjects. What struck Elder was that the information collected did not always match what he and others wanted to know about the participants: "How did they make it to middle age? Did they go into the military, into college? What kinds of careers did they pursue? And what about the impact of social change?"

Before the 1970s, most studies were organized around comparisons. Researchers could scan a list of facts describing a person on his tenth birthday, and then his twentieth, thirtieth, and fortieth, but they did not know why or how he moved from one to the other. The research offered a series of snapshots, not a moving picture. What happened in between was anyone's guess. "The intervening years remained a black box, open to speculation, not scientific understanding," Elder said, reflecting on this first wave of work.

Elder was intent on opening that box. Individual psychological development was important, but so were circumstances. Midlife could not be studied in splendid isolation but had to be located in the context of an entire life, grounded in a particular time and place, and situated in a mesh of family and community ties. "If historical times and places change, they change the 'way people live their lives,'" he realized. "And this change alters the course of development and aging. Likewise, changing people and populations alter social institutions and places."

Elder started by looking at a group of men in the early years of middle age, but his research led him to widen his frame and fit middle age into a larger panorama. The problem with theories that divided a human life into stages was that they missed the connective tissue. Erikson was sensitive to history and culture, but his Eight Stages of Man did not account for them. Elder wanted to construct a theory that would.

Other social scientists, including Bernice Neugarten, expressed similar reservations about age-based stages that uniformly proceeded in an orderly progression. She had only to look around. Feminism was propelling middle-aged women in new directions. Social strictures surrounding the timing of sex, marriage, parenthood, and careers were loosening. Better health and longer life spans were altering the customary path toward old age. In 1974, the same year that *Children of the Great Depression* appeared, Neugarten labeled the cluster of active, engaged people between 55 and 75 the "young-old" and distinguished them from the middle-aged and the "old-old." The emergence of the "young-old" was interfering with the familiar social clock, which she predicted would eventually help create "an age-irrelevant society." Neugarten built on Erikson's seminal work but eventually moved beyond a rigid notion of sequenced steps. "The psychological themes and preoccupations of adults, although they are often described by psychologists as occurring in succession do not in truth arise at regular moments in life, each to be resolved and put behind as if it were a bead on a chain," she observed. "It is therefore a distortion to describe the psychology of adulthood and old age as a series of discrete stages, as if adult life were a staircase."

Other kindred spirits also stepped away from the staircase. Pioneering psychologists like K. Warner Schaie and Paul Baltes, to name just two, were already at work constructing a more encompassing alternate theory of lifelong development.

The person who ultimately brought many of these leading thinkers together in the 1970s was Bert Brim, the man who would later spearhead the world's largest study of middle age.

8

Middle Age Under the Microscope

The original members of the MacArthur Foundation's Network on Midlife, 1992. Bert Brim, top row, far right.

Stage theories are a little like horoscopes. They are vague enough so that everyone can see something of themselves in them. That's why they are so popular.

—Bert Brim

The research revolution that gained momentum in the 1970s among social scientists studying the middle decades culminated in 1989 with the creation of the MacArthur Foundation's nearly $10 million, ten-year investigation into midlife. Sundry theories about middle age had been floating through academic circles and the popular culture for nearly a century: it was the prime of life, it was a depressing low point; it was stagnant, it was crisis-ridden; it was ruled by genetics, it was governed by circumstance. None, however, had been scientifically verified. Finally, here was a comprehensive, scientific, and interdisciplinary search for hard evidence that could clear away the thicket of conflicting assumptions.

The ambitious undertaking was largely the work of Bert Brim. Seated at his dining room table in Old Greenwich, Connecticut, Brim, now retired, talked about the path that led him to become the impresario of research on middle age. He was born in 1923 in Elmira, a small town in the northeastern part of New York, the baby of the family and the first boy after three girls. He enrolled at Yale, but left in 1943 when World War II spread to America's shores to join the air force and fly B-24s, the cumbersome long-range bombers. Brim, lean with white hair, paused for a moment as he remembered his days soaring over the Pacific more than sixty-five years ago. "Sometimes you look back at your different selves," he said, peering through the glass patio doors at the Long Island Sound as if searching for the younger Brim. "I don't recognize that self at all."

Brim returned to Yale after his military service and pursued his plan to become a novelist. He finished a tale of wartime adventure and, filled with confidence, took the train from New Haven to Grand Central to deliver his freshly typed manuscript to Random House's midtown office.

"Put it on that stack behind you," the receptionist said, pointing to a mound of tumbling boxes, envelopes, and towers of paper already creeping up the wall. A polite rejection soon followed.

He put aside his aspiration to be the next Fitzgerald and got a PhD in sociology at Yale in 1951. Later, he joined the staff at the Russell Sage Foundation, a nonprofit devoted to strengthening social science methods and theory, and became its president in 1963. Brim wondered how children internalize the values and behavior of their family and community. As he watched his young subjects, he realized that their parents were going through a similar process of socialization, learning how to be mothers and fathers. Adults increasingly claimed his attention, and as president of Russell Sage, a post he held until 1972, Brim directed research dollars toward establishing middle age as a bona fide field of study. One seed he planted was at the nonprofit Social Science Research Council, which organized committees to focus on cutting-edge topics. In 1973, he chaired a panel on Work and Personality in the Middle Years. This committee and others that followed gathered leading scholars like Paul Baltes and Glen Elder, who were trying to devise a better model to explain the continual process of growing up.

The approach that ultimately took shape has come to be known as life course or life span development theory. Despite many variations, at its core is the idea that human development is flexible and never-ending. Over a lifetime, shifts in behavior and personality are powered by an unpredictable combination of biology, timing, choice, chance, relationships, history, and geography—the decision to move to a city, the unplanned third child, an unforeseen financial bubble or military conflict.

None of these elements is particularly surprising. Common sense would lead most people to the same conclusions, but as a theory the notion was messy and unwieldy, spilling over the boundaries of any single discipline and any defined age group, characteristics that made it extremely difficult to research, test, or prove. Over time, however, it has capsized our understanding of how human beings develop. In 1998, the psychologist Anne Colby called the establishment of life span theory "one of the most important achievements of social science in the second half of the 20th century."

The idea nonetheless encountered stalwart resistance. Brim remembered the reaction to a 1980 collection of essays he co-edited with the psychologist Jerome Kagan titled *Constancy and Change in Human Development*. "Most Western contemporary thought" rejects the possibility of growth in adults, they wrote, but "in the new field of life span development, research on middle-aged and older persons indicates that personality and behavior are more malleable than most people think."

Their colleagues who studied children responded as if they were evolutionary biologists who had just been told that *Homo sapiens* evolved from chickens instead of apes. When Brim and Kagan presented their ideas at a large conference on child development after the book came out, Eleanor Maccoby, the field's grande dame and a proponent of biological influences, stood up. "You and Jerry Kagan are fouling the nest of child development," Brim recalled her saying with contempt. The audience clapped enthusiastically. "And as we were leaving the room," Brim added, "no one would speak to us."

The insistent debate over how much people are capable of changing in middle age was as much about human nature as it was about academic theory. Which holds sway: God or man, nature or nurture, biology or environment? The questions reflect two divergent views of humanity: one that maintains we are prisoners of our genetic inheritance; the other that sees an enormous potential for change.

Nineteenth-, twentieth-, and twenty-first-century thinkers have frequently held that human beings are bound by inborn limits. The neurologist Pierre-Paul Broca, the man who founded the Anthropological Society of Paris in 1859 (the same year that Darwin published *On the Origin of Species*), was convinced the size of the brain limited intelligence. After spending months in the dark morgues of Paris hospitals weighing autopsied brains, Broca used his measurements to support the conventional wisdom that men were smarter than women. Freud's theory that adult personality was permanently formed in the first years of life similarly rested on a belief in natural limits, as did the notion that men should not squander their finite supply of the vital "male principle" (semen), or that a human being was physiologically incapable of running faster than one mile in four minutes. Assumptions about natural limits underlay negative views of middle age and beyond—"the fixed period" that Anthony Trollope lampooned in his 1882 novel and that William Osler called the "fifteen golden years of plenty."

Notions of preprogrammed limits, often referenced to genetics, remain popular. A theory bandied about in the late 1990s was that the brain's critical wiring was completed by age three. At a 1997 White House conference on this issue, Hillary Clinton, then first lady, declared that early experiences "can determine whether children will grow up to be peaceful or violent citizens, focused or undisciplined workers, attentive or detached parents themselves."

Evidence may prove the fallacy of inherent limits as when Roger Bannister broke the four-minute-mile barrier in 1954, or when scientists discovered men did not run out of semen. But the belief often persists in spite of the facts because it is based on philosophy or politics. Liberals and conservatives both invoke theories of intrinsic limits, either to argue that there is no point in trying to improve immutable characteristics, as Charles Murray and Richard Herrnstein, the authors of *The Bell Curve,* said about IQ, or to press for greater government intervention, as Hillary Clinton did on behalf of young children.

Ideas about middle age can be just as stubborn, for they, too, are influenced by intellectual fashion and unrecognized bias.

Middle Age Is Official

As the eighties progressed, middle age, the neglected wallflower of development, attracted more and more attention. In 1980, the year Brim and Kagan's book *Constancy and Change* came out, four hundred scholars signed up to receive a nationwide list of research projects on midlife that the Social Science Research Council compiled. By 1984, the sign-up sheet had grown to eight hundred.

During those years, Brim and Baltes recruited ninety-five scholars to contribute to a six-volume series on lifelong development. "They were the first new publications of their time. There was no professional journal then about midlife and they were the principal resource around the early 1980s for ideas about midlife development," Brim said. "This work was the avenue that led to the MacArthur Foundation program in 1989." That was when Brim, who was receiving money for research on human development from MacArthur, noticed that the foundation had a task force—what it labeled a network—on children, another on adolescents, and a third on successful aging in older Americans. Absent from that lineup was middle age.

"It's obvious," Brim recalled telling the director of MacArthur's health program. "You guys are missing the whole midlife period. I mean it's not there. You need a network on midlife development."

The foundation agreed to create one, with Brim at the helm. Life span theory informed the research design, methods, and goals. No other significant national survey linked information-gathering to a particular psychological and social theory. To accomplish this task, Brim enlisted scholars from fields that had never bothered with midlife before. This cocktail of different disciplines produced a unique national survey. The team combined techniques to acquire breadth and depth. They gathered a large random representative sample of the population to question (an approach favored by sociologists, epidemiologists, and demographers), and arranged for small groups to be interviewed and observed at length (as is preferred by psychologists and anthropologists).

Interest in midlife had been percolating for a while, but securing the MacArthur Foundation funding was a turning point. The emerging political significance of a particular segment of the population can be traced through its mention in public pronouncements and programs. Political parties in the nineteenth century adopted platforms that promised to provide specific protection for children, citing their unique needs and vulnerabilities. In 1909, the same year that Ellen Key's *Century of the Child* was published in English, President Theodore Roosevelt hosted the first White House conference on children, which led, a few years later, to the creation of a federal Children's Bureau. By 1944, both political parties had added teenagers as a group deserving special consideration. The elderly's addition to the public agenda was signaled by the Kennedy administration's decision in 1961 to hold a presidential conference on the status of seniors. By 1962, every state in the nation had an agency on aging, and in 1963 the White House designated May as Senior Citizens Month.

In the 1980s, foundations took the lead in directing research and establishing new fields of study, and the MacArthur project sent a signal. "That really did put middle age on the map," Brim said. It was as if a fringe hobby suddenly turned into an Olympic event. Brim deserves a lot of the credit. David Featherman, a leading expert on aging and a former president of the Social Science Research Council, pronounced that "this enterprise established the legitimacy of a new developmental life period."

Midlife Without the Crisis

The intensive information-gathering from the nearly 7,200 participants between the ages of 25 and 76 occurred in the mid-1990s as researchers distributed questionnaires, conducted phone interviews, ran lab tests, and convened roundtables for intensive discussions.

At the end of the ten-year period, the MacArthur project—later included under the MIDUS banner—offered a detailed snapshot of midlife in America. The results reflected the more comprehensive and fluid life course perspective. "Midlife is more flexible than are childhood and old age," Brim reported. "It is less driven by a biological clock that causes the changes in childhood and old age. The same events of midlife can occur at different ages for different people. We know, too, that there is no set order, no series of stages, in which these familiar events may occur. There are different sequences for different people. Thus, though most of us will share the events of midlife, there is no single path that we all take."

Brim's team discovered that middle age wasn't so bad after all. The despondent empty nester, the crisis-ridden sports-car buyer, the stubborn closed-minded matron turned out to be much rarer than depicted in the world of prime-time television, films, and advertisements. "New Study Finds Middle Age Is Prime of Life," the *New York Times* announced when the results were released in 1999; "Study finds midlife 'best time, best place to be,'" the *Chicago Tribune* wrote. The *Washington Post* devoted part of a special section to the results titled "Midlife Without the Crisis." The ambitious project helped to transfigure the way we think of the middle-aged mind and body.

The research debunked a number of popular shibboleths. The notion that men abandon middle-aged spouses because they are programmed by evolution to pursue fertile, wrinkle-free maidens was discredited by the fact that most breakups occurred during the first eight years of a marriage. Divorce in midlife was relatively rare; when it did happen, women were more than twice as likely as men to have initiated it. Eight out of every ten men in middle age rated their marriages good or excellent, as did more than seven out of ten women.

For most women, menopause was a nonevent, just as Beauvoir predicted it would be once women were no longer confined to maternal roles. Nearly sixty-two percent said they felt "only relief" when their periods stopped, while fewer than two percent said they felt "only regret." Another twenty-three percent said they had no particular feelings about it one way or the other. Women also appreciated having greater control of their sex lives in midlife, with less pressure from men and fewer worries about getting pregnant, something often overlooked when the passing of youthful sex is lamented. Virtually no evidence existed that women experienced a diagnosable "syndrome" when children left home. An empty nest was simply another one of the stresses of parenthood, like hearing your baby cry herself to sleep or allowing your teenager to borrow the car, and one that has eased in recent years with the proliferation of cell phones and Skyping. In many cases the pangs of loss were countered by newfound opportunities for mothers to develop their own talents and interests. Men and women in the survey celebrated the independence and freedom they gained when their children left and noted that their marriages often improved.

The MacArthur network's innovative search for positive experiences enabled researchers to see how a narrow focus on disease and dysfunction had skewed results in the past. By testing for the six components of well-being, or *eudaimonia,* discussed in chapter two (a feeling of control, positive relationships, personal growth, a sense of purpose, autonomy, and self-acceptance), they discovered that pluses could counteract minuses. So while middle-aged women might have higher rates of depression than men, they also reported better relationships and more personal growth, which strengthened their psychological resilience.

Although many people made it through middle age in good health, problems with high blood pressure, cholesterol, arthritis, and expanding waistlines sometimes made their debut. Not having enough energy, sleep, and time were also frequent complaints. Offsetting these deficits, though, was delight in the feelings of control, experience, and being settled that middle age brought. For most adults, the largest source of satisfaction came from their friends and family.

MacArthur and the Midlife Crisis

MacArthur confirmed the skepticism that George Vaillant and other researchers had about the scourge of the midlife crisis. Less than ten percent of those between 40 and 60 underwent a turning point or crisis related to a looming sense of mortality, its defining characteristic. Turning 30 was actually much more disruptive for most people than 40 or 50 (an observation Daniel Levinson had made). Among respondents who claimed to have had a midlife crisis, the trauma often turned out not to have occurred during middle age at all. Like the phony psychics whose one accurate prediction is remembered out of hundreds of incorrect ones, the occasional midlife crisis perpetuates the belief that the phenomenon is an inescapable ritual of middle age.

Brim told me he believes that people have an internal thermostat they use to adjust their ambitions in order to maintain a happier outlook. The point at which motivated people seem most content is what he calls "just manageable difficulty," which he estimates to be a job that demands you work at about eighty percent of your capacity. "This intuitive process by which we constantly reset our goals in response to ups and downs is one of the most overlooked aspects of adult development."

"Middle age is not the period of high anxiety that we've been led to believe," he added. "For most people, midlife is the place to be."

Today, more than a dozen years after extensive discussions of these results in the media, what remains surprising is the tenacity of this fiction. The *idea* of a midlife crisis has persisted despite the lack of evidence that most people ever go through one. Initially, mistaken assumptions about the pervasiveness of midlife crises may have been due to researchers' tendency to study people who had come to a specialist for treatment. It was like surveying an orthopedist's patient list and concluding that nearly everyone in the population had suffered a broken limb. Alice S. Rossi, a sociologist and MacArthur investigator, suggested that the classic portrait of the sad-sack midlifer "may strike a future developmental researcher as burned out at a premature age, rather than reflecting a normal developmental process all men go through so early in life." The middle-aged men that Daniel Levinson wrote about in *The Seasons of a Man's Life,* for example, had dutifully climbed the social and career ladder in the fifties and early sixties, hitting middle age at the height of the countercultural rebellion when young people accusingly branded their generation as conformist, complacent, and inauthentic.

Their feelings of dislocation and unease may have been triggered by the social upheaval occurring at the time.

We have become conditioned to use the midlife crisis as the default explanation for any discontent or unusual decision. Ninety years ago, G. Stanley Hall recognized how age, like the older sibling who should know better, always got the blame: "Shortcomings that date from earlier years are now ascribed to age." So David Foster Wallace, a deeply insightful author, described a breakdown he had in college by saying, "I had kind of a midlife crisis at twenty." Media pundits in 2011 who described the actor Charlie Sheen's drug abuse, fights, and rants at age 46 as a midlife crisis ignored similar episodes that occurred in his youth, including shooting his fiancée in the arm when he was 25. And the Danish director Lars von Trier, already notorious for outrageous statements, suddenly blamed a midlife crisis for declaring himself a Nazi at the 2011 Cannes Film Festival. As David Almeida, a psychologist at the University of Pennsylvania and MacArthur researcher, argues: "Many of the stereotypical hallmarks of a midlife crisis, such as the sudden purchase of the expensive sports car, likely have more to do with middle-age financial status than with a search for youth."

There is, however, another way to think about the midlife crisis. The bare-bones outline matches an archetypical plot: a hero encounters an obstacle or turning point and is shadowed by thoughts of death, yearns for an Edenic past, and then emerges from the crisis with new insight. Stripped of its ageist sentiments, this heroic journey fits adolescents, and 20- and 30-somethings—like David Foster Wallace—better than it does those in middle age. Trying to return home from Troy, Odysseus has the equivalent of a twenty-year midlife crisis (or crises) before reuniting with his wife, Penelope. This universal theme could explain why the midlife crisis narrative has resonated so deeply and has been so hard to dislodge. Everyone creates a story about their lives, fitting events together in a way that makes sense. These tales are modeled on plots that we have heard since childhood. We choose which events are significant and how they mesh with our overall experience. "One spends a lifetime reconstructing one's past," the writer Brendan Gill observed, "in order to approach some tentative, usable truth about oneself by ransacking all the data that have hovered dimly somewhere 'out there,' helping to form one's nature."

The midlife crisis provides such a powerful narrative that people shoehorn their experience into that story line even when it is not true—labeling all significant crises as "midlife" no matter when they happened. People rewrite the past to fit their current understanding.

Not Your Average Middle Age

The MacArthur study constructed a portrait of the typical middle-aged American. That "average" creature, however, is only one character in midlife's story. America is vast and complex, and its inhabitants don't progress in lockstep. Thinking of the 1960s only in terms of radical youths without any reference to conservatives, for example, presents a distorted picture of that decade. Ultimately, "people," "Americans," "adults," "men," and "women" are always generalized stand-ins for a collection of quirky, distinct individuals whose experience of the middle decades varies widely.

In 2004, the *Annual Review of Psychology* asked Margie Lachman, a psychologist at Brandeis and a MacArthur veteran, to write a status report about the emerging field of midlife development, a kind of State of the Union address for the discipline. One of the biggest challenges facing researchers, she noted, is that adults in midlife have such diverse and varied experiences. Compared with previous generations, this group of middle-aged men and women is at the center of a much more intricate and sprawling web of social roles and responsibilities. The variety is compounded by differences in backgrounds, income, and geography. Divorce, aging parents, gay marriage, adoptions, and fertility drugs are contributing to the construction of novel family arrangements that are both stressful and enriching. "For investigators trying to sort their way through the growing stacks of new information, discerning patterns can be frustrating," Lachman concluded.

MacArthur researchers found responses often varied with location. When it came to describing the ingredients that contribute to a sense of well-being in middle age, New Englanders emphasized control, having no constraints on their ability to do what they want. Inhabitants of the West South Central region (Texas, Oklahoma, Arkansas, and Louisiana) reported feeling less nervous and restless, and more cheerful and happy. Residents of the West North Central region (Minnesota, North

Dakota, South Dakota, Nebraska, Iowa, Kansas, and Missouri) weren't as cheery but felt calm, peaceful, and satisfied, a level of contentment that researchers thought might explain the region's marked unconcern with personal growth. And in the East South Central region (Tennessee, Mississippi, Alabama, and Kentucky), saddled with the lowest levels of personal income and education, participants were in worse physical and emotional health, and felt less in control of their lives. The one area that Southerners reported feeling good about was their contribution to other people's welfare.

The network also underscored the stark gaps in health and well-being that class, wealth, and schooling produced. The poor aged much faster than their middle-class contemporaries. Like a coastal town punished by salt water and rain, impoverished people in midlife were battered by the cumulative effect of mediocre or curtailed education, joblessness, single-parent families, ill health, and poor care.

Educational divisions revealed other unexpected differences, as in definitions of "the good life." Everyone between 40 and 59 agreed that relations with others was the most important element of well-being, followed by feeling healthy, being able to enjoy oneself, and experiencing a sense of accomplishment and fulfillment. Financial security and having a positive outlook on life were also common responses. But college grads in their middle years emphasized being "able to make choices" and having a goal and purpose. High school graduates in the midsection of life tended to talk instead of doing the right thing and not giving up. It's about "endurance," said one respondent. "If things get bad, I just feel God is testing me to see what I am capable of . . . just hang in there, hang tough."

A similar class divide showed up in the MacArthur data on the topic of responsibility. Meeting obligations and attending to the needs of others were elements that nearly everyone mentioned. But middle-aged high school graduates frequently added "being dependable to others" and "adjusting to circumstances" on their short list. By contrast, those who attended college emphasized balancing numerous responsibilities and taking the initiative. "I am good at juggling multiple tasks. I have a family life that demands that, I have a personal life that demands that, and I have a professional life that demands that," said one mother. A man put it this way: "Life should be a balance, you know, of work, of fun, of commitments."

"Doing what I don't want to do" and "taking care of myself" showed up much more frequently on the list of social responsibilities cited by college graduates. "I take on the responsibility and I complete it, which is the reason, for instance, why I have stuck with being treasurer at church," said one college-educated respondent.

These definitions of social responsibility reveal a sense of self-entitlement among the college-educated group, who groused about interferences with their own happiness and their ability to control what happens in their lives. Underneath many of the answers lay the assumption that taking care of others depended on taking care of oneself first. "Typically what gets lost for me is . . . a sense of responsibility to myself, which would be, you know, just take a weekend off and go sit under a tree," said one overworked woman. Responsibility includes being "good to myself, responsible to myself," said one man. Without the gym and down time, "[I] build up a lot of passive-aggressive resentment." Compared with high school graduates, the college graduates were much more likely to draw a link between responsibility and self-improvement—twenty-nine to two percent.

Differences between men and women were evident in many corners of midlife, including the experience and effects of marriage. From their early 30s through their mid-80s, three out of four men had a ring on their finger; between the ages of 55 and 64, that figure rose to eighty percent, peaking among 65- to 74-year-olds, when eighty-two percent of men were married.

The marriage curve for women had a radically different shape, in part because men typically marry younger women. Roughly seven out of ten women between 32 and 44 were married. That proportion dipped slightly for women between 45 and 54 before sliding down a steeper incline. Sixty-four percent of women between the ages of 55 and 64 were married; for women between 65 and 74, the figure dropped to fifty-eight percent. By the time women reached the 75- to 84-year-old interval, only forty percent were married compared with seventy-four percent of men that age.

The glaring marriage gap between elderly men and women was primarily due to health. Men die earlier than women, leaving many more widows than widowers, although the gap is closing. Perhaps reinforcing this differential was women's ability to weather the death of a spouse better than men: about half of women over 55 who lost a husband reported being in good health compared with thirty percent of men whose wives had died. And while women over 55 who never walked down the aisle were somewhat more likely to be in good health than their married counterparts, the opposite was true for men.

Women and men with college degrees had a better chance not only of getting married but of having a happy relationship. Researchers also found a link between marriage and health, but they have not yet sorted out whether marriage causes people to be healthier or whether healthier people are more likely to get married. Either way, miserable couples lost out on any possible health benefits; they were no healthier than adults who never married.

Life Without a Middle Age

The MacArthur project attempted to probe more deeply into what life was like for racial and ethnic minorities, so in addition to the general pool of survey respondents, the investigators collected information from nearly fourteen hundred Mexican-Americans, Dominicans, Puerto Ricans, and African Americans who lived in either Chicago or New York City. Data about minority groups was still sketchy, but the information illustrated the unpredictable variety of midlife experiences.

Minorities tended to be in worse physical health than their white counterparts. Heart disease, cancer, diabetes, and high blood pressure visited middle-aged African Americans much more often than whites, for instance. They smoked more, slept less, ate badly. Death also knocked more frequently and earlier for blacks than for whites over 45. When it came to the psychological side of the equation, however, racial and ethnic minorities tended to be in better shape than whites. Confounding expectations, minorities enjoyed a greater sense of well-being, personal growth, and contentment with the way life turned out after the negative effects of discrimination or lower education and income were taken into account. Latinos who embraced their ethnic identity were similarly in better physical and mental health than those who did not. Trying to explain this apparent paradox, some researchers have suggested that the challenges minorities face sharpen their confidence and abilities—as the saying goes, what doesn't kill you makes you stronger. Racial and ethnic pride, embedded in tales of overcoming persecution, apparently offered a protective veil against life's knocks. Interpreting suffering as building resilience and offering redemption infused it with meaning.

Blacks over 40 who were surveyed also greeted the prospect of their middle decades with a sense of accomplishment. For poor black men, the pressure to prove oneself on the street eased and there was satisfaction in having made it this far without getting killed. "When you get to be 40," said Geoffrey Powers, a black man from Harlem, "life changes for the better. No more hotdogging. No more running around. I think it's time to settle down and just look after family." Katherine Newman, a sociologist at Princeton University, oversaw a pilot study in the mid-1990s funded by the MacArthur network that included extended interviews with working-poor African Americans in their 40s and 50s in Harlem. She found that residents of troubled and dangerous neighborhoods "look upon success as the absence of major failure. A middle-aged parent is to be congratulated if she or he has managed to raise a family where the children are not in trouble."

In Harlem, stable middle-aged men were in great demand but in short supply. A black woman in her middle decades who managed to maintain a job and save for retirement might discover that her relative security was accompanied by unexpected stresses. She was besieged by her children and an extended network of friends and family for help in paying for a doctor, a broken carburetor, or a new winter coat. A refusal to assist was often met with anger and disappointment. Being poor and single in late middle age frequently brought loneliness, guilt, and worry. In addition to their personal travails, African Americans in midlife felt as if they had to account for the social problems of their community in a way their white counterparts never did.

Many of the Harlem women found their strongest bonds at midlife not with a partner but with a daughter (rather than a son) and grandchildren.

Some had their first child as teenagers, an event that rippled through the family—an example of Glen Elder's injunction that one generation's decisions can have a fateful impact on others. That mother often found herself a grandmother in her 30s or early 40s; a great-grandmother before she hit 60. If their children were swallowed by addiction and joblessness, women in middle age had to raise their grandchildren. Many of the people Newman interviewed had migrated from the Jim Crow South and had opportunities their parents never dreamed of, yet they also saw fragile economic and social gains crumble when inner-city black communities were slammed in the 1980s by the crack epidemic and a recession. In this respect, these women were thrust back into the circumstances of early nineteenth-century farmers' wives whose burdens of childcare did not cease until they died.

Perhaps this is one reason that in this neighborhood black men and women in their 40s and 50s "never mentioned 'middle-age' as a period in the life cycle, preferring instead a long period of undifferentiated adulthood," as Newman observed. They had not adopted the "cultural fiction" of middle age, because it was not a useful benchmark. Much more important to them were history, place, and race—three elements that had been neglected before the advent of life course theory. This middle-aged generation was bound to look very different from the one that followed because their histories were so different.

The decade-long MacArthur project filled in many of the gaps and corrected long-held misconceptions about middle age in America. But absent from this still photograph was a story with a beginning, a middle, and an end—an unfolding narrative. That required following the same people over a number of years, as was done in the Oakland and Berkeley studies. More biological and neurological information from the survey participants and comparisons over time were also needed to answer puzzling questions about why some people remained healthy and engaged as they grew older and others did not. Did behavior in the decades between 40 and 60 mean the difference between a long, healthy life and a short, afflicted one? And if so, was there anything one could do about it? With middle age finally established as a legitimate field of social scientific research, in 2002 the National Institute on Aging took over from the MacArthur Foundation, rechristened the project Midlife in the United States, or MIDUS, and gave $26 million to turn it into a long-term study.

In this second phase, the reconstituted research team could take advantage of sophisticated cutting-edge tools to track the neurological mysteries of the brain that were sparking a flood of new research by scientists like Richard Davidson in Madison, Wisconsin. MIDUS II was in a position to expand the already impressive database by exploring the effects of aging on the brain and the intricate neural links between emotional and physical health.

9

The Middle-Aged Brain

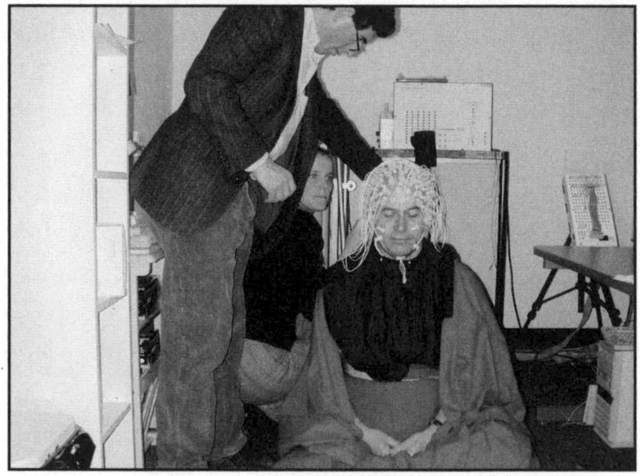

The Buddhist monk Matthieu Ricard gets his brain scanned by Richard Davidson.

"If you believe," he shouted to them, "clap your hands; don't let Tink die."

—J. M. Barrie, *Peter Pan*

In 2004, ten years after Bert Brim's team had started telephoning and mailing questionnaires for the MacArthur-funded study, now renamed MIDUS I, researchers began to reconnect with the more than seven thousand people who participated to ask if they were willing to continue with the second wave. Brim had retired and Carol Ryff, the head of the University of Wisconsin's Institute on Aging, sat in the director's chair. For the next five years, through 2009, MIDUS II researchers gathered information, building on the storehouse of data already collected. Five thousand of the original participants—now between the ages of 35 and 86—agreed to cooperate, while researchers recruited a few hundred more to replace those who had quit. Once again the volunteers fielded intensive and detailed questions. Researchers returned to the group that kept exhaustive daily stress diaries during phase one to see how their load had changed and what toll the previous ten years had taken on their mental and physical health.

The MIDUS II team also added a new series of assessments in order to more closely examine the traces of wear and tear that experience leaves on the body. Three times a year, 1,255 of the survey group journeyed to one of three testing laboratories at the University of Wisconsin, Georgetown University in Washington, D.C., or University of California Los Angeles to be measured and monitored so that a full series of physiological assessments could be added to the database. Immune and cardiovascular systems; nerves and hormones; blood, urine, and saliva were all tested. The volunteers were also asked to keep daily sleep diaries. Others wore what is known as an activity watch, or Actiwatch, to record sleep patterns during their visit to the lab. In addition to the hundred-page survey that all the MIDUS participants completed, this troupe answered a detailed, twenty-six-page-long questionnaire about how they had felt over the previous week or month. Were you happy, depressed, crying? Did you have diarrhea, a dry mouth? Were you able to control irritations in your life, or were you upset because something happened unexpectedly? Do you generally fly off the handle, say nasty things when you get mad, consider people who think they are always right irritating?

MIDUS II also launched two new studies focused on the brain that explored the links between cognitive ability and aging, and between emotional and physical health. By learning more about the brain's functioning, investigators hoped to uncover clues about keeping the mental gears smoothly turning and the body spry and diseaseless in later years.

One brain study was led by Richard Davidson, a professor of psychology and psychiatry at the University of Wisconsin. His research was the reason that I had traveled to Madison and lay inside an fMRI machine on that sweltering summer day discussed in chapter two. Davidson was interested in exploring the mind's inner workings to discover the links between emotional resilience and health. What he refers to as "affective style"—the various ways in which people respond to significant emotional events—is something that has been studied at every age, from babbling infants to the elderly. He had not intended to focus specifically on the affective style of middle-aged adults, but when the MIDUS headquarters relocated to Madison he saw an opportunity. The more he thought about it, the more midlife appeared to be the ideal age to study the connection between emotion and health. Despite claims that emerged in the 1990s that the critical window of brain wiring closed after age three, the brain continues giving birth to neurons, padding its insulation, and enlarging the maze of undulating pathways into adulthood. And the prefrontal cortex—located right behind the forehead; the place where judgment, personality, impulse control, conscience, and critical self-appraisal reside—is the last part of the brain to mature, sometimes not until a person's 30s.

What appealed to Davidson about studying the middle-aged was that they have had their share of life experiences. Their resilience has been tested. They have had the opportunity to learn how to better cope with adversity, and their reactions, repeated thousands of times over the years—to a delayed train, a child's accident, an overdue bill, a lost wallet, a split pair of pants—have etched themselves in the body. It is the perfect time to observe the diverse patterns of emotional reactions that people develop.

Davidson believes that coping effectively with adversity is at least one element of staying healthy. Chronic stress has been linked to cancer, type 2 diabetes, and cardiovascular disease. Recent experiments have demonstrated that just the perception of intense stress can make the body's cells age more rapidly—perhaps as much as ten years—by eating away the tips of each cell's chromosomes. The pressing question is whether people can learn to control their emotions and anxieties. Such composure is particularly important for people in their middle decades, when the stresses of family, work, and finances are at their peak and the physical wear that plays out in later years first surfaces.

MIDUS II offered an unusual opportunity to marry the bird's-eye view that large-scale surveys deliver with the detail and intimacy of laboratory research and in-depth interviews. Davidson could attach a hairnet of electrodes to the scalps of survey respondents to record electrical activity in the brain or slide them into his fMRI when they came to the university for other lab tests. "That's been a spectacular strategy," he explained. "I don't think that MIDUS has at this point even come close to realizing its potential as a unique research enterprise."

Davidson and his colleagues plan to follow their sample of 331 MIDUS subjects over the next five, ten, twenty years, and beyond. The process is comparable to one of the most famous and ambitious long-term health studies, the Framingham Heart Study, begun in 1948 by the National Heart Institute (now called the National Heart, Lung, and Blood Institute). By tracking the men and women who lived in Framingham, Massachusetts, and then their children and grandchildren, scientists have been able to explore the roots of heart disease. Over the years more than fifteen thousand participants have dutifully submitted to medical examinations, lab tests, and interviews every four years, helping scientists learn, for example, that high blood pressure in middle age was a risk factor for cardiovascular disease later on. Davidson essentially wants to do the same thing, but instead of blood pressure he is looking at emotional responses. "I am particularly interested in how life experience may play a role in modulating brain function, which then will be associated with physical health and illness," he said. The brain works on every organ in the body, and every organ sends messages back to the brain; we just don't know the pathways. By discovering the biological connection between the head and heart, Davidson hopes to detect whether the way in which individuals respond to adversity at 50 will predict whether they develop cardiovascular disease at 60.

"I've been interested in emotion my entire life," Davidson told me during my first visit to his office at his laboratory at the University of Wisconsin. Davidson is trim in khakis and a crisp button-down shirt. A wave of gray-speckled black hair surfs across his forehead. He has a low, husky voice that on certain words reveals his Brooklyn roots.

How, he wondered, were these insubstantial, immaterial feelings—

fear, anger, guilt, joy—produced? At 14, he was volunteering in the sleep lab at a local hospital, cleaning electrodes and trying to decipher electroencephalography (EEG) recordings of electrical activity in the brain. In high school, he read voraciously and became deeply interested in meditation. While at Harvard working toward a PhD in psychology, he took three months off to travel through India and Sri Lanka. In 1974, as most Americans watched Richard Nixon resign from the presidency, the 22-year-old Davidson and his soon-to-be-wife, Susan, were on a mountain in northern India for a meditation retreat.

He came to teach at the University of Wisconsin in 1984, and has since won a shelf full of awards for his psychological and neuroscience research, as well as a spot on *Time* magazine's 2006 list of the hundred most influential people in the world. In 1992, Davidson was surprised and thrilled when Tenzin Gyatso, the fourteenth Dalai Lama, got in touch with him. He had heard of Davidson's work through the Mind & Life Institute, a nonprofit organization in Boulder, Colorado, where Buddhists and scientists research the brain's abilities and contemplation. Davidson was on the board of directors.

"He was interested in having neuroscientific research on Tibetan monks who had spent years cultivating their minds," Davidson said. Behind his desk is a photograph of him with the Dalai Lama in his recognizable saffron and maroon robes. The Dalai Lama wondered whether the monks' deep and extended meditative training could generate compassion and more positive thoughts. Davidson accepted the invitation to visit Dharamsala, the Dalai Lama's residence in northern India during his exile from Tibet. In the psychologist's considerable load of baggage were portable electrical generators, laptop computers, and EEG recording equipment.

After the trip, Davidson said, "I made a commitment to myself . . . that I was going to come out of the closet with my interest in meditation." He had kept this passion a secret ever since his Harvard professors scorned it. "They patted me on the knee and said, 'Richie, this is not a good way to start a scientific career.'"

In the years that followed, the scientist and the monk have collaborated on a variety of studies as robed lamas have journeyed to Davidson's lab to lie on the scanner bed, as I did, and have their brain circuitry scrutinized.

Descartes versus Spinoza

Davidson is bringing the full arsenal of advanced technology to bear on the centuries-old mind-body problem. Since the Enlightenment, Western civilization has hewed to the model that the Parisian René Descartes set forth in the seventeenth century, with the immaterial mind in one realm and the physical body in another. "This I (that is to say, my soul by which I am what I am) is entirely and absolutely distinct from my body, and can exist without it." Davidson was dissatisfied with this formulation. Emotions were incorporeal, but something in the body had to generate them. They had no substance, yet they could cause your hands to sweat and the back of your neck to tingle. "I was interested in emotion when emotion was in the dustbin of American psychology," Davidson said of the 1970s and 1980s. "There were probably three people in the academy who were studying emotion and it was considered a real backwater, not at all tractable and really uninteresting. And it just seemed to me that was really an off-base view, because emotions seemed to be so central to everything that is important about our behavior. . . . People thought I was completely off the wall."

The twentieth century's infatuation with behaviorism—we are what we do—led scientists to view the brain as a miniature computer, an infinitely sophisticated mechanism for reasoning, calculation, memory, and language. Feelings were unscientific.

The very notion that emotions could be measured or studied in laboratory experiments seemed ridiculous. Besides, who cared? Most scientists did not assume there was any link between one's emotional state and one's physical health. And if one existed, the body was the source.

When Davidson embarked on studying the brain in graduate school in 1972, EEGs were state of the art. But in the last fifteen years, neuroimaging, particularly functional magnetic resonance imaging (fMRI) and other imaging methods, have revolutionized the field. Indeed, the influence of fMRIs has been compared to the impact of the telescope on astronomy. Of the sixty-one people employed in his lab, about one-third are physicists who work on new technology and methods. Brain imaging gives neuroscientists a much fuller picture of what goes on in our heads. Although our understanding of how the layer of gray and white matter works is still in its infancy, the glimpse inside has convinced most scientists that the brain and the body are much more intertwined than anyone suspected.

Descartes, it seems, was wrong after all—at least from the standpoint of today's neurologists. It looks like Baruch Spinoza, the moody seventeenth-century Dutch philosopher and excommunicated Jew, who never lived to see most of his work published, was right to argue that the mind and body are not two separate entities but simply different expressions of the same thing. In Spinoza's cosmology, there is only one unique infinite and indivisible substance, and that is God or Nature. "Spinoza prefigured in a remarkable way some of the ideas on emotion, feelings, and ethics that are now taking shape as a result of modern neuroscience," said the neurologist Antonio Damasio, author of the book *Looking for Spinoza.* Our emotions are, in fact, bound to our physical health and critical to our survival.

How that connection operates is still a mystery. What happens inside your body to produce that feeling of frustration when you get stuck in traffic, and how does that frustration cause your blood pressure to rise? How can the circuitry in the brain accelerate heart rate or weaken the immune system? Health psychology is the field that studies the link between emotion, stress, and physical health, but to Davidson "health psychology is a brainless enterprise."

"These events happen to you in the outside world and somehow they affect your health," he said. "But what are the mechanisms for how that occurs—that's never really been asked. From where I sit, the brain has to be in the equation, because the way the social world gets under the skin is via the brain."

Emotional Resilience

Through a series of experiments, Davidson and a handful of other neuroscientists have helped to upend more than three hundred years of thinking about the dualism of mind and body. In 1996, he and his colleagues published one of the first studies to show that disturbing pictures caused a response in the human amygdala. Davidson found that neural circuits in that region of the brain became particularly busy when people got angry, upset, or depressed. He discovered that negative emotions and stress set off the right prefrontal cortex, while joy and enthusiasm set off circuits in the left prefrontal cortex.

Davidson's early experiments with monks and meditation suggested it might be possible to purposefully alter the neurological activity in the brain and gain control over one's emotions. In one study, monks who had spent at least three years alone or about ten thousand hours on a retreat—the "Olympic athletes of meditation"—were monitored as they meditated in a state of "unconditional loving-kindness and compassion." They all showed an unusually strong pattern of synchronized gamma-wave activity, a movement of brain cells that is generally associated with concentration and emotional control.

Scientists interested in meditation were exploring whether it could induce physiological changes in the brain and the immune system. In 1997, Davidson convinced a few dozen workers at a biotechnology company outside Madison to learn mindfulness meditation, a method rooted in Buddhist practices in which a person trains to control his thoughts, and then identifies and banishes those that produce anxiety. Once a week, for two months, Davidson's associate brought meditation tapes and Tibetan chimes to the office and led a group of scientists, marketers, lab technicians, and managers in meditation for three hours. Before each session, their brains were wired and measured. Davidson's team found that the average emotional state of the employees had shifted into a more positive zone—that there were significant increases in activity in several areas of the left prefrontal cortex, the joy center, compared with workers who did not receive any training. One possibility, Davidson hypothesizes, is that neurons in the left prefrontal cortex are capable of blocking disturbing messages sent by the amygdala. Even more intriguing, participants showed signs of strengthened immunity; the number of antibodies they produced after a flu shot were higher than that of the control group. The experiment did not prove that meditation caused the boost to the immune system, but it did suggest that the experience of meditating might accomplish the extraordinary feat of modifying the brain's structure.

Stephen Kosslyn, a Harvard psychologist who has collaborated with Davidson, said this study "fits into the whole neuroscience literature of expertise . . . where taxi drivers are studied for their spatial memory and concert musicians are studied for their sense of pitch." Kosslyn was referring to an experiment involving London cabbies, whose famously rigorous training requires that they master 320 routes comprising 25,000 streets. Brain imaging showed that the posterior hippocampus, the peapod-shaped area related to memory, was enlarged. The more experienced the driver, the larger the rear hippocampus. Those drivers might have had bigger hippocampi all along, but Kosslyn believed there was another cause: "If you do something, anything, even play Ping-Pong, for twenty years, eight hours a day, there's going to be something in your brain that's different from someone who didn't do that."

Davidson is convinced that a cause-and-effect connection exists. "Neuroplasticity"—the ability of the brain to change—"is the most important idea in neuroscience in the last decade," he said. "More than any other organ in our body . . . the brain is built to change in response to experience." Scientists agree that the brain is more adaptable than anyone thought. What no one knows is how much more. Davidson argues that with practice people can learn to modify their brain activity through mindfulness training or meditation like the monks, who seemed able to control their concentration and emotions by generating synchronized gamma waves. These "neurally inspired behavioral interventions," as Davidson calls them, may reduce the danger of stress-related diseases like cardiovascular illnesses and diabetes later in life, as well as the premature aging of our cells. An experiment published in 2009 and financed by the National Institutes of Health suggested this might be possible. Researchers found that high-risk African American patients who meditated over five years were roughly half as likely to suffer heart attacks, strokes, and deaths compared with a group of similar patients who were counseled about diet and lifestyle.

In 2011, a group of scientists at Massachusetts General Hospital reported that they found direct proof that meditation was the cause of alterations in the brain's structure. People who meditated half an hour every day for eight weeks developed more gray matter, the densely packed outer layer of nerve cells, in the hippocampus and other regions of the brain associated with learning and emotional regulation. At the same time, the density of gray matter in the amygdala, the stress center, decreased. "This study demonstrates that changes in brain structure may underlie some of these reported improvements and that people are not just feeling better because they are spending time relaxing," said Sara Lazar, one of the study's authors at the hospital's Psychiatric Neuroimaging Research Program.

In Davidson's eyes, "there is no more effective way to produce localized and specific changes in the brain than behavioral or mental interventions."

The Middle-Aged Brain and Intelligence

Until the twenty-first century, the prevailing view was that mental decline started in midlife. There were reasons to think so. At around 40, the brain, with its 100 billion neurons, begins to shrink in both weight and volume by about two percent every decade. The ventricles, which contain the fluid that surrounds and cushions each part of the brain, protecting it from knocks and jolts the way an amniotic sac cradles a fetus, grow larger as gray matter disappears. At the same time, the spaces or fissures between the undulating grooves on the brain's thin outer layer become more defined. Connections between neurons thin out like male-pattern baldness, and the synapses—the places where neurons fire chemical transmitters—become increasingly sparse. The flow of blood and oxygen to the brain also begins to contract ever so slightly. Across the brain's white matter—those bundles of nerve cell transmitters that are wrapped and insulated in a fatty molecule called myelin—small lesions can sometimes appear. Myelin itself can deteriorate and the brain's ability to repair the DNA inside weakens. Most vulnerable of all is the prefrontal cortex, the brain's executive office, where high-level planning and organization of complex behaviors take place.

Such physical alterations sound ominous and seem to point to irrevocable loss. But that is far from the whole story. If mental agility declines with age, why then is wisdom, one of the most valued measures of brain functioning, consistently associated with old age?

Scientists began questioning assumptions about aging and mental decline in the late 1920s and early 1930s. Edward Lee Thorndike, a psychologist who helped found the modern field of educational psychology, was one of the first to challenge conventional thinking about declining brainpower. Drawing on his experience with testing subjects for the U.S. military in World War I, Thorndike later conducted research on adult learning, asking people between 14 and 50 to perform different tasks like memorizing passages of poetry. He concluded that there were no meaningful differences in the abilities of 25- and 45-year-olds, the early years of middle age.

In the 1970s, a handful of psychologists pointed out that conclusions about aging and mental losses were often based on the frailest and most impaired segment of the population, the five percent of elderly people who lived in nursing homes. Like the originators of the MIDUS strategy, they decided to examine what extra abilities might accompany aging instead of searching only for deficits—to look at the half of the glass that was full.

Other studies had design flaws. Some differences in test results between younger and older adults were due to the particular vocabulary used on an exam or a familiarity with certain professions rather than with age. Testing memory in the elderly and college students by asking them to remember pairs of nonsense words skewed against older people. Students, accustomed to competing in all sorts of tests, were keen to do well, while the elderly were not especially motivated to work hard to remember meaningless terms.

A more fundamental problem that has always bedeviled researchers is how to measure what is variously called brainpower, wisdom, mental acuity, or general intelligence. Embedded in all the political fights about bias in standardized tests is a conceptual question: Should intelligence be thought of as a single item that can be cleanly measured on a scale like a pound of beef?

Over the last three decades, research has established how simplistic much of the theorizing about intelligence has been, and that it cannot be accurately defined by a series of questions social scientists make up and label "intelligence tests." When people talk about wisdom, they generally include numerous attributes in the definition, including knowledge, analytic capability, open-mindedness, resilience, empathy, humility, and adaptability. This is why some leading theorists in the field, like Robert J. Sternberg, Howard Gardner, John Horn, and Mihaly Csikszentmihalyi, have promoted what has been called alternative or more flexible theories of intelligence. Wisdom is not simply having the ability to handle complex calculus; it requires practical and emotional savvy as well. Brainpower does not exist in a vacuum, sealed off like a computer in a climate-controlled room. That is the problem with intelligence testing. Most people do not naturally put the everyday objects and materials they use or are surrounded with into abstract categories, which is the type of thinking that characterizes a modern scientific perspective. This was an insight that Alexander Luria, a Soviet psychologist, had after traveling to Central Asia in the 1930s to study cognitive development. Luria asked subjects whether a "log" belonged in the same category as an "ax" and a "hammer." City dwellers tended to say no, that a log was not a tool. But in the Uzbekistan countryside, the residents said yes. "We say a log is a tool because it works with tools to make things," one responded. Another added, "We have a saying, take a look in the field and you'll see tools." On a modern IQ test, the Uzbek's answer would be marked incorrect, even though it points to a more flexible and perhaps more creative understanding of what a tool is.

Paul Baltes, one of the originators of life span theory and a member of the MIDUS I team, thought wisdom meant expertise in everyday life, what he referred to as "wisdom in action." In 1980, Baltes joined the Max Planck Institute for Human Development in Germany to help found the Berlin Wisdom Project and conduct research on what it means to be wise and how wisdom might be nurtured. His method was to pose hypothetical situations: "A 15-year-old girl wants to get married right away. What should one/she consider and do?" The wise response, according to Baltes, is: "Marriage is typically not a good idea for 15-year-olds, but there are certain instances—if the girl is an orphan, say, or has a terminal illness, or lives in a different historical period or culture than our own—when marriage might work out, depending on the girl's state." Observers may question just how meaningful these vignettes are, but they do illustrate an expanded notion of brainpower. In addition to intelligence, Baltes's definition of wisdom emphasized an individual's awareness of particular historical circumstances as well as the vast range of values and cultures that co-exist with one's own. The Wisdom Project chose the early 60s as the age when wisdom most likely peaked. Baltes, a frequent collaborator of Brim's who died in 2006, believed that in the brain experience could outrun biology. The notion that the brain is capable of continually changing in response to practical knowledge mirrors the underlying assumption of their life span theories that experience shapes one's psychological development.

Sternberg, a former president of the American Psychological Association and an editor of *A Handbook of Wisdom,* stressed that a quality like wisdom can be understood only in a particular context. Wisdom rests on values that are aimed at achieving the common good, a point of view that sounds remarkably like Erikson's definition of generativity, the caring stage of life reached in middle age. In Sternberg's eyes, wisdom is about balancing various interests and circumstances.

Such a definition has as much to do with a particular value system as it does with any ostensibly scientific explanation of intelligence. The influential Harvard psychologist Howard Gardner, who came up with a "theory of multiple intelligence" in 1989, insists that language and logic intelligence, which are generally what can most easily be tested, are not superior to the five other types of intelligence he identified: musical, spatial, personal, environmental, and bodily intelligence. Other researchers have turned to more metaphysical definitions and talked about "higher awareness," merging the spiritual realm with the intellectual. "Wisdom is a process versus a state of being," as one psychologist put it. This perspective on human intelligence differs dramatically from the one George Miller Beard gave in the nineteenth century, when he examined the accomplishments of history's geniuses and determined that their best work was done before age 40 or 45.

New ideas about intelligence have painted a much more positive view of middle age. One by-product of the widening definition of wisdom has been to jettison the belief that youth and cognitive ability always walk hand in hand.

"While the theme of youth is flexibility, the hallmark of adulthood is commitment and responsibility," Gisela Labouvie-Vief, a psychologist at Wayne State University, argues. "Careers must be started, intimacy bonds formed, children raised. In short, in a world of a multitude of logical possibilities, one course of action must be adopted. This conscious commitment to one pathway and the deliberate disregard of other logical choices may mark the onset of adult maturity." Looked at from an evolutionary perspective, perhaps there is a reason that particular mental skills improve in midlife while others fall off; the mature brain is confronted with a different set of tasks and problems that require another set of abilities.

The notion of the developing brain contradicts the assumption, held for most of the twentieth century, that the brain stopped progressing in adulthood. Just as psychologists assumed personality was fixed before school age, so did neurologists mistakenly assume nerve cells in the brain stopped growing in childhood, another iteration of the theory of inborn limits. With fMRIs, scientists can now see what differentiates youthful and mature judgment in the brain's circuitry, and, as it turns out, the passage of time endows the brain with certain advantages. Recently, neuroscientists have found that myelin losses in middle age can be offset and possibly superceded by increases elsewhere. Meanwhile, experience imprints itself into the mass of cells, carving new neural pathways and cataloging responses that can be called up as templates when needed, whether you are a London cabbie or a stranded tourist. Recognizing patterns that you have encountered before is one of the brain's most powerful tools.

Gene D. Cohen, the former director of the Center on Aging, Health & Humanities at George Washington University, illustrated the kind of original, creative thinking that can come only from experience. His in-laws, both in their 70s, got stuck in a snowstorm on their way to visit the Cohens in Washington, D.C. They couldn't find a cab and were unable to reach either their daughter or her husband by phone. Then they spotted a pizzeria and his father-in-law had an idea. The couple went inside, ordered a pizza to be delivered to their daughter's home, and then made an unusual request: Could they ride with the delivery man to the house? This type of thinking—the ability to extract a new strategy from a vast repertoire of previous experiences—is what is known as "pragmatic creativity in everyday problem solving," or, to use a more technical term, "crystallized intelligence." Heavily influenced by education, crystallized intelligence is distinguished from the more biologically based "fluid intelligence," which involves quick reasoning and abstract thinking. This may be why middle-aged people are often better in the face of adversity than 20- and 30-somethings; they have been through it before. What might have floored someone in her early years is taken in stride by someone in her middle decades.

MIDUS Looks at Brainpower

About a thousand miles east of Madison, where Richard Davidson is peering inside the skulls of test subjects, Margie Lachman and Patricia Tun, two psychologists at Brandeis University in Waltham, Massachusetts, are conducting the second of MIDUS II's brain studies. Lachman and Tun wanted to explore what activities or circumstances—from attending college to running laps to playing Sudoku—might protect mental abilities, or for that matter, diminish them. They reviewed the array of mental skills and selected the ones most vulnerable to aging. The duo devised a fifteen-to-twenty-minute phone interview consisting of several quick memory, verbal ability, and reasoning tests to measure these thinking processes, which they administered to 4,500 of the survey participants.

A trained interviewer initiated each assessment by saying: "We suggest that you close your eyes while you are doing these to help you concentrate. . . . Some of the questions will be easy for you, and some will be harder. We do not expect anyone to get all of these correct—just do the best you can." She then recited a list of fifteen words:

Drum
Curtain
Bell
Coffee
School
Parent
Moon
Garden
Hat
Farmer

Nose
Turkey
Color
House
River

Ninety seconds later, the interviewer asked: How many of those words can you remember? Numbers were next, only this time the subject was asked to repeat the series of digits backward. So for "2, 4" the correct answer is "4, 2." Now repeat these eight numbers in reverse order: "9, 4, 3, 7, 6, 2, 5, 8." Another test was like a version of the television game show *$100,000 Pyramid.* The interviewer named a category, and the respondent had one minute to list as many items as possible. Fruit? Pear, apple, grapes, and so on.

At the end of the handful of tests, the researcher once again asked how many of the fifteen words from the original list the subject remembered. Sometimes respondents were embarrassed when they could not recall very many, or worried they had failed. So interviewers were advised to reassure them: "Remember, we do not expect anyone to get all of these questions correct," or "Don't worry. We have deliberately made these questions challenging. If people could get them all right, we would not learn anything. We're trying to find which questions are harder than others."

As they expected, Lachman and Tun found that younger people performed better than the middle-aged on tests involving speed and memory. The middle-aged brain, it seems, is more easily distracted and has more trouble retrieving information. Where people in midlife excelled was in decision-making skills and verbal ability, tasks in which their experience and accumulated knowledge, their crystallized intelligence, could be put to use. Financial planning and vocabulary are two areas that show marked improvement in midlife, Lachman told me.

The preliminary results from their tests are not quite as upbeat about the abilities of the middle-aged brain as other recent research. The Seattle Longitudinal Study that K. Warner Schaie launched in 1956 has been tracking the mental abilities of six thousand people every seven years. The 2005 check-in showed that after repeated tests of six important cognitive abilities, middle-aged subjects from age 40 to the early 60s scored better on four of the six (vocabulary, verbal, spatial perception, and the most complex skill, inductive reasoning) than people in their 20s (who scored better on number ability and perceptual speed). Sherry Willis, a psychologist at Penn State University who co-directs the project (and is also Schaie's wife), reported: "For both men and women, peak performance . . . is reached in middle age." In those categories, people in midlife functioned at a higher level than they did at 25.

"Contrary to stereotypical views of intelligence and the naïve theories of many educated laypersons, young adulthood is not the developmental period of peak cognitive functioning for many of the higher order cognitive abilities," she said.

The discrepancy with MIDUS's results is puzzling. Perhaps one test is more sensitive than another at detecting a fall-off in ability; in timed tests, for example, younger subjects tend to perform better. The Seattle study did not add some of the most age-sensitive tests until 1997. Where the subjects came from and what generation they belong to may also make a difference. The Seattle participants all lived in the vicinity, whereas the MIDUS sample comes from across the nation (in which case Seattle may shoot up on Rand McNally's list of most desirable places to live).

"We just don't know why yet," Lachman said from her office at Brandeis. Some researchers think the brain may be capable of devising ways to compensate for a drop in memory retrieval and other tasks as it ages. Recalling a word or recognizing a face is an activity that occurs on the left side of the brain in young adults. Some lucky, high-performing middle-aged and older adults may be able to recruit both hemispheres or another region to accomplish the same task. Perhaps the brain is reorganizing its neural networks to compensate for weaknesses, just as a right-handed person might, after an injury, learn to carry out more tasks with his left hand.

Lachman and Tun, like Davidson, hope to discover what people in middle age can do to protect and strengthen both their mental and physical health. That task has taken on greater urgency in recent years as more and more middle-aged adults watch loved ones struggle with Alzheimer's and dementia and worry that their own mental powers might fail as they move into old age. The Brandeis professors are examining why some people in their 60s are as quick on fluid intelligence tests as those in their 40s, and vice versa. Is there something the fast-responding 60-year-olds are doing to keep their brains fit, or are the slow-responding 40-year-olds engaging in behavior that impedes their skills? How important is innate intelligence or education? So far, the professors have found that up to the age of 75, "people with college degrees performed on complex tasks like less educated individuals who were ten years younger." In other words, for those in midlife and beyond, a college diploma subtracted a decade from one's brain age. One theory is that native intelligence or education, or both, act like weatherproofing and add a protective coating against mental deterioration.

Most encouraging was evidence that people without a college diploma could build up this mental weatherproofing in middle age by regularly stimulating their minds—attending lectures, reading, writing, and playing word games. "They looked very different from other low-education counterparts," Lachman said; their brains appeared younger. The mental exercises seemed to hone the responsiveness of the brain's neural circuits. Using a computer was also associated with better brain functioning, particularly among people with less education. Those who spent more time in the digital world had better memory and reasoning skills, and they could process information and switch tasks more quickly, an element of making CEO-type decisions. It could be that searching the Internet or even playing video games requires people to multitask, shift attention, and coordinate motor, sensory, and cognitive skills in a way that bolsters brain functioning. People who were disadvantaged in terms of income and education seemed able to make up some of the mental workout they had previously lost out on, and therefore, showed the most progress.

Lachman cautioned that there is still a lot more research to be done, but she was buoyed by the results: "Many of the previous studies have focused on people who already have a good memory. One of the new pieces our study uncovered is that there is hope for those who need it most, those with less formal education, who are at greater risk for memory problems."

She and Tun also discovered another unexpected brain booster: confidence that you can influence what happens in your life. People who *believe* they are able to protect their mental functioning end up doing exactly that. The belief operates in a self-reinforcing loop: you do more to keep your brain healthy (like diet, exercise, and playing word games) because you think it will make a difference; and it makes a difference because you do more.

Lachman found the same phenomenon more widely when the latest batch of survey data from MIDUS II came in and she compared what subjects did over the course of ten years to stay healthy and happy. Feeling in control of your life (one of the six components of *eudaimonia,* that full-bodied flourishing) works on the emotional, physiological, and behavioral levels simultaneously by enhancing your self-esteem, lowering your levels of stress hormones, and spurring you to adopt a healthy lifestyle. After analyzing thousands of survey responses, Lachman discovered that, along with a satisfying network of relationships and physical exercise, a sense of control in midlife can dramatically reduce disability and preserve one's health and independence for years to come. Like Tinkerbell, whose existence depends on a belief in fairies, improving your health in middle age and beyond depends on the belief that you can improve your health in middle age and beyond.

Thanks to MIDUS and other research efforts focused on midlife, nearly every day brings new revelations, trivial and significant, about middle age. Unlike experts in the 1920s, who had a narrow physiological view, researchers have discovered just how multidimensional middle age is. In unexpected ways, MIDUS I and II have overturned the stereotypical view of midlife as a time of shrunken possibilities. Faith in self-improvement as a path to happiness has been a recurrent theme in American life. It powered consumer-driven prosperity in the twentieth century; it motivated people to surgically alter their noses; and it inspired Erik Erikson and other scientists to argue that human development continued throughout adulthood. Now we discover it is also an essential source of well-being in midlife. Trust in self-help is what makes self-help effective. People have more control than they realize over their physical health, their emotions, and possibly the structure of their brains—and the very awareness of that control is in itself a significant mainspring of happiness.

The directive to take charge of your middle age is increasingly heard in the popular culture as well, but in that arena, too often the message is about buying $100-an-ounce antiwrinkle cream or enduring hormone injections.

Part III

The Midlife Industrial Complex

10

Consuming Desire

Consumerism and self-help meet in modern advertising. A 1928 ad for Lysol in *Ladies' Home Journal*.

Middle age doesn't exist, Fast Eddie. It's an invention of the media, like halitosis. It's something they tame people with.

—Walter Tevis, *The Color of Money* (1984)

Millions of boomers who grew up with tired, compromised, and unappealing portraits of the middle decades marched into their 40s, 50s, and 60s determined to rehabilitate middle age. Their campaign has managed to mobilize more people and more resources with more singularity of purpose than the War on Poverty, the civil rights campaign, or the feminist movement. The advertising and entertainment industries and the medical establishment have been eager collaborators in the enterprise. In two decades, the concentrated effort has refashioned common expectations about middle-aged faces, bodies, and behavior.

These days, middle age on-screen and in magazines frequently looks good. Sometimes too good. It is thinner, smoother, sexier, wealthier, happier, and hipper. Women are as lustful as hormone-addled teenage males; men are boyishly charming and irresistible to women half their age. These perpetually improving midlifers tone their triceps and deltoids at daily six a.m. workouts, freeze their faces during discreet trips to the dermatologist, lunch at expensive restaurants, and hop into bed for multiple orgasms. Fictional middle-aged women look more like the affluent runway-ready sex addict Samantha Jones (Kim Cattrall) in the *Sex and the City* series and films than her fleshier, middle-class, similarly aged precursor Blanche Devereaux (Rue McClanahan) in *The Golden Girls*. Middle-aged men in films like *Wild Hogs* and *Grown Ups* can be adolescent, but their immaturity is endearing. This imagined middle age is certainly better than the cliché of a defeated man in a gray flannel suit with a frigid, nagging hausfrau, but it is not one that is meaningful to most people. As *GQ* noted when it featured a nude photo of 40-year-old Jennifer Aniston on its cover in 2009, "that body—well, as you can see it defies both time and nature." In reality, middle age is brimming with opportunities and disappointments that include the size 6 and the size 16, the enthusiastic entrepreneur and the anxious laid-off worker, the new mother and the veteran grandmother. These multiple middle ages are all part of the aging process, that "estuary that spreads and enlarges itself grandly as it pours into the great sea," as Walt Whitman called it. By comparison, the media-produced middle age is a tidy puddle, more suited to Stepford, Connecticut, the seemingly idyllic town where husbands replaced their wives with shapely, perfectly groomed robots as conjured up by the novelist Ira Levin.

The Stepford middle age for both men and women is unforgiving and narrow in its perfection, a standardized, 1,200-calorie-a-day, nipped-and-tucked version that is defined primarily by its appearance. It, too, is a "cultural fiction," one of the varied stories a society tells about the course of a life. And like its predecessors, this one has its own set of drawbacks, for it creates unrealistic expectations about the way sex, bodies, workers, and social status are supposed to look in midlife.

At the Corner of Self-Help and Macy's

The source of today's idealized archetypical midlife lies at the intersection of self-improvement and mass consumption, two of the most powerful movements of the twentieth century. Faith in the perfectibility of man through his own efforts, combined with the promise of the marketplace's transformative abilities, have molded our current conception of what it means to be middle-aged. Intimately connected, these two forces have formed—to crib President Dwight Eisenhower's phrase—the Midlife Industrial Complex.

This amalgam is a complex in both the institutional and emotional sense: a massive industrial network that manufactures and sells products and procedures to combat supposed afflictions associated with middle age; and a mental syndrome that exaggerates angst about waning powers, failure, and uselessness in one's middle years. Zeroing in on the physical body, the market whips up insecurities, creating a sense of inferiority, then sells the tools that promise to allay those fears.

The origins of the Midlife Industrial Complex date back to the 1920s, when America became a visual culture—what the poet Vachel Lindsay called a "hieroglyphic civilization"—and consumerism attached itself to the growing self-help movement. "She looks old enough to be his mother," two women remark about a friend in a 1928 advertisement for Lysol disinfectant. "And the pity of it is that, in this enlightened age, so often a woman has only herself to blame if she fails to stay young with her husband and with her women friends." The poor Lysol-less woman was not fated to a life of neglect and aging; she could have done something about it. In this democratic arena, youthful beauty is not confined to genetic luck or wealthy pampering; it is within everyone's reach, part of an individual's inalienable right to pursue happiness. As Helena Rubenstein reputedly said, there are no ugly women, only lazy ones. In the language of self-improvement, middle age doesn't simply happen to you; it is what *you* make of it. Here, self-improvement is more than a path to happiness; it is a responsibility. Pauline Manford in Edith Wharton's *Twilight Sleep* was a prototype, enduring "months and years of patient Taylorized effort" to ward off "the natural human fate"—aging.

Since mass marketing took off after World War I, youthful images have paraded across screens, billboards, publications, and imaginations. Two things have changed in the twenty-first century, however. Cosmetic medicine has advanced so much that less invasive treatments are able to effect startling alterations in appearance. At the same time, our digital world incessantly assails us with artificially maintained images of youth. The combination has ratcheted up disdain for signs of aging to an unmatched degree. "We have become so used to seeing perfect, unwrinkled faces," a 45-year-old woman from New Jersey commented to the *New York Times,* that "now when you see someone who looks like a raisin or a prune, it seems so unusual that you are almost repulsed." In the 2008 film *The Women,* Candace Bergen's character explains why she got a face-lift: "There are no 60-year-old women. I was the only one left." In some affluent circles, there is an antiaging arms race among women, described in Orange County by one competitor as involving "big boobs, blond hair, and Botox."

The combination of America's youth obsession and revised expectations about the new and improved middle-aged face have strengthened the link between employability and a youthful appearance. In Silicon Valley, Hollywood, and on Madison Avenue, employees feel added pressure to appear younger—just like the boilermakers and bricklayers who purchased hair dye a century ago. A 2005 Harris survey found that most men and women think it is important to try to look younger. Half of those polled agreed that a youthful appearance is necessary for professional success and for personal happiness.

The deep recession that gathered force in 2008 intensified fears of the "age deadline," bolstering the belief that middle age is a detriment. One Virginia clinic located near the Pentagon "donated" free Botox injections to unemployed workers in June 2009, an investment in publicity and future customers for when the economy picked up. Colleen Delsack, 47, was one of dozens who stood on line for the free facial freeze. The single mother had been out of work for eighteen months and her home was in foreclosure. "Age is a handicap," she said plainly.

As early as 1929, the German sociologist Siegfried Kracauer argued that cosmetics and other products created to improve one's appearance were a necessity for middle-class job seekers. Decades later, self-help authors make the same argument. "Looking hip is not just about vanity anymore," Charla Krupp advised in her 2008 book, *How Not to Look Old*. "It's critical to every woman's personal and financial survival." The women who make up half of the labor market are repeatedly informed that their economic worth as well as their sexual desirability are tied to a youthful appearance. "I have to look young," a Botoxed 50-year-old woman who works at an investment bank confided. "I work on Wall Street."

During the health-care debate in 2009, the National Organization for Women spoke out against a proposal to help finance universal health care with a five percent tax on elective cosmetic surgery—nicknamed the Bo-Tax. "They have to find work," Terry O'Neill, the NOW president, said of middle-aged women. "And they are going for Botox or going for eye work, because the fact is we live in a society that punishes women for getting older. . . . Now they are going to put a tax on middle-aged women in a society that devalues them for being middle-aged?"

When confronted by critics, O'Neill insisted, "The women's movement is not overly concerned with the more superficial aspect of clothing or beauty or fashion trends. I know a lot of women whose earning power stalled out or kicked down as they entered into their 50s, unlike their male counterparts', whose really went up." The numbers told a different story. The first year of the recession came down hardest on men, who accounted for three out of every four job losses. But O'Neill's argument reveals a troubling assumption that affects both men and women: that the middle-aged must employ artifice to deceive potential employers about their age. They must pass.

Assuming an identity that is not your own—passing—was once considered a desperate act that entailed profound sacrifice for society's most oppressed members. Blacks who passed as white sometimes cut off ties to their family, their heritage, and their true identity to gain opportunities that were otherwise not available. They were frequently seen as quietly complicit in a system that discriminated against them. Men and women who pass themselves off as young, however, are praised for their success rather than pitied for a lack of authenticity or moral resolve.

Passing can also be seen as offering moral redress. It undermines a system of prejudice by circumventing its dictates. It opens up opportunities that should rightly be available but are not. Still, whether as moral compromise or moral justification, passing involves a loss—the inability to openly embrace one's singular identity and originality. Gays may have been justified in passing for straight in order not to be dismissed from the military during the days of Don't Ask, Don't Tell, and educated blacks may make a rational calculation to hide ethnic names or "whiten" their résumés in order to get a job interview, but the question of why they should have to don a mask in the first place persists.

In an era of unwonted diversity and pluralism, the standardized conception of beauty has narrowed. Recent studies have found that more people preferred "a 'generic' face, a computer-composed *average* beauty rather than an *exceptional* one." William Ewing, the director of the Musée de l'Elysée in Lausanne, Switzerland, sees this as evidence that "a new form of homogenized beauty seems to be emerging as the norm." "A hundred years ago people demanded that photographs reflect what they saw with their own eyes: the standard was physical reality," he said. Now that retouching of photographs has become routine, "they demand that the material face and body conform to the standard of the image." Television series that offer plastic surgery makeovers or ridicule abashed participants' clothing while redesigning their wardrobes contribute to a contracted aesthetic and style. No one wants to look middle-aged.

The Power of Persuasion

The strength of the Midlife Industrial Complex derives primarily from the ability of the media and advertisers to set standards and manipulate tastes. In 1873, the *Bazar Book of Decorum* declared: "No devices to give a deceitful appearance of youth can be justified by the sense of fitness and good taste." But by the 1920s, women were embracing makeup to look youthful. Persistent marketing combined with glamorous images of penciled eyebrow arches and bee-stung lips that flickered from movie screens ultimately reversed the perception that middle-aged women should not use cosmetics to roll back the years. Recall that Gertrude Atherton, the author of *Black Oxen,* chastised the "fools" who refused to take advantage of science's marvels, saying they "deserve the worst that malignant Nature can inflict upon them."

This was the same strategy Clairol and other companies used a couple of decades later to alter the disreputable taint associated with hair coloring. For most of history, as P. G. Wodehouse once observed, the only cure for gray hair was the guillotine. Clairol offered an alternative and employed a two-pronged campaign to convince women of its benefits. One aim was to send the message that coloring hair was socially acceptable. "Nice women do color their hair," a 1943 Clairol ad declared. "Remember when rouge spelled 'hussy,' when lipstick meant 'brazen,' when nail polish branded you 'common'?" An ad for Eternol Tint Oil Shampoo said, "Lipstick was once considered daring . . . so was tinting your hair." Early Clairol advertisements offered Hollywood beauty secrets and endorsements by glamorous stars such as Joan Crawford.

The second prong was aimed at denigrating gray. "Because of her prematurely gray hair, Miss H was fast becoming known as 'the old maid aunt' . . . at the age of 32!" Clairol grimly related in a 1943 ad. Then Miss H "Chases Gray Hair! . . . Joins Younger Crowd!" Advertisements did whatever they could to promote the notion that aging was regrettable and gray hair its stigmata. In the 1940s, Clairol ran a series of ads suggesting gray hair was the cause of a wide range of exclamation-pointed social failures: "UNPOPULAR!" "WALLFLOWER!" "LOSING FRIENDS!" "PITIED!" all followed by the parenthetical question "(because your hair is gray?)."

In 1956, when Clairol came out with a new twenty-minute color treatment without peroxide, its memorable slogans—"Does she or doesn't she?"; "Is it true blondes have more fun?"; and "The closer he gets, the better you look"—did much to dilute the disgrace and artificiality associated with hair dye. Instead of glamorous movie stars, advertisements featured unknown models who were supposed to resemble the slightly more attractive woman next door—someone like you. Without color photographs to remind us, we have forgotten that gray was the color of middle age before the mid-1950s. Previously, roughly seven percent of adult women over 40 dyed their hair. Now nearly seventy-five percent do.

Fifty years ago, Clairol aimed to alter the views of women. Today, advertisers are working to revise the perception of hair dye for men. Commercials seek to build positive associations by using athletes and sex symbols such as the actor Patrick Dempsey. In one Grecian Formula spot, a man gets a job after ridding his hair of gray.

Edward L. Bernays, who is credited with founding the public relations industry in the 1920s, brought extraordinary perceptiveness and creativity to the job of molding tastes. A nephew of Sigmund Freud, Bernays had an intimate connection with psychological theories about subliminal desire and persuasion. He worked on the Committee on Public Education during World War I, stoking popular support for military action, and at the Paris Peace Conference in 1919, where the Treaty of Versailles was signed. He was impressed by the French people's responsiveness to pro-democracy slogans and recognized how susceptible the public was to manipulation. Like the adman Bruce Barton, Bernays was as much of a philosopher as a marketer. "This is an age of mass production," Bernays wrote in a 1928 article, "Manipulating Public Opinion." "In the mass production of materials a broad technique has been developed and applied to their distribution. In this age, too, there must be a technique for the mass distribution of ideas." But while Barton saw marketing as an engine of democracy, Bernays was an unapologetic elitist with a dim view of the general public. He believed a small group of elites, the "intelligent few," were necessary to oversee opinion-making in a democratic society. The new class of public relations professionals would use the principles of psychology, economics, and sociology to oversee "the conscious and intelligent manipulation of the organized habits and opinions of the masses" for the overall good. It was the only way to get "vast numbers of human beings" to cooperate in a "smoothly functioning society" and enjoy continued economic prosperity. In his book *Propaganda,* Bernays explained that it was impossible for each person to individually investigate every political, economic, and ethical issue or test every product in the market. Instead, we have agreed to let an "invisible government" do it for us. From our leaders—be they essayists, teachers, ministers, or "prevailing opinion"—"we accept a standardized code of social conduct, to which we conform most of the time," just as factory workers were expected to conform to Taylorized standards. Bernays's views were widely adopted by the industry. As one trade press put it: "Those in control *can* improve the taste of the mob."

When George Washington Hill, the president of the American Tobacco Company, discovered that women weren't buying Lucky Strikes in the early 1930s, he called Bernays. Women told surveyors that the cigarette's dark green packaging clashed with their outfits, but having spent millions branding Lucky's green design, Hill was not about to switch to a different one. Bernays's response? "If you won't change the color of the package, change the color of fashion—to green." And so he did, organizing a Green Ball in 1934 with a society figure who commissioned Paris fashion designers to create emerald-colored gowns. He put together a Color Fashion Bureau that fed stories to the press about the new green trend, and sponsored a Green Fashions luncheon for fashion editors, with art and psychology experts to expound on the significance of the color.

Bernays understood how effectively marketing could guide opinions about what is normal, rude, desirable, or deviant. Ads can exploit long-standing urges (the quest for youth), establish new ones (being hip), and fan free-floating worries, impressions, and biases (do I look too old to get this job?). They can make a commonplace item seem outdated and turn disdain into desire. Objects, even trivial ones, are animated with meaning. Marketers provide the narratives. They create fairy tales, in which a flask of hair tonic or a bowl of oat bran functions as a handful of magic beans; and cautionary fables, in which the failure to use a stick of deodorant or a teeth whitener loses you the girl, the job of your dreams, and the approval of your friends. Science makes magical transformation possible. The modern marketplace expanded from quantifiable materials and services to intangibles like beauty, confidence, and social conscience until desire and imagination supplanted necessity as the mother of invention.

The consultant Paco Underhill describes shopping as "a method of becoming a newer, perhaps even slightly improved person. The products you buy turn you into that other, idealized version of yourself: That dress makes you beautiful, this lipstick makes you kissable, that lamp turns your house into an elegant showplace."

In moderation, the power of consumption to enrich daily comfort and sensibility is one of the great luxuries capitalism provides. Yet there is a danger in infusing products with too much meaning. In his classic 1979 critique *The Culture of Narcissism,* Christopher Lasch perceptively argued that consumers want "to find a meaning in life," and advertising "upholds consumption as the answer to the age-old discontents of loneliness, sickness, weariness, lack of sexual satisfaction." Sixties radicals expressed a rebellious individualism by buying mass-produced goods, and in the nineties "Bourgeois Bohemians" flaunted a commitment to environmental sustainability—"conspicuous conservation"—by buying expensive products with ecofriendly labels.

The middle-aged version combines happiness with virtue. This connection is one that surfaced when college graduates talked to MIDUS researchers about social responsibility, mentioning that taking care of themselves was a prerequisite for taking care of others. Taking responsibility for personal health should be vigorously encouraged, but the Midlife Industrial Complex transforms this impulse into anxiety about aging. Responding to the pressure to mask signs of middle age and look more youthful is cast as a civic obligation, as when Rubenstein scolded women for being lazy if they did not utilize the market's bounty to make themselves beautiful.

Consumption as activism has obvious appeal. For one, it infuses our daily transactions with meaning, elevating them above the narcissistic function that Lasch excoriated. It also satisfies a fundamental need: the very act of buying can give people a sense of control, not only because financial resources are a tangible buffer against bad fortune but because it can create the illusion of potency. Even if the wrinkle cream doesn't work or the drooping stomach remains under the camouflage of clothing, at least you have the satisfaction of knowing you took action instead of sitting passively, listening to the clock tick. As MIDUS studies demonstrated, a feeling of control is both a source of satisfaction and a spur to improve your health.

Middle age is hardly the first vehicle that marketers have used to turn happiness, respect, youth, and self-confidence into commodities. But the number and power of the generation who currently occupy this tier have given midlife's consuming desire a new prominence and influence. Products and procedures that once lay outside the glossy ring of everyday consumption have been pulled inside. Many surgeons and clients consider plastic surgery a kin of any other luxury commodity available to aspiring Americans. One Beverly Hills plastic surgeon recounted, "One of my patients said: 'I financed my car. Why shouldn't I finance my face?' . . . Plastic surgery is another high-ticket item you put on credit and pay for later." Among their clients are working-class people who would not have considered such expensive treatments without the lure of easy loans. ("Don't wait to enjoy the benefits of plastic surgery," one website urged. "You can qualify for a loan in as little as 30 seconds.") After the financial crisis tightened credit, some surgeons offered layaway plans.

Reality makeover shows normalize the idea of plastic surgery and other extreme cosmetic treatments in the pursuit of a youthful appearance. The overwhelming majority of American women, seventy percent, say they would never consider plastic surgery. That figure seems surprising given the operation's ubiquity on-screen. Four out of five patients who went under the knife said they had been "directly influenced to have a procedure by the plastic surgery reality-television shows they watch." Although viewers see the bandaged, pained expressions of patients, the brief summary of their recovery (followed by further alterations effected through makeup and clothes) minimizes the surgical risks. A perfectly sculpted middle age, no matter the physical, financial, and emotional price, is promoted as a universal dream.

Plastic surgery, an expensive luxury, bounced back during the recession, according to the American Society for Aesthetic Plastic Surgery. The number of operations grew to 1.6 million in 2010, a hike of nearly nine percent in one year. Newer nonsurgical treatments, including Botox and facial fillers, are far more popular, although they were more affected by the economic downturn. The number of these procedures dropped by nearly nine percent to 9.5 million in 2010. (Although the percentage of male customers has been growing, men still accounted for fewer than one in ten procedures.) Altogether, Americans, most of them middle-aged, spent nearly $10.7 billion on cosmetic procedures.

Companies that manufacture these pharmaceutical products, not to mention over-the-counter cosmetics, invest millions of dollars to convince people that wrinkles and sagging skin, like nearsightedness or a chipped tooth, should be treated or repaired as a matter of course. High-end sports clubs have cosmetic dermatologists on staff to suggest laser facials and injections to clients. "You do your hair, right?" a doctor at a day spa asks. "Why wouldn't you do your face?"

Botulinum toxin type A, more commonly known by its brand names Botox and Dysport, is a neurotoxin that eliminates lines by temporarily interrupting the connection between the nerves and muscles. It is the number one minimally invasive cosmetic procedure in the country. The widespread use among actors over 35 has directors bemoaning the eerie absence of facial expressiveness. More troubling is a 2011 study that found Botox reduces a person's ability to empathize with others because it erases the ability to mimic facial expressions.

For Allergan, the manufacturer of the biggest seller, Botox, middle age has proved to be an enormous marketing opportunity. Originally created to treat strabismus, a condition in which the eyes are not properly aligned, Botox was first used in the mid-1990s to paralyze facial muscles, even before the FDA formally approved it for cosmetic use in 2002. Since then, purchases of the injectable have leaped up year after year with total net sales expected to pass $1.5 billion in 2011. More than a name, the brand has become a signifier for a lifestyle and an attitude. Allergan was eager to repeat its success with a product it introduced in 2008, Juvéderm, an injectable hyaluronic acid used to fill in or plump out lines and wrinkles. Its ad campaign serves as a case study of how a company goes about redefining the look of middle age.

Consumerize It

"Forty is the sweet spot," says Caroline Van Hove, Allergan's director of marketing. That's when women and, to a lesser extent, men become interested in what Van Hove calls "middle age" cosmetic treatments.

Dressed in a lapis blue blouse and black pants, Van Hove is thin, with blond hair and eyelashes as thick and long as spider legs. They are, she reveals with a conspiratorial smile, the result of using Latisse, the company's new eyelash lengthener. "Juvéderm was a challenge to the marketing team in the U.S.," Van Hove explained. While Botox had completely dominated the market for more than a decade, Juvéderm was a newcomer. A competitor, Restylane, was already well established as a popular alternative to more radical surgical procedures. Other firms were similarly trying to wriggle their way into the American market. Allergan not only had to get Juvéderm noticed, it had to differentiate it from other skin plumpers.

"The beauty of this is that it is still medicine, but you can consumerize it," Van Hove said of Juvéderm. In other words, sell it like a bar of soap.

Allergan launched Juvéderm with a sponsorship of the U.S. Tennis Association. Many fans are affluent women in or nearing middle age. Allergan signed Lindsay Davenport, a singles champion, and Tracy Austin, the former top tennis player in the world, to be the faces of Juvéderm.

The Decades of Smooth campaign, created by Grey Advertising, portrayed Allergan as a well-meaning mentor. "The project's goal," copywriters wrote, "is to educate women and men about the best skin care routines for the various decades of life, taking into account lifestyle choices, environmental factors, and individual approaches to aging." The tennis players were described as partners in a "health education campaign." "What I like about the campaign is that it's just educating people that there are choices out there," Austin declared during the rollout in 2008.

Juvéderm wove information about the product into what appeared to be a public health message, except in this account signs of natural aging were a cause for alarm: "Continued exposure to the environment, coupled with repeated facial expressions such as frowning, squinting, and smiling may make wrinkles and lines apparent even when your face is relaxed." In other words, laughing and smiling are damaging to one's appearance because they create wrinkles; they are characterized as agents of physical deterioration rather than as emblems of a life well lived.

Instead of directly urging people to use Juvéderm, the ad phrased its message as a form of medical advice: "Your doctor may recommend Juvéderm dermal filler to treat the 'parentheses' lines between the nose and mouth and other wrinkles and folds on the face where volume has been lost over time." These cosmetic treatments are precisely the ones from which doctors make the most money. At an annual meeting of the American Academy of Dermatology, one speaker pronounced 14 as the age when "a girl's lips reach their peak of fullness." After that, "it's an uphill battle." (At this rate, only newborns will have desirable skin, and mothers will be advised to slather on antiaging cream along with baby lotion.) No wonder women in their 20s are anxious about whether they should start eliminating the first signs of aging.

At a press conference for the campaign launch, Austin, then 45, said seeing her face on high-definition TV is what convinced her she needed work. She mentioned her mother's skin cancer. Although Juvéderm has nothing to do with disease prevention, by linking the two, Austin sent the message that healthy living (applying sunscreen to prevent cancer) is associated with looking younger (using Juvéderm). At another point, Austin referred to how the stigma associated with these treatments has faded, an echo of Clairol's forties-era ads about hair dye. "I was secretive at first about it, only telling a few friends," Austin said, "but now I'm proud to talk about it."

Thirty-one-year-old Davenport, her dark hair cut in a bob, said she wanted to let women know they have options their mothers did not. She, too, emphasized health. "I am a proponent of healthy aging, which can involve different approaches at various points in your life, especially when it comes to skin care, eating right, and exercise," she said. In this telling, injectable treatments are unrelated to vanity, but simply a sign of healthy living and taking charge of your life, like going to the gym.

The themes of responsibility, happiness, and empowerment are combined in the advertising campaign's narrative. Juvéderm places itself within the familiar frame of self-improvement, helping people to become their best selves. "I'm celebrating the 'big 4-0' this year so there's no better time than now to switch up my routine to help me look and feel like the best version of myself," Dayna Devon, a former television host, tells visitors to Juvéderm's website.

The campaign repeats the same "take responsibility" message that Lysol and other products pitched in the 1920s, albeit with a gentler tone: "Over time the natural volume of youthful skin begins to diminish as wrinkles and folds form. But with Juvéderm injectable gel, you don't have to just sit back and let it happen!"

Juvéderm later instituted a frequent flier–like rewards program that allows repeat users to earn points to spend on more Allergan products.

Feminists have embraced such products not only out of necessity, as in NOW's justification for fighting the Bo-Tax, but also as a measure of empowerment. "In 1985, I saw a tape of myself where my eyes were puffy," said Faye Wattleton, president of the nonprofit Center for the Advancement of Women. "I looked very tired and bedraggled and not as youthful as I would like to have been." Then 41, Wattleton had an eye-lift. Twenty years later, she had a lower face-lift. "I didn't do it because I was worried I would lose my job," she said in 2008. "I did it to make a better appearance, a fresher appearance, a more youthful appearance."

Wattleton chastised others for judging cosmetic procedures harshly: "Being a person who has had plastic surgery and goes to the gym five days a week to work my muscles up so they don't look atrophied as a 60-year-old, I don't disparage people who want to maintain their appearance. But what I don't want is a society that tells me I have to." Disdainful comments from respected public figures about "atrophied" skin, however, contribute to the pressure. Wattleton's comments are evidence of a wider shift in judgment about the way women and men are supposed to look. Even AARP, a group created to fight ageism, urged readers on the cover of its magazine to "Look Younger Now: Erase Ten Years (or More)."

In the summer of 2011, Indiana instituted a law requiring anyone over 40 to show identification when buying alcohol, motivated by a concern about curbing teenage drinking and the difficulty of trying to estimate someone's age in this era of agelessness.

The cultural critic Margaret Morganroth Gullette, who has written extensively about "middle-ageism," notes in her 2011 book *Agewise* that since the 1990s, a narrative of decline—"the entire system that worsens the experience of aging-past-youth"—has become more prevalent and powerful. One effect has been to convince people that the middle-aged body "once located within the huge range of normal, has become substandard or even deformed."

Confronted with a demand to conform to the market's image of beauty, middle-aged women have internalized the judgment and transformed the pursuit of beauty into an exercise in self-improvement and autonomy. Marketers encourage that perception. "I love that L'Oréal is a company known for empowering women," Diane Keaton said in a television ad. Taking steps to look younger by erasing wrinkles is converted into an act of self-expression, an exercise of control.

Equating female empowerment with purchasing a product was a strategy pioneered by Edward Bernays. His first job for American Tobacco was convincing people that smoking in public was socially acceptable for women. Recalling that suffragettes smoked while marching for enfranchisement, Bernays hired ten fashion models to light up during the 1929 Easter Parade on Fifth Avenue in New York and called the cigarette a "torch of freedom." A headline in the *New York Times* the next day read: "Group of Girls Puff at Cigarettes as a Gesture of 'Freedom.' " Within a year, women were commonly seen smoking outside. Philip Morris successfully repeated Bernays's tactics in the late 1960s and 1970s, when it employed the slogan "You've Come a Long Way, Baby" for a new skinny cigarette designed for women, Virginia Slims. By emphasizing that objections to women smoking once signified sexism, the ads suggested that puffing on a Virginia Slims was an empowering symbol of independence. Never mind the increased risk of cancer, a fact the tobacco industry was doing everything possible to conceal. Light up a skinny cigarette and declare yourself a feminist.

Today, the challenge facing both men and women in their middle years is to manage self-help's exuberant possibilities and its tyrannical dictates, to take responsibility for improving physical and mental health without succumbing to the compulsion to deny middle age.

11

Middle Age Medicine

"Search for the Fountain of Youth,"
1898

Youth is a silly vapid state
Old age with fears and ills is rife
This simple boon I beg of FATE—
A thousand years of Middle Life!

—Poet and author Carolyn Wells

Before Alex Comfort became spectacularly famous as "Dr. Sex," author of *The Joy of Sex,* he was known for his work on the biology of aging. Throughout the 1950s and 1960s, Comfort wrote about the process of growing older in mollusks, mongoose, and man, and in 1969 predicted that within twenty years average life expectancy would reach 120. What Comfort and other biologists were aiming for was not simply an extension of life but of midlife in particular. No one wants to stretch out old age with all its frailties and debilities. As the political philosopher Harvey Wheeler pointed out. "The aim, and the promise, is instead to add the additional years to the prime of life. So-called middle age would last for forty or more years."

An elongated middle age is now offered by another branch of the Midlife Industrial Complex—the sprawling antiaging and hormone replacement industries. For all the evocations of "youth," a prolonged midlife certainly seems to be what Ronald Klatz, co-founder of the American Academy of Anti-Aging Medicine, is describing when he says, "We believe that there can be an end to aging," a way of "achieving optimal health and optimal performance at age 55 . . . and staying that way for another 50, 60, 70, 80 years or perhaps even longer." We are "ushering in a new reality," he adds, "in which 75 years old may well be considered middle age." As adults in their middle years witness in their family and friends the physical and mental frailty that accompanies longer life spans, deep fears of creeping decrepitude strike more acutely, priming them for these sorts of messages.

Part industry, part movement, part philosophy, antiaging is really middle age medicine, with all its promise and its perils.

A Modern Fountain of Youth

Myths about halting or reversing aging have been told by ancient Greeks and contemporary science-fiction writers. The magic has taken the form of restorative springs, alien cocoons, hidden cities, and clones. But the current, institutionalized, IRS-registered industry is of much more recent vintage. Today, antiaging products include everything from mesotherapy's "medicinal bullets" to untested hormone therapies that purport to slow or reverse the biological process of aging. This modern partnership between commerce and science emerged in the 1990s, when the first wave of boomers hit their mid-40s, and grew into a nearly $90 billion industry in little more than a decade. The American Academy for Anti-Aging Medicine is both a mainstay and an emblem of this wide-ranging and mostly unregulated industry. The official-sounding "academy" goes back to 1992, when a dozen doctors met in Mexico to explore the antiaging effects of human growth hormone (HGH). Two osteopaths, Klatz and Robert Goldman, were its founders. Their partnership has bloomed into a huge global operation with more than twenty-two thousand members and a series of conferences hosted around the world that attract thousands of practitioners even though the trade group is not recognized by the American Medical Association. The continuing education courses in "anti-aging regenerative medicine" and the international conference business that the academy sponsors bring in millions of dollars each year.

Las Vegas is an apt site for the academy's annual world congress. It is a place of wild dreams and desperate failures, high rollers and low-rent con artists, utopian fantasies and cold, unyielding statistics. A place where reality can smack you in the head, where scams knock on your hotel door, where young, voluptuous flesh beckons from sign boards and stage shows, and where regional quirks and particularities fade in the shadow of the overpowering American drive for quick success, instant gratification, and promised happiness. The academy conferences bring together an equally colorful assortment of characters, passions, and eccentricities: Harvard-trained scientists and slick quacks, multimillion-dollar pharmaceutical companies and husband-and-wife teams who cook up nutritional supplements in their kitchens. Here, the Midlife Industrial Complex works overtime.

Middle age medicine is a biological four corners, an intersection of traditional Western practice, alternative therapies, the beauty and fitness industries, and quackery. Science has never been so frequently invoked and so frequently abused. In Las Vegas, the Anti-Aging Academy takes up residence at the Venetian Hotel, where the conference rooms are a short stroll from the hotel's faux St. Mark's Square. There, under a perpetually blue sky, cheerful baritones in red-and-white-striped shirts navigate their gondolas down a mini-canal near sidewalk cafés that occupy faux sidewalks. The resort's exhibit hall serves as a village square and town market. On display are examples of the "new," "revolutionary," "pioneering," "miraculous," "scientifically tested," "science-based," "doctor-approved" wonders and wares that fill today's antiaging department store. I strolled through the aisles of the cavernous hall at the 2008 meeting to sample Cleopatra's 24K gold skin cream ($55 for five ounces), Brain Longevity capsules ($40 for a month's supply), and a miniaturized paint roller with 192 tiny needles that prick the skin for better absorption of skin-care products ($120). I lay in an oxygenating home hyperbaric chamber, a blue cylindrical pod that looked as if it could hold an astronaut in suspended animation ($20,000 for the canvas home unit; $72,000 for metal), and exposed my cheeks to a chilly "facial workout" with a cryotherapy set that resembled a pair of lightbulbs filled with blue curaçao—in reality, antifreeze ($30 a pair, or $9.49 a gallon at your local gas station, bulbs not included).

Technical jargon and unproved claims are common. And since most of these products are not advertised as diagnosing or treating anything, they do not need approval from the Food and Drug Administration. The brochure for the Ondamed, a biofeedback system, includes a brief history of "great innovations in non-invasive medicine." On its pages are portraits of Gabriel Fahrenheit, the inventor of the first mercury thermometer in 1714; René Laennec, who introduced the first stethoscope in 1816; Wilhelm Conrad Roentgen, who discovered the X-ray in 1895; and Rolf Binder, unshaved and wearing a scruffy T-shirt, the man who introduced the Ondamed. The makers of Ion Magnum muscle builder and Perfector electronic face-lift suggest their products can reverse aging by making time go backward, Einstein be damned. A thick, shiny booklet in robot-silver declares that "microscopic laws of physics allow for time reversal," referencing a study that "found a single substitution in the amino acid sequence of an enzyme seemed to turn the clock 2.5 million years back." Taking ten years off a face should therefore be a snap.

One can discern a path from the conference back to the period when plastic surgery expanded medicine's portfolio from treating diseases of the body to supplying happiness. Indeed, the atmosphere at these gatherings is similar to that of a nineteenth-century Age of Science exhibition, when the astonishing leap forward in knowledge was accompanied by gross misinformation and false promises. Although the medical establishment rejects the belief that aging is a disease, the notion has nonetheless been revived by leaders of today's antiaging and beauty industries, from Ronald Klatz to the beauty and health guru Nicholas Perricone. "Wrinkled, sagging skin is not the inevitable result of growing older," Perricone advises. "It's a disease, and you can fight it." To capitalize on the faith in science, companies have invented a new vocabulary to suggest a scientific pedigree. They sell "cosmeceuticals" and "nutriceuticals." "We're trying to connote the fact that there's serious scientific research here, even though it's a cosmetic or a vitamin," Perricone said when asked about his own line of antiaging products. "Buzzwords like these give people a way to identify products that are moving in the direction of science-based rather than marketing-based."

According to a 2006 Harris poll, nearly six out of ten people surveyed incorrectly believed the FDA regulates antiaging products. It does not. As Goldman and Klatz themselves advise in collections of antiaging articles they edit: "Under no circumstances is the reader to construe endorsements by the academy of any specific companies or products. Quite to the contrary, *Caveat Emptor.*"

The Not-So-Magic Bullet

If there is a single item that embodies the contentiousness of the antiaging movement, it is human growth hormone, or HGH. The pituitary gland, the pea-sized CEO of the endocrine system that is located at the base of the skull, is its natural producer. In 1971, biochemists figured out how to isolate and synthesize growth hormone in the laboratory, and doctors can now legally prescribe it for children and adults with severe deficiencies or muscle-wasting diseases. The hormone has also been popular among athletes, who use it to bulk up and speed their recovery from injuries, and antiaging enthusiasts, who believe it restores youthful vigor—although it is illegal to use the substance in the United States for these purposes and it is banned worldwide in most athletic competitions. Assessing the assertions of both the disciples and the scarred evokes the 1985 dystopian fantasy *Brazil.* In the film, one woman goes to a brilliant new plastic surgeon and becomes miraculously younger with each treatment, a glamour-puss swirling around the dance floor in a red dress, until she eventually looks younger than her son. The same treatment, meanwhile, leaves her friend progressively more crippled and mutilated, a wheelchair-bound biddy insisting that the doctor will manage to successfully adjust her treatment any day now. "There's been a little complication with my complication," she explains, until she finally wastes away, not even leaving a body for her coffin.

Growth hormones gained notice in the 1990s after a *New England Journal of Medicine* article reported that twelve men between the ages of 61 and 81 had more lean body mass and less fat after six months of taking the substance. Since then, claims for its fountain-of-youth-like effects—increasing bone density, smoothing skin, improving one's outlook and mental acuity—have tumbled from the mouths of enthusiastic supporters. Yet our understanding of what HGH will do to the body in the long term is sketchy, and the government as well as various medical societies have issued warnings about its use. Dr. L. Stephen Coles, a gerontology researcher and lecturer at the University of California–Los Angeles, was one of the dozen doctors who was in Mexico with Klatz and Goldman but is no longer associated with the movement. "I remember saying [HGH] is really important; this is what medicine will be in the next five years." He has since revised his opinion, stating, "Growth hormone is risky, and I'd like to see long-term studies."

A 2007 review of thirty-one randomized, controlled studies published in the *Annals of Internal Medicine* concluded, "risks far outweigh benefits when it is used as an anti-aging treatment in healthy older adults." Side effects include diabetes, high blood pressure, hardening of the arteries, abnormal growth of bones or internal organs, and carpal tunnel syndrome.

To many antiaging practitioners, HGH is part of the solution to aging itself. In their view, aging is by definition a hormone deficiency condition, since the body produces less growth hormone as the years go by. But human biochemistry is in constant flux. Cells start dying off while we are in the womb, programmed to "commit suicide" so that their healthy brethren can mature and develop. The only human cells known to reproduce indefinitely are cancer cells. No direct link between HGH and cancer has been established, but some scientists think there is evidence of a troubling connection. They hypothesize that the body cranks down the production of growth hormone in adults to curb the abnormally rapid growth of malignant cells; dosing on growth hormone may eviscerate that protection.

Advocates contend such dangers are exaggerated, and either dismiss the research or argue that low doses of hormones are safe and effective. For many Gen Xers and boomers over 40, the promise of strength and energy is too seductive to worry about the risks. Many of the doctors who push HGH are true believers, and they inject themselves and their spouses, arguing that it makes as much sense as restoring insulin to diabetics. The academy is a heavy promoter of growth hormones—something that has not gone unnoticed by the FDA. Half of the twenty people indicted in 2007 for Internet trafficking in human growth hormone and anabolic steroids belonged to the Anti-Aging Academy or promoted products at its conferences. (The law requires a doctor to examine a patient before prescribing the hormone.) The academy was not charged, but Klatz, who co-authored a book on human growth hormones, *Grow Young with HGH: The Amazing Medically Proven Plan to Reverse Aging* (1997), disdains the restrictions: "By the time the F.D.A. researches and approves these drugs, we'll all be dead."

In rare instances, the FDA has gone after a physician, as it did in 2004, when Dr. James Forsythe, the owner of a Las Vegas clinic, was indicted for prescribing HGH as an antiaging treatment. Prosecutors charged that he gave an unfounded diagnosis of adult hormone deficiency to a patient in order to administer the steroid. He was acquitted. At 70, Forsythe is an avuncular man, with a round head and gray hair. He has been injecting himself with hormones six days a week since 2002 and tells me he has never felt better. An entire day of panels at the academy's 2008 conference was devoted to Dr. Forsythe's battle with the FDA, and he was cheered as a hero in battle with a villainous bureaucracy.

The academy has aggressively attacked critics in the medical establishment. "Simply put, the death cult of gerontology desperately labors to sustain an arcane, outmoded stance that aging is natural and inevitable," Klatz declared. "Ultimately, the truth on aging intervention will prevail, but this truth will be scarred from the well-funded propaganda campaign of the power elite who depend on an uninterrupted status quo in the concept of aging in order to maintain its unilateral control over the funding of today's research in aging." Fears about debilitating side effects from other hormone treatments like testosterone and estrogen were similarly dismissed by promoters at the conference.

No one knows precisely why the human body ages, whether it is the result of natural wear and tear, a genetically determined life cycle, environmental pressures, or an evolutionary adaptation. People live longer than they used to because sewage is not dumped on the streets, meat, fruit, and vegetables are plentiful, houses are heated, and doctors can prescribe antibiotics and chemotherapy. But whether human beings can extend the life span a couple of additional decades, let alone the eighty years Klatz imagines, without attendant deterioration is unknown.

The name that Klatz and his colleagues have chosen to represent their efforts to prolong life has an ironic edge. Think of the term itself: antiaging. Literally, against aging. It is labeled "the enemy," a scourge to be eliminated rather than life's natural progression, and women and men are depicted as being at perpetual war with it. "Antiaging" today is like "antiwar" in the 1960s, a term that encapsulates opposition to everything we hate and fear, said Nina Jablonski, the head of the anthropology department at Pennsylvania State University. "'Anti-aging' is one of the words that have slipped into the language in this decade, because everything connected to natural aging is anathema."

The Customer Is Always Right

Antiaging entrepreneurs often make incomplete and inaccurate claims, but it is not simply a matter of a shrewd puppet master pulling the strings of a gullible public. Middle age medicine has a strong grassroots element. Many doctors at the Las Vegas conference said they were motivated to explore antiaging strategies by requests from their patients. Companies, of course, have been quick to capitalize on these desires, reinforcing and expanding them. The movement is a by-product of an empowered patient who refuses to meekly accept the pronouncements of a man in a white coat. That is both its virtue and its vice. It has prompted patients to demand more information and better service. Consumers like its emphasis on prevention and wellness, and its attention to the entire patient, which runs counter to the increasing specialization of modern medicine.

Joseph Maroon, like James Forsythe, has the perspective of both a physician and patient. The vice chairman of the Department of Neurological Surgery at the University of Pittsburgh Medical Center, Maroon is one of the academy's two senior vice presidents. At 68, he arrived at the conference after finishing an Iron Man triathlon in Hawaii. Maroon is well known in the sports world for helping to develop a computerized system to determine the severity of concussions and the recuperation time an athlete needs before returning to play. It has become the standard of care for concussion management in the NFL, NHL, Major League Baseball, and NASCAR, and it is used in more than twenty-five hundred American colleges and high schools. During the Las Vegas meeting, Maroon described his first academy conference as "an Archimedes-like Eureka experience, a mind-blowing event."

Like many other proponents, Maroon was inspired by personal experience. With dozens of Iron Man competitions under his belt, Maroon was feeling the pain by his seventh decade. The Advil he had taken regularly over the years had given him an ulcer. He recalled that at his first conference some of the speakers were talking about fish oil as a natural anti-inflammatory with its beneficial effects on heart function. He tried it and was amazed by how much better he felt.

"There are things presented at this meeting that are clearly controversial, that you don't agree with," he acknowledged to the early-morning Vegas crowd. Maroon later told me he understands that the academy, in the wake of negative press, had recently created the vice presidential posts to bolster its credibility by associating with respected doctors. But he maintains it is "the only scientific organization" that is devoted to the healthy extension of life. If he had his way, he would replace the term "antiaging" with "preventive medicine." "We're so busy treating diseases, very little is spent on prevention unless you're in the highest socioeconomic class," he said.

Nicholas DiNubile, an orthopedic surgeon at the Hospital of the University of Pennsylvania, is the other vice president. A sports medicine specialist, DiNubile counts among his patients towering players from the Philadelphia 76ers and willowy dancers from the Pennsylvania Ballet. It was the middle-aged clerks, salesmen, and lawyers who limped into his office after a weekend of tennis, soccer, or a prolonged workout at the gym, however, who pushed the doctor into middle age medicine. These patients were demanding help for a whole series of injuries that had not traditionally been associated with the 40-plus crowd. Knee and hip replacements, cartilage tears, ligament damage, stress fractures, tendonitis, arthritis, bursitis—what DiNubile calls "fix-me-itis" and ultimately named (and trademarked) "boomeritis."

"The number one reason people go to the doctor is musculoskeletal problems," he told the crowded hall. "Our frame is failing us because we're aging." In DiNubile's view, a good deal of the physical decline that has long been associated with age can be blamed on a La-Z-Boy lifestyle. "You have some control over aging's time clock," he said. "You can change the aging curve." Researchers believe that lack of use accounts for about half the functional losses that usually occur between the ages of 30 and 70, with some claiming that exercise in middle age can set the clock back by as many as twenty-five years.

Like Maroon, he knows that medical advances can have as much to do with scientific breakthroughs as with consumer demand. "Boomers are the first generation that grew up exercising, and the first that expects, indeed demands, that they be able to exercise into their 70s," DiNubile has said. "But evolution doesn't work that quick. Physically, you can't necessarily do at 50 what you did at 25. We've worn out the warranty on some body parts. That's why so many boomers are breaking down. It ought to be called Generation Ouch."

The rising number of such sports-related injuries among middle-aged Americans is altering medical practices, from prognoses to interventions. "When I first started practicing, ACLs had a cut-off at 40," he said, referring to operations that reconstruct the knee's anterior cruciate ligament. "Now 60-year-olds get it. They want to keep skiing moguls." This motivated surgeons to develop less invasive procedures like arthroscopy and pharmaceutical companies to develop new instruments. An ACL surgery used to mean being in a cast for six weeks, with a stiff knee and a long rehabilitation afterward. Today, the operation can be done with a small incision and a short rehab. Other common sports-related operations, like rotator cuff or complex elbow and ankle repairs, which were once limited to patients 40 or younger, have similarly become commonplace for the middle-aged. That is a great boon for people in midlife.

To DiNubile, the medical establishment still lags in serving its middle-aged patients when it comes to education. "I've been trying to put exercise on the medical school curriculum for ten years," he told me. Doctors know that exercise is good, but "they are not comfortable in outlining programs for their patients over the age of 50. . . . It's the weak link." Ambitious novices go to a gym without having a good understanding of what they can and cannot do, sometimes injuring themselves. He noted that SilverSneakers, a fitness program established in 1992 for people over 50 and offered at more than nine thousand gyms and fitness centers, has been underwritten by a number of health insurance companies because they recognized the preventive benefit.

The pressure from consumers has both its positive and negative sides. Demand for better treatments from middle-aged patients encouraged scientific advances and helped shift the mind-set of many orthopedists from treating injuries to prevention and lifestyle. At the last boomeritis gathering he attended—an annual conference that the American Academy of Orthopedic Surgeons established in 2007—DiNubile marveled at the lack of sessions pushing surgery. "There wasn't one bloody picture during the whole conference," he said. "That's a dramatic shift."

On the downside, people often have unrealistic expectations of their own abilities as well as the medical limits on fixing what breaks, which can result in a reckless run-up of costs.

Well-insured patients can shop for a doctor until they find the one who says yes to surgery. Some midlifers have had more than a dozen to repeatedly fix faltering parts. "This is a highly motivated group of people," DiNubile noted. "And sometimes you just have to inject a sense of realism."

No distinction is made between reasonable optimism and magical thinking. Self-improving middle-agers can easily end up indulging in frivolous and dangerous treatments because they believe the stories of miraculous regeneration they hear from pitchmen, doctors, and the Internet. Just as baseball players and cyclists want steroids to power their batting or increase their stamina in spite of the long-term dangers, people want thinner bodies, smoother skin, and more sexual vitality regardless of the higher risk of developing cancer or having a heart attack at some unspecified time in the future.

12

Middle Age Sex

Love in the prime of life

Life begins at forty
That's when love and living start to become a gentle art
A woman who's been careful finds that's when she's in her prime
And a good man when he's forty knows just how to take his time

Conservative or sporty, it's not until you're forty
That you learn the how and why and the what and when
In the twenties and the thirties you want your love in large amounts
But after you reach forty, it's the quality that counts
—"Life Begins at Forty," music and lyrics by Jack Yellen and Ted Shapiro

H. L. Mencken was famous for his hard-nosed skepticism about religious, political, and medical claims. In 1924, the *American Mercury,* the monthly magazine he co-founded, published an article ridiculing Eugen Steinach's vasectomy and X-ray rejuvenation treatments: the facts "seem to shatter this theory completely." Yet, in 1936, at age 56, Mencken himself succumbed to the lure of Steinach's age-prolonging vasectomy. He may have been encouraged by a breakthrough the previous year that enabled scientists to isolate and manufacture testosterone, a discovery that generated fevered excitement about the possibility of rejuvenation. The predecessors of today's antiaging researchers promoted the hormone as a youth serum for middle-aged men and the supposed problems of "male menopause," also referred to as andropause. Oreton, a drug manufactured by the Schering Corporation in 1934, claimed to be "a highly effective means of 'finding' the man who is 'lost in his forties.'" An ad for Perandren, another testosterone drug, showed a photograph of a downcast man dressed in a tux titled, "The Fifth Age of Man," and explained that "the male decline" meant sexual decline.

During the Depression, when middle-aged men were desperate for any edge in the job search, the potential of hormonal youth-inducing "miracle drugs" sparked interest. Henry Harrower's Gonad Tablets, concocted by the endocrinologist Dr. Harrower in his California-based laboratory, promised to elevate physical and mental energy. Efforts to restore male vigor focused on performance, strength, and other physical attributes of masculinity. As drug companies made versions of testosterone, estrogen, and cortisone, hormones were added to the physician's menu of aids. Commerce and medicine established an alliance that was high in profitability and low in ethics and efficacy. Some doctors struck deals with pharmaceutical manufacturers to be the sole dispenser of a particular drug, which they then sold out of their office at a substantial profit.

In 1939, the prestigious *Journal of the American Medical Association* ran an article that claimed men went through a "climeratic" that included hot flashes, low sex drive, crying, and memory problems. Severe cases led to psychosis. Testosterone produced a "remarkable clinical improvement" that included a marked increase in the "sex urge and in the capacity to respond with proper emotions not only to intercourse but also to other acts such as kissing or embracing."

The culture found inspiration in the news. An issue of the science-fiction magazine *Amazing Stories* featured Gland Superman, a regular guy enhanced by hormones. Satirizing the hormone mania, Ray Bourbon, a gay performer, released a record in 1941 called *Gland Opera*:

Ain't science marvelous, ain't science grand?
It'll make worn-out libidos lib by grafting on new glands.
Now a certain worn-out bachelor, who had gone from
frail to frailer,
They had no stevedore's glands in stock,
So they gave him a ladies tailor's.

The Male Sex Hormone, a 1951 film produced by Schering, advocated using testosterone to address the ills of male menopause. But the medical establishment ultimately denounced the treatments and declared andropause did not exist. Hormone therapy for men didn't catch on until the antiaging industry of the 1990s revived interest in it.

In 2002, the Commission of the European Communities sponsored the European Male Aging Study, an ambitious effort to identify and measure symptoms and disabilities associated with aging and settle the question of whether there is a clinical condition similar to female menopause. In June 2010, the *New England Journal of Medicine* published a preliminary account of the 3,219 men between 40 and 79 who were participating and concluded that reports of andropause were highly exaggerated. Testosterone levels naturally drop about one percent a year beginning at age 30. Researchers, for the most part, found that there was barely any connection between levels of testosterone and falloffs in physical, mental, and sexual health. Low sex drive, depression, and sagging energy levels were more likely to be caused by stress, poor eating habits, and laziness than diminished hormone levels. Indeed, another set of scientists made headlines in 2011 when they discovered that fatherly activities from changing diapers to playing peekaboo lower testosterone even in 20-somethings.

Discussions of "male menopause" and andropause nonetheless continue to proliferate, particularly on the Internet. Advertisements for topical forms of testosterone, like AndroGel, promote the idea that men who put on a few pounds and notice a dip in sexual drive may suffer from a medical disorder. As one critic put it, these hormonal products have become "an all-out escape hatch for middle age." Replacement therapy sales increased with a compound annual growth rate of more than twenty-five percent between 2005 and 2009, surpassing $800 million at the end of the four years. In November 2010, the FDA approved Axiron, a topical testosterone applied under the arms. Testosterone supplements are enthusiastically hawked at Anti-Aging Academy conferences.

Testosterone falls into the same category of anabolic steroids that have been at the heart of drug-doping scandals in sports, yet they have escaped censure because of shrewd marketing and willing believers. Promoters in Las Vegas and elsewhere dismissed the medical establishment's concerns about links to cancer and side effects like lowered sperm count, shrunken testicles, increased risk of heart attack and stroke, enlarged prostates, and swollen breasts. The long-term effects of additional testosterone on healthy men are still unknown. The National Institute on Aging undertook a study in 2009, recruiting eight hundred men over 65 with low testosterone levels who had difficulty walking, low vitality, and sexual or cognitive problems. Results will not be available until 2015. That has not deterred advocates, who frequently appear on news programs and daytime talk shows to praise testosterone therapy. Even without a doctor, anyone who wants to take testosterone can get it from the hundred or more "rejuvenation clinics" now operating, or order it on the Web. "Beat the Ban," a headline in the online bodybuilding magazine *Flex* announced, referring to an article advising how to get around the FDA's prohibition of prohormones, substances that act like steroids.

Middle Age and Menopause

Menopause has always elicited conflicting responses in the medical community. Gynecologists and psychoanalysts frequently portrayed menopause as a scary, disfiguring ailment that occurred when the ovaries met their "inevitable demise." In the 1930s, the advice writer W. Beran Wolfe claimed that many large hospitals had sections for mentally disturbed menopausal women. So-called pathological conditions like "vaginal atrophy" were identified. Although there were physicians who derided such pronouncements, others warned that menopause amounted to a rehearsal for death and endorsed hormone therapy.

A range of female hormonal therapies using artificially synthesized progesterone and estrogen was offered in the 1930s in an assortment of combinations and potencies, but treatments did not really catch on until the following decade, when less expensive versions could be administered in a pill instead of by injection at a doctor's office. In 1942, the FDA approved hormone replacement therapy to treat hot flashes, mood swings, insomnia, and other menopausal symptoms. Because of regular gynecological and obstetrical visits, doctors had many more opportunities to persuade their patients to take hormone supplements and women ended up embracing replacement therapy more eagerly than men. (A similar dynamic encouraged women to try surgical and chemical youth treatments at the end of the twenties.) And unlike the vague symptoms and timing of purported andropause, menopause was clearly marked by the end of menstruation and fertility. The substances were also cheaper.

In their book *The Pursuit of Perfection,* David and Sheila Rothman recount how hormone therapy, like plastic surgery, pushed medicine to expand its purpose to include promoting happiness. In the 1930s and 1940s, Emil Novak, a gynecologist at Johns Hopkins, enthusiastically prescribed estrogen for menopausal patients who were depressed. Most gynecologists believed the psychological benefits outweighed the potential risk of cancer. Withholding estrogen because of "a slight theoretical possibility," said Novak, was "carrying conservatism and caution to an extreme." The failing of medical hormones has always been that its claims outran the evidence.

Therapies were marketed with the familiar combination of appeals to empowerment and self-improvement. In the fifties, ads for estrogen featured photographs of kicking showgirls and beauty queens, suggesting that prolonged youth was possible. "There Goes A Happy Woman," one ad trumpeted above a picture of a woman exiting her doctor's office. *Charm,* a magazine for working women, promoted hormone treatments in advertisement and articles. "After 35 you can fool all of the people all of the time by treating your face, throat and hands regularly with a hormone cream or lotion," an article in 1954 gushed. "There are hundreds of other 'miracles' made possible by the progress of science and chemistry."

In the 1950s, William Masters, who later won worldwide fame for the sex research he conducted with Virginia Johnson, fervidly promoted hormone therapy to reverse women's aging. Like Elie Metchnikoff and others before him, Masters believed aging was a disease, and one that science should attack with the same enthusiasm it mustered in the fight against polio or tuberculosis. "One of the greatest public health problems of the present and future, is the rapid increase in our aging population," he wrote in a 1955 paper. Masters laid out an ambitious plan at the 1957 annual meeting of the American Gynecological Society. "The only known member of the female gender to live past her period of reproductivity is the human female," he told doctors who gathered at Washington University School of Medicine in St. Louis. "The postmenopausal years represent, for her, a socially conditioned phenomenon." Medical advances, along with social progress, had increased the human life span far beyond what Masters considered normal; now it was science's obligation to undo the side effects of their success and care for these middle-aged women.

Masters's campaign to correct what he characterized as a defect gained many adherents in the profession in the 1960s and 1970s. Middle-aged women, frequently dismissed by doctors as they went through "the change," were suddenly alluring to physicians and pharmaceutical companies once hormone therapy became widely available. The boundless fortune that could be made by convincing every middle-aged woman to buy a preparation to cope with menopause was an irresistible incentive for drug companies. Psychotropic drugs were similarly marketed as menopausal aids to women in midlife. Between 1966 and 1971, doctors prescribed tranquilizers and antidepressants to seventeen percent of all women (compared with eight percent of men). Their median age was 44. A drug marketing executive explained the general process of building a consumer base: "It's not just about branding the drug; it's branding the condition and, by inference, a branding of the patient. . . . What kind of patient does a blockbuster create? We're creating patient populations just as we're creating medicine, to make sure that products become blockbusters."

The end of fertility was commonly portrayed as marring women's desirability so that unattractiveness and frigidity revolved around menopause like satellites. Simone de Beauvoir observed that a woman "is still relatively young when she loses the erotic attractiveness and the fertility which, in the view of society and in her own, provide the justification for her existence and her opportunity for happiness. With no future, she still has about one half of her adult life to live. . . . The crisis of the 'change of life' is felt much less keenly by women who have not staked everything on their femininity."

Conversations about menopause took place in whispers, as if the subject were unseemly or distasteful. It is "probably the least glamorous topic imaginable; and this is interesting, because it is one of the very few topics to which cling some shreds and remnants of taboo," wrote the feminist novelist Ursula Le Guin. "A serious mention of menopause is usually met with uneasy silence: a sneering reference to it is usually met with relieved sniggers."

Physicians made authoritative pronouncements about the dire physical and psychological effects of menopause, even though barely any research had been done. (Only in 1991, when Dr. Bernadine Healy, the first woman to run the National Institutes of Health, launched the Women's Health Initiative, a $625 million study on middle-aged women, did researchers shift their gaze from men to women.) The gynecologist Sherwin Kaufman wrote in the January 1965 issue of *Ladies' Home Journal*: "It is perfectly natural for women to wish to slow up the aging process and to remain more attractive. They don't hesitate to use contact lenses for failing eyesight, color rinses for drab-looking hair or caps for their teeth. Then why should they put up with the discomforts that afflict about half of them in middle age, when the menopause begins? . . . Treatment doesn't make a woman younger, but it does make her younger-looking."

A year later, in 1966, the British-born gynecologist Robert Wilson published *Feminine Forever,* arguing that menopause was "chemical castration." The title was a swipe at Friedan's 1963 seminal work *The Feminine Mystique*. In his eyes, femininity was not the problem but the answer. A menopausal woman becomes the "equivalent of a eunuch," he wrote. "The entire genital system dries up. The breasts become flabby and shrink, and the vagina becomes stiff and unyielding. The brittleness often causes chronic inflammation and skin cracks that become infected and make sexual intercourse impossible. . . . Multiplied by millions, she is a focus of bitterness and discontent in the whole fabric of our civilization." Menopause was a disease, he declared in his bestselling account, which convinced millions of women to sign up for hormone replacement therapy.

Throughout the sixties and seventies, gynecologists encouraged every woman approaching menopause—and many younger women as well—to down an estrogen pill. Wilson suggested using estrogen from "puberty to the grave." If relief of menopausal-related symptoms like hot flashes and night sweats were not enough to persuade middle-aged women to buy the drug, then the promise of looking younger might. If your doctor disagreed, Wilson counseled, then find another doctor. Only after his death did documents—and his son—confirm that Wilson had been paid by a pharmaceutical company.

The elitist bias that infused the work of rejuvenation specialists in the 1920s was discernible in the 1960s. Wilson saw hormones as a tool for the wealthy to maintain class differences, writing a nasty, mean-spirited description of those who were unable to afford hormone treatments after menopause. These undeserving women gradually sink "into a state of almost bovine passivity," he wrote. "Such women generally flock together in small groups of three or four. Not that they have anything to share but their boredom and trivial gossip. Clustering together in monotonous gregariousness, they hid themselves from the rest of the world. They go together to the same hairdresser to have their hair tinted purple. As though they were schoolgirls again, they dress alike and buy the same little hats."

To Wilson, class differences were what made estrogen socially meaningful. He implied that regular hormone treatments kept one's social status intact, and personally recommended Estradiol, which he called the "Cadillac of hormones." His animosity is reminiscent of the British prime minister in C. P. Snow's dystopian novel *New Lives for Old,* who urges doctors to keep their discovery to elites, "those of the highest gifts, of the finest aims."

In 1975, doctors wrote 27 million prescriptions for hormone replacements, which generally consisted of estrogen-only pills given in a variety of high dosages. Then, in December of that year, the *New England Journal of Medicine* published a series of articles that reported women who used estrogen for five years were five times more likely to develop endometrial cancer; those on the hormone for seven years were fourteen times as likely. A few weeks later, the Food and Drug Administration issued a warning about prolonged use, particularly in women without debilitating menopausal side effects.

As the women's movement rippled out from radical feminists to thousands of small discussion and consciousness-raising groups organized by suburbanites and professionals, women encouraged one another to reclaim responsibility for their health from the medical profession. The Boston Women Health Care Collective published *Our Bodies, Ourselves,* which became a female health bible. Here the empowering aspect of self-help was effectively employed to challenge the patronizing and paternalistic attitudes of mostly male physicians. Wilson's idea of questioning your doctor was one they supported, though not for the reasons he listed. Feminists were critical of the hormone push; they argued the body would naturally reach a new hormonal balance as it aged. Different medical specialties reacted differently to these ideas. By the end of the 1970s, for example, standard psychological texts had discounted menopause as a direct cause of depression or crisis, and prescriptions for estrogen dropped to 14 million as evidence mounted that it led to a higher risk of uterine and breast cancer.

In the 1980s, estrogen-only formulas were replaced by a combination of estrogen and progestin, and many gynecologists recommended their use for postmenopausal women, hoping additional benefits, such as preventing heart disease, memory loss, and the bone-weakening effects of osteoporosis, would surface. (Few did.) The platoons of female baby boomers, more outspoken about menopause and more committed to retaining their youth, constituted a large pool of consumers. "More than 30 million women in the baby boom generation . . . will pass age 40 over the next two decades," the *Los Angeles Times* noted in a story on the "meno boom" in 1989. Whispers about menopause were replaced by public discussion. Gail Sheehy, Gloria Steinem, and Germaine Greer published books on the subject in 1992 and 1993. The following year, a workshop sponsored by the National Institutes of Health concluded that menopause has unfortunately been associated with illness and was often "treated" as a medical problem rather than as a normal part of a woman's life. For most women, menopause was not a watershed event but more like hair growth, something that happened gradually over a period of years. Hormone therapy was what the medical sociologist John McKinlay called "a treatment in search of a disease." Conflicts over dosages, treatment length, and benefits continued, but through the close of the century, hormones remained a huge business, if not for the supposed miseries of menopause, then as an antiaging treatment—just as Sherman Kaufman had suggested in *Ladies' Home Journal* in 1965. MIDUS I researchers found that women most frequently cited concern over a youthful appearance as the reason for taking the pills.

Attitudes abruptly veered in 2002. The National Institutes of Health unexpectedly halted the Women's Health Initiative's clinical trials of a hormone therapy that combined estrogen and progestin because of the stunning news that the treatments increased the risk of breast cancer, heart disease, blood clots, and stroke. Sales of hormones plunged.

Many doctors and antiaging practitioners still recommend hormone therapy in lower doses, and public confusion about the benefits and drawbacks persists. In April 2011, the Women's Health Initiative created a new muddle when it announced that women from the study who had hysterectomies and had taken an estrogen-only pill were significantly less likely to suffer from breast cancer and heart attacks. (About one-third of American women in their fifties have had their uteruses removed.) Experts reacted to the news with wariness, especially because the older women in the study had taken a prescription, Premarin, which is not used much anymore. The health initiative repeated that its recommendations were unchanged: a woman with a uterus should take a low-dose combination of estrogen and progestin only if she had severe symptoms and for as short a period as possible.

The expert reversals and qualifications can have the unfortunate effect of undermining confidence in scientific findings, as people come to expect that today's cutting-edge pronouncement will be contradicted by tomorrow's. Perhaps more usefully, the tangle of information should instill caution about astonishing medical claims, reminding us of how little we know about the human body's mysteries.

The Business of Sex

The gradual decline in regular, heart-pounding sex is a familiar midlife regret. Fifteen, twenty, or thirty years into a marriage or relationship, it is not surprising that sex can become, as the novelist William Kennedy put it, like "striking out the pitcher," satisfying though predictable. The impression fostered by the current lineup of wet-lipped women and randy men on display in print and on-screen, however, is that ubiquitous desire is common and normal. Twenty-something or 60-something, these knowledgeably carnal adults eagerly hop into bed whenever possible, enjoying multiple partners and orgasms. In the popular culture, female independence is often signaled by sexual aggression rather than accomplishments, financial security, or intelligence. Openness about sex is certainly preferable to the Victorian era's embarrassed silence, yet today's overexposure to standardized portrayals of Stepford sex asserts its own form of tyranny, raising expectations and anxieties about sexual performance and appetite at all ages, especially the middle decades. *What's wrong with me? Why am I missing out on all the fun?*

In 1998, when the Food and Drug Administration for the first time approved a treatment for male impotence, Viagra, doctors developed hand cramps from responding to requests for prescriptions. The market for male libido lifters reached $2 billion in 2010. Drug companies reportedly spend $100 million each year on advertising treatments for male impotence or flagging desire, rebranded as erectile dysfunction (or preferably by its nonrevealing initials, ED).

After the phenomenal financial success of Viagra, the feverish hunt for a female counterpart was on. Within a year of the drug's approval, scientific and professional conferences sprang up in the United States and abroad about female sexual dysfunction (FSD), an abnormal absence of desire frequently mentioned in connection with middle-aged women, both pre-and postmenopausal.

The effort to find a pharmacological answer to FSD was further energized by a 1999 article in the *Journal of the American Medical*

Association about a study which estimated that forty-three percent of women between the ages of 18 and 59 suffered from sexual dysfunction. Drug companies and women's groups seized on the results to protest that female sexual problems deserved as much attention as male ones.

This examination of the sex lives of 1,749 women and 1,410 men had serious flaws. Anyone who reported problems with sexual desire, arousal, orgasm, pain, pleasure, or minor anxiety about sexual performance over a period of two months was included in the sexual dysfunction category. Such troubles were often reported by women who were dissatisfied with their partners or single, had physical or mental health difficulties, or had experienced a recent social or economic setback. Any woman who might have mentioned a disappointing sex life because she had just lost a job, developed a painful backache, was contemplating a divorce, or suffering from depression was labeled as having a sexual disorder. Two of the study's authors had links to Pfizer, which was in the process of developing a drug for FSD.

A series of scientists challenged this research, arguing that female sexual dysfunction was essentially a newly concocted syndrome fabricated by the drug industry. Writing in the *British Medical Journal* in 2003, Ray Moynihan called female sexual dysfunction "the freshest, clearest example we have" of a disease created by pharmaceutical companies. "A cohort of researchers with close ties to drug companies are working with colleagues in the pharmaceutical industry to develop and define a new category of human illness at meetings heavily sponsored by companies racing to develop new drugs."

More recent surveys have estimated that seven to fifteen percent of women between 20 and 60 are distressed about problems related to drive, arousal, and orgasm, significantly fewer than the forty-three percent trumpeted by the 1999 study. Even these figures may exaggerate the problem. All the studies that found more than one in ten women were affected were financed by drug companies. In truth, research on female sexuality is sparse and ambiguous. It is not at all clear how many of these problems are signs of a sexual disorder and how many are related to other physiological dysfunctions or social pressure. Nor do scientists know how many middle-aged women might be affected.

Viagra and its competitors essentially work on a mechanical problem. The drug increases blood flow to the penis to produce an erection. The effect of a treatment can be measured. That isn't the case with female sexuality, a combination of desire, arousal, and gratification that cannot be gauged with a ruler. As a Harvard Medical School newsletter put it: "Without an empirical standard by which to assess female sexual function, it would seem difficult, if not impossible, to come up with criteria for female sexual dysfunction."

Judgments about what a disease or disorder is reflect social and historical currents as much as they do science. Moral pronouncements have always had a hand in demarcating the border between sickness and health. In 1898, James Foster Scott warned men over 50 that sexual overexertion was bad for their health. Until it was removed in 1987, homosexuality was classified as a disorder in the *Diagnostic and Statistical Manual of Mental Disorders,* or *DSM,* the handbook published by the American Psychiatric Association. Changing norms and the development of the gay rights movement put muscle behind empirical evidence to bring about the reclassification. The level of female desire that certain doctors, advocates, and television writers consider normal would have been labeled nymphomania in previous eras. In the eighteenth and nineteenth centuries, lascivious glances from a woman were considered a sign of sexual madness, possibly brought on by masturbating, spinal lesions, an enlarged clitoris, reading novels, or eating too much chocolate.

Female sexual dysfunction was added to the manual in 1980 and is essentially defined as "persistently or recurrently deficient (or absent) sexual fantasies and desire for sexual activity." No clear diagnostic keys distinguish someone who has it from someone who doesn't, and the process of updating the manual for the fifth edition, scheduled to appear in 2012 or 2013, has sparked vigorous arguments over how to improve the diagnosis.

The distress that plagues many people about their sex lives may be as much of a cultural phenomenon as a physiological one. Media portrayals of consuming, aching desire in the middle years have become common. Leonore Tiefer, a clinical associate professor of psychiatry at New York University Langone Medical Center, criticizes what she sees as "the mandatory participation in high frequency, high pleasure, high desire culture," or the pressure to have "sex—womb to tomb." Some plastic surgeons have said that widespread images available on-screen, on the Internet, and in magazines have inflamed concerns about the aesthetics of female sexual organs. They have been visited by women who say they have become self-conscious about the appearance of their genital features. Though there are no verifiable statistics on the emergence of genital plastic surgery, some doctors have reported that women are coming in for "vaginal rejuvenation." "I was very, very self-conscious about the way I looked," one middle-aged patient explained. "Now I feel free. I just feel normal." In 2010, the first global symposium on a "new subspecialty," genital cosmetic surgery, was held in Orlando, Florida.

Lori Brotto, a psychologist who is overseeing the *DSM*'s revised entry on female sexual disorder, is wary that conceptions of normal desire often reflect a male perspective. Persuaded by research from Rosemary Basson, a clinical professor in the Departments of Psychiatry and Obstetrics & Gynecology and one of her collaborators at the Center for Sexual Medicine at the University of British Columbia, Brotto believes that a focus on urges may be misleading. For women, desire is triggered by arousal. A decision to have sex, to be responsive to a partner's touch, may be at the core of the female sexual response, rather than an inescapable impulse.

In 2010, researchers who analyzed the latest MIDUS results reported evidence of a gender gap in middle age sex. At age 55, men can expect an average of 15 more years of an active sex life, while women can look forward to 10.6 years. One explanation the researchers offered was that many more men in their late 60s have regular partners than do women of the same age. Another is the increased use of drugs that stoke men's sexual capacity. Tiefer believes the push for a "female Viagra" follows men's artificially induced sexuality.

Pfizer initially undertook testing to prove that Viagra could work for women as well as men, but admitted in 2004 that this was not the case because female sexual disorders were the result of "a broad range of medical and psychological conditions." Procter & Gamble's attempt to get the FDA to approve a testosterone skin patch for some women was rejected that same year because of a possible increase in the risk of breast cancer and cardiovascular disease. Other variations are in the works. The Illinois-based BioSante Pharmaceuticals has been developing a testosterone patch, while Acrux, an Australian company, has tested a testosterone-based spray for women.

The German pharmaceutical company Boehringer Ingelheim announced in November 2009 that it had completed the pivotal Phase III clinical trials of the drug flibanserin, used to treat the most common form of FSD, hypoactive sexual desire disorder (HSDD). The company reported that North American women in the trial had an average of 4.5 "sexually satisfying events" a month, compared with 3.7 by women who took a placebo and 2.7 by those who did not take any pills. Interestingly, European women did not register any significant change, an indication of how "cultural fictions" play an important role in expectations about sex.

Flibanserin was meant to treat depression but was ineffective. That meant it was a drug in search of a disease. The process brings to mind Latisse, the eyelash lengthener released in 2009 by Allergan, the maker of Botox and Juvéderm. Initially developed to treat glaucoma, Latisse turned out to have a much more profitable side effect: longer lashes. Before it could be sold as a prescription drug, however, Allergan needed the Food and Drug Administration's stamp of approval. But the FDA found itself in a quandary: What disease or condition was this new drug purporting to treat? None existed, so the FDA created one: hypotrichosis of the eyelashes, or not having enough hair. (The company is currently investigating how to treat hypotrichosis of the scalp—also known as baldness.)

Finding a disease to fit the cure is similar to what advertising copywriters did in the 1920s, when they invented hundreds of syndromes, like bromhidrosis (sweaty foot odor) and acidosis (sour stomach). It is what the cosmetics and dermatology industries are currently trying to do to wrinkles—to get consumers to see them as a form of dermatosis, a skin disease. The American Society of Plastic and Reconstructive Surgeons employed the strategy in 1983 when it used the term "micromastia" for small breasts. A memo sent by the society to the FDA declared that "a substantial and enlarging body of medical information and opinion" believes "these deformities"—small breasts—"are really a disease," since they create "a total lack of well-being." Plastic surgeons assured patients that "normal breasts" could be achieved through augmentation surgery.

As the 2010 date approached for the Food and Drug Administration's ruling on flibanserin, Boehringer Ingelheim launched a publicity campaign that included a website, Twitter feeds, and a documentary about the supposedly widespread problem of HSDD, declaring that six out of ten premenopausal women suffer from it—a claim disputed by a number of independent researchers. As part of a medical education class sponsored by the German pharmaceutical, doctors and nurses were asked to diagnose a 42-year-old working mother who cares for three children and her sick mother, and has no desire for sex. The correct response, the company instructed, was to evaluate her for a sexual-desire disorder.

"This is really a classic case of disease branding," said Dr. Adriane Fugh-Berman of Georgetown University's medical school, who frequently testifies on behalf of plaintiffs in lawsuits against pharmaceutical companies. "The messages are aimed at medicalizing normal conditions, and also preying on the insecurity of both the clinician and the patient."

Michael Sand, director of clinical research at Boehringer Ingelheim, conceded the company has no idea how flibanserin works. "We don't understand the pathways," he said. "What we think is that in women with HSDD there is likely an imbalance of serotonin, and that flibanserin is balancing the imbalance in these neurotransmitters." With flibanserin, the company has shifted the focus from hormones to psychology. Boehringer Ingelheim is guessing that brain chemistry is at the root of the problem. A Kinsey Institute survey found that general well-being was the most frequently cited contributor to female sexual satisfaction, followed by emotional reactions, attractiveness, physical responses to lovemaking, frequency of sexual activity with a partner, the partner's sensitivity, one's own state of health, and a partner's state of health. This is not to say that middle-aged women and others do not suffer from sexual problems, only that a pill may not be the cure-all. Mindfulness training and cognitive therapy have also had success in raising low sexual desire.

In June 2010, the FDA recommended against approval of flibanserin. Its assessment was that the benefits did not outweigh the side effects, which included dizziness, nausea, and fatigue, and that the company had not proved that the drug increased women's desire (though panel members urged Boehringer Ingelheim to keep trying).

Social, commercial, and political forces can have as much to do with decisions about treatments as they do with scientific advances and health concerns. From miraculous hormone therapies to drugs that instill sexual vigor, many of the pitches and promises of middle age medicine echo those of the previous century. What is different today is the existence of better and safer treatments, an established scientific methodology to test them, and the means to communicate the results. What has not changed is the will to believe.

The Flip Side of Self-Improvement

Attempts to remodel middle age have exposed the tension between authenticity and social acceptance, between the democratizing and coercive aspects of the market, between self-help and social responsibility, and between biological determinism and environmental influence.

Distorted information from advertisers and the media promote unrealistic expectations, whether about pills that ignite sybaritic sexual pleasure or sprays that promise to instantly and imperceptibly cover bald spots. Skeptics are chastised for failing to do everything they can to help themselves before it is too late.

Self-improvement is a wonderful tool, helping people to stay sober, finish an education, or feel happier. But there is a flip side: blame. Success may be yours for the taking, but so is failure; the fault does not lie with society, the system, nature, or history—only with you. And because failure is personal, personal effort is expected to fix the problem. If you were unhappy in a job, early advertisements admonished, individual flaws were the cause. Those who fail to take advantage of the commercial aids, as Helena Rubenstein suggested, have no one to blame but themselves. In the 1920s, Williams Shaving Cream told men: "It's the 'look' of you by which you are judged most often." Listerine advised readers to "suspect themselves first." Today, the self-help guru Dr. Phil (Philip McGraw) reminds his fans that "there are no victims, only volunteers."

Refusal to partake in consumerist self-improvement promoted by the

Midlife Industrial Complex is perceived as a moral failure rather than as a sign of independent thinking. The motivational entrepreneur Tony Robbins captures the essence of the self-help imperative in his directive: "Commit to CANI—Constant And Neverending Improvement." The relentless burden to improve becomes more curse than counsel.

Attributing success and failure solely to individual effort can distract people from working on social and political issues, or from pursuing other aspects of well-being. A relentless focus on self-help reinforces the notion that society has no responsibility for any negative treatment of middle-aged people, and no obligation to take any remedial action on a broader scale. Economic restructuring, income inequality, institutionalized layoffs that hit workers in their middle years (not to mention others) are the result of national policies and global forces, but effort is put into individual self-improvement like Botox rather than social change.

There is a built-in contradiction to the logic of self-help. The solutions bought in the marketplace are not the individual's but those of a copywriter or product manager. In the freewheeling capitalist bazaar, individual power can be turned on itself, allowing others to decide what the model for *your* self should be. As George Carlin joked: "The part I really don't understand is if you're looking for self-help, why would you read a book by someone else? That's not self-help, that's help."

The contradiction is particularly sharp for middle-aged women. As engineers of the feminist movement, they personified self-empowerment, crashing through age-old barriers to positions of power. Their success in the workplace and on college campuses has even sparked debate about affirmative action for men. Yet once they hit middle age, women are under more pressure than ever to conform to narrowing definitions of attractiveness and beauty. Anorexia, bulimia, and other eating disorders have increased enormously among middle-aged women over the past decade. "In our culture, remaining cute throughout midlife is a problem," Debra Benfield, a clinical nutritionist from Winston-Salem, North Carolina, said. "Our mothers didn't stay cute. It was okay to look like a mother when you reached fifty." No more. Even though the extra ten to fifteen pounds that women tend to put on in middle age increases bone density and protects them against fractures, women don't want them. Jean

Kilbourne, the creator of the 1995 documentary *Slim Hopes: Advertising and the Obsession of Thinness,* observed: "The hope was that as the baby boomers grew old, aging would finally be in, that it would be sexy to have wrinkles and gray hair. But that did not happen."

Self-help has created a conundrum: at the very moment consumers exercised their power, they also surrendered it.

13

Complex Accomplices

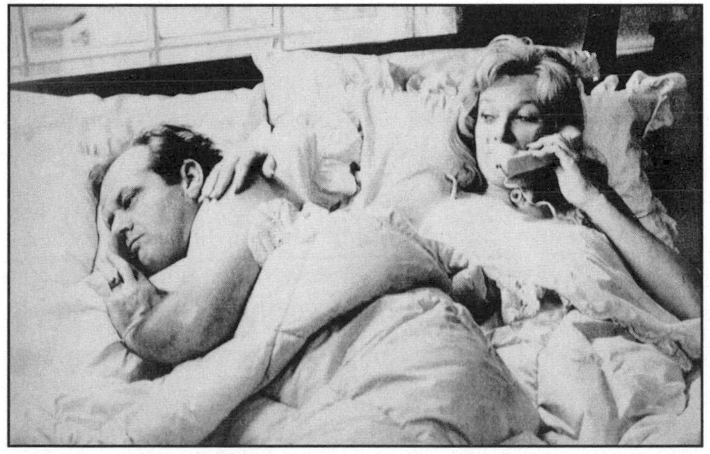

Jack Nicholson and Shirley MacLaine in *Terms of Endearment,* 1983

There are only three ages for women in Hollywood: babe, district attorney, and Driving Miss Daisy.

—*First Wives Club* (1996)

Since *Harper's Bazar* and other middle-class periodicals began accepting national advertising from cosmetics companies in the 1920s, magazines have been an integral part of the Midlife Industrial Complex. Publications that had virtually ignored the subject of beauty, like *Ladies' Home Journal,* redirected their editorial content as they partnered with cosmetics manufacturers. Pages were dedicated to discussing the benefits of soothing balms and eye-catching lip colors, while the staff assisted advertising agencies with market research. Some columnists and editors sold their endorsements to particular brands.

Expert in the language of empowerment, magazines today have perfected the promotional art and dispense advice on how to fend off the indignities of middle age, counseling that the threat of old-style dowdiness is averted by well-timed purchases. *Vogue, Bazaar, Glamour,* and others produce special aging issues every year. A *Vogue* cover promises advice to those "19 to 91," from "conquering your first wrinkle at 29 to the perfect Yoga body at 52." One writer offers a "lesson in age-appropriate makeup," confessing that in her mid-40s "the ravages of age" have finally caught up with her. On the "cruel cusp" of 50, she can get help for her "droopy" eyes and "withered" lips by attending a "Fabulous at 40 and Beyond" makeup class. What has this new midlife experience taught her? Makeup is about "confidence and knowing who you are." Buying into the stereotypical attitude toward an aging face is spun here to represent personal insight and strength. And the story ends happily: "Ever the consumer, I have gleefully purchased a whole new arsenal of products."

O, The Oprah Magazine seemed to offer a refreshingly frank appraisal in its May 2011 issue, devoted to the theme "Love the Age You Are." Oprah wrote a rousing editor's note. "For sure we live in a youth-obsessed culture that is constantly trying to tell us that if we're not young and glowing and 'hot,' we don't matter," she declared. "I refuse to let a system, a culture, a distorted view of reality tell me I don't matter. . . . People who lie about their age are denying the truth and contributing to a sickness pervading our society—the sickness of wanting to be what you're not." The message, however, was strangely at odds with some of the inside copy. In "How Do You Feel About Your Face?," an attractive middle-aged woman with the normal complement of lines, creases, and brown spots was pictured in retouched before-and-after-style photographs to illustrate how five progressively more intensive antiage treatments turned her from young to younger. Choose makeup or Botox or go all the way with a full-scale face-lift.

Men's magazines offer a similar if toned-down message. The June 2010 issue of *Esquire* included a year-by-year guide to aging that told readers their forty-second birthday was the time to stop "worrying that you're starting to look old" and start "doing something about it." The magazine suggested Un-Wrinkle Night Cream and Men Age Fighter face moisturizer, and for those with brown spots and wrinkles, chemical peels or Fraxel laser technology.

Advertisers have been extolling "the younger crowd," as Fatima cigarettes put it, as the standard-bearers of beauty and taste since the twenties. What has changed is a vastly enlarged media that has extended the impact of youth-centered appeals much further, faster, and more powerfully than ever before.

Television Advertising and Market Segmentation

"Change Your Life Television" programming, like the series *10 Years Younger* and daytime talk show episodes that promise "New Ways to Look Younger," directly encourages viewers to purchase self-improving products and treatments. In general, though, television's partnership with the Midlife Industrial Complex operates more subtly.

The notion of young viewers as a kind of commercial grail has been based on two beliefs long taken as gospel: that buying habits are formed early, and that middle-aged and older consumers have buying patterns as rigid and immovable as the faces on Mount Rushmore. The reasoning holds that capturing an audience when it is young guarantees a lifetime of brand loyalty. That is why a television program with younger viewers can charge more than twice as much for commercials as one with older viewers, and why the phrase "coveted 18- to 49-year-olds" or "18- to 34-year-olds" is practically an amen to every conversation or story written about television viewers. That preoccupation has driven programming toward youthful themes and characters.

Abbe Raven, the president and CEO of A&E Networks, remembers how some in the industry wrote A&E's obituary in 2002 after the median age of its viewers hit 61. One trade paper "called us 'a sinking ship.' Another said we were 'rearranging chairs on the Titanic.'" Raven was then 48 and the general manager of AETV, a joint venture of the Hearst Corporation,

Disney-ABC Television Group, and NBC Universal. Created in 1984, it featured BBC network productions and highbrow arts programming that included telecasts of plays, concerts, operas, and documentaries. Raven, who joined A&E in the mid-eighties answering phones and Xeroxing scripts, quickly concluded that an extreme makeover was needed. "We wanted to be a network that had a mission of welcoming younger viewers, and that's what we did," she said shortly after the network embarked on an overhaul.

Attracting younger viewers became the prime directive and reality television seemed a quick way to accomplish the goal at a low cost, Raven told me. In 2004, A&E introduced *Growing Up Gotti,* starring Victoria, the daughter of the deceased boss of the Gambino crime organization, and *Dog, the Bounty Hunter,* about a convicted murderer in Honolulu who tracked down bail jumpers.

"Almost overnight, the median age dropped twenty years," said Raven. In the first two years of the makeover, A&E TV introduced seventeen real-life shows.

Raven has wrought a marketing miracle. But she is not completely convinced that the assumptions on which her success is built are meaningful. Neither the 18-to-34 nor the 18-to-49 grouping has any intrinsic meaning. They sprang nearly five decades ago from the minds of marketers who created these age segments to show off a particular network's strengths and downplay its weaknesses. The obsession with these younger age groups "is a little outdated," Raven confessed. "I spend more today than I did at 25. I didn't own a car at 25." But Toyota, which advertises on A&E, doesn't think that way, she continued.

Now in her mid-50s, she has aged out of the demographic group that she so successfully brought to her network.

The hallelujahs to youth grew out of the quest for a competitive advantage. With the advent of television in the 1950s, advertisers could reach directly into people's living rooms and bedrooms at the same time that postwar affluence was converting them into eager consumers. The fledgling networks wanted to capture as many viewers as possible across generations. No one considered a 25-year-old more valuable than someone 45 or 65. Competition among individual programs intensified when the business model shifted from having a single sponsor (Texaco presents Milton Berle on NBC) to several sponsors. The more viewers a show had, the more a network could charge for each minute of ad time. CBS, the largest and most successful of the networks, adopted a something-for-everyone strategy. *The Ed Sullivan Show* was the model. Other variety shows were set up to offer a smorgasbord of entertainment for children, parents, and grandparents. Even if you didn't care for the Beatles, you might stick around for Frank Sinatra. The network stocked its comedies and dramas with characters that spanned different generations. The formula was easily adaptable to a family of monsters (*The Munsters*) or a family of astronauts (*Lost in Space*).

The multigenerational strategy made sense for CBS, which was solidly in first place. But what about last place? That was where ABC, the youngest and smallest network, was in the late 1950s and early 1960s. ABC was built on a series of affiliates in large cities like Los Angeles, Chicago, and New York, with a somewhat younger audience. Its string of failed and canceled shows gave rise to the joke that the quickest way to end the Vietnam War was to put it on ABC. Burdened by these handicaps, the struggling network was looking for a way to distinguish itself at the same time the trend of sorting consumers into categories was spreading through the industry.

The idea of dividing the population of buyers into separate segments in the 1950s, the art of demographics, was the work of marketing consultant Wendell R. Smith. Born in 1911, Smith grew up in Shenandoah, Iowa, where he worked in his parents' shoe store after graduating from college. He completed Florsheim Shoes' trainee program in Chicago and decided to get a PhD at the College of Commerce at the State University of Iowa. During World War II, he joined the Office of Price Administration, later returning to Iowa to teach at the university and, eventually, chair the school's marketing department. He left the academic world in 1954 after meeting Wroe Alderson, one of the most innovative marketing theorists of the postwar era. At Alderson's management-consulting firm, Smith became director of research.

It was from this perch that he published a jargon-studded article titled "Product Differentiation and Market Segmentation and Marketing as Alternative Marketing Strategies" in the 1956 *Journal of Marketing*. Businesses and consultants had practiced segmentation before. In the twenties, the marketing consultant and *Ladies' Home Journal* writer Christine Frederick had advised her clients to tailor appeals to different age groups. In the thirties, department stores and clothing manufacturers created the toddler stage by segregating children's clothing in separate sections, and in the forties the word "teenager" was popularized by marketers who recognized the buying power of these nascent consumers. But Smith put this tactic into a larger conceptual framework. He argued that the strategy of selling the same item to as many people as possible had reached its limit. Consumers had different needs and desires, which businesses had ignored. A better approach was to break down the single mass of consumers into assorted segments and then adapt merchandise accordingly. For the first time, industrial processes had the efficiency and technical ability to diversify a company's products, which made segmentation profitable in a way that it previously was not.

In Smith's view, "The emergence of market segmentation as a strategy once again provides evidence of the consumer's preeminence in the contemporary American economy and the richness of the rewards that can result from the application of science to marketing problems." Advertisers had adopted a scientific approach when they employed strategic polling. As early as 1940, Elmo Roper modified his job description from "Poll-Taker" to "Marketing Consultant," telling businesses that survey data could open up the "mass mind" to them. Like the PR mandarin Edward Bernays, who wanted to apply scientific management to marketing, Smith wanted to marry advertising and science. Taylorites would have been proud.

Smith's ideas rippled through the industry. The Alpha Psi Kappa Foundation, a nonprofit group devoted to educating business leaders, named his piece the most important marketing article of the year. Companies immediately took notice and earnestly began to cut up the mass of consumers based on income, gender, geography, ethnicity, and age to more precisely target their message to potential buyers. Instead of putting resources into publicizing the benefits of a product, Smith argued that advertisers should create a community of like-minded consumers, and then heavily advertise to that group. As the business historian Richard Tedlow explained: "Segmentation based not on logistics or on some genuine product characteristics, but on demographic and psychographic groupings carved out of the general population is an invention of late 20th century American marketing."

When ABC decided to pursue a younger market, it had demographics on its side. By 1966, nearly half of the American population was under age 25 and their influence surged through the culture. Soon it became clear that some viewers were more equal than others. Advertisers drilled deeper into the youth market, further elevating viewers in the 18-to-34 bracket.

The spirit of youthful nonconformity and rebellion that the Beats embodied was already infusing advertisements by the late 1950s and early 1960s. There was a qualitative shift in the mid-sixties, however. Rather than target an isolated age group, advertisements proffered a characteristic sought by everyone—youthfulness. Or perhaps it would be better to call it "youthiness," a cousin of the word "truthiness" coined by the television-show host Stephen Colbert to satirize the political discourse on the Iraq war. Colbert was referring to rhetorical devices that were used to appeal to people's emotions rather than intellect—"something that seems like truth, the truth we want to exist." Marketers were not going after an existing youth demographic but manufacturing a segment of consumers who wanted to feel youthful. Pepsi's slogan was not "the drink for those who are young" but the "drink for those who think young."

"The old fragmentation was based on realities, but this new segmentation springs wholly from the imagination of the marketer," Tedlow argues. "There was no such thing as the Pepsi Generation until Pepsi created it." Manufacturers and advertisers were attempting to "create group identities where before there had been nothing more than elementary feelings and survey answers."

Since the sixties, corporations and political parties have increasingly used survey techniques to break the public into finely graded segments and cluster them in novel formulations. But while some of these consumer-oriented surveyors revealed affinities that people were unaware of, many others created group identities where none previously existed. In recent years, marketers and consultants have created categories like early adapters, techies, metrosexuals, soccer moms, cougars, angry white men, and Sam's Club voters—some of them based on perceived similarities that seem critically important one moment and dissipate the next.

Throughout the late sixties and seventies, the cult of youth dominated the country and the airwaves, nudged along by Nielsen's attention to a younger demographic. The feminist movement inspired a couple of popular exceptions, like the TV character Maude, an outspoken, Mack truck of a middle-aged protagonist. But advertisers continued to dismiss viewers in their middle years. "I went to Hollywood in 1979 and asked television executives if they were bringing out anything for older audiences," Landon Y. Jones, the author of the 1980 book *Great Expectations: America and the Baby Boom Generation,* recalled. "They looked at me like I was from Mars."

In the mid-1980s, baby boomers moved into middle age and positions of power in broadcasting just as cable was restructuring broadcast television. By 1990, viewers were abandoning the networks in droves. The prime-time cable audience had increased thirty-five percent, while the networks' had shrunk by twenty-five percent. The trend continued through the end of the century.

The obsession with age had created a double bind. "The worse TV nets perform at getting large audiences, the more they emphasize segments, and the more they emphasize audience segments, the more they lose audience," John Polich, a professor of communications at Fordham University, observed. In surveys, the vast majority of respondents over 40 complained that they had a hard time finding television shows that reflected their lives.

As cable stations proliferated, many sought to target a niche of viewers. This both fragmented the culture and reinforced the notion that each age group has its own distinct interests, stories, and styles. MTV and Nickelodeon sought to siphon off younger audiences and children; ESPN went after sports fans. The WB network, launched in 1995, was created in response to ad buyers' continuing hunger for youthful programming (it was later swept up by the newly constituted CW network). The Super Bowl may be the only regularly scheduled program left that can count on drawing in large numbers from every generation.

Throughout the 1990s and early 2000s, advertisers and ad buyers continued to crown the younger consumer as king. "If you were 50, you were dead," said Matt Thornhill, the founder of the marketing firm the Boomer Project. "You just didn't exist. We could care less about you. If we cared about you at all, you were part of this group called seniors, and we wanted to sell you Geritol and Depends."

The preference showed up in ad prices. In 1997, thirty seconds of ad time on Fox's *The Simpsons* (thirty-second in the ratings) commanded $168,100, while *Walker, Texas Ranger* (in thirty-fourth place but with an older audience) cost $85,400. For *Melrose Place,* a show popular with teenagers, Fox got $17.28 for every thousand viewers who watched compared with $5.10 that CBS received for the same number of middle-agers who tuned in to *Touched by an Angel.*

The head of sales for Fox at the time described older viewers as "common currency, copper as opposed to gold," adding, "Who do you think are the early adapters? They set the style and determined what was trendy."

The predilection for youth has persisted despite demographic shifts that bulked up the middle-aged public. In 1993–94 the median age of prime-time viewers topped 40; in 1997, it inched past 42; in 2010, it passed 51. During the past two decades the television audience has aged twice as fast as the general population. Television is the favored medium of middle age, but it has been a case of unrequited love.

A&E's Raven thinks the 20-somethings who buy ad space further denigrate the value of middle-aged viewers. "When you go to an ad agency, the people who are making the decisions are my son's age," said Raven. "It's hard to make the case to advertisers that baby boomers are an important demographic." No one knows that better than David Poltrack, who came to CBS more than four decades ago, and since 1994 has been vice president of research and planning. CBS's audience is typically a few years older than its competitors, and for more than twenty-five years,

Poltrack has consistently argued that the 18-to-49-year-old slice of the audience is not the nirvana that most advertisers and television executives assume. He says that all the truisms about middle-aged viewers—that they spend less, avoid switching brands, and formed their lifelong habits at the dawn of time—are exaggerated, if not altogether wrong. He maintains it is a mistake to neglect the vast swath of 50-plus Americans who are television's most loyal viewers. "We should really be paying attention to the baby boomer market," Poltrack explained from his no-nonsense office on the twenty-fourth floor of Black Rock, CBS's granite headquarters in Manhattan. "We're leaving this age group at a point when wealth is great, consumption is greater, and their consumer power is greatest." He has made that argument hundreds if not thousands of times. As is explained in the next chapter, only recently have advertisers and buyers begun to heed his message.

The neglect of middle age in the movies is due to a different constellation of economic interests than that of television and magazines. The industry caters to youthful audiences not because advertisers demand it but because filmmakers and studios believe that young audiences will buy more tickets. In the late fifties and sixties, that assumption was true. Middle-aged parents spent their movie and popcorn money on shoes and accordion lessons for the first baby boomers. In 1957, three-quarters of theater audiences were under 30; half were under 20. A decade later, the same kids who had kept their parents home on Saturday nights were filling seats themselves. Half of the film audience was between 16 and 24. "To catch the greatest audience you had to zero in on the 19-year-old male," American International Pictures concluded in a 1968 report, arguing that female and younger viewers deferred to the male teen's movie selection. AIP was an independent company specializing in exploitation films, but its analysis was extraordinarily influential.

Today, movie audiences look very different. Forty percent of frequent moviegoers are over 40; twenty-one percent are between 18 and 24. But movies are still geared toward 19-year-old males. Teenagers are more likely to rush to theaters on that crucial opening box-office weekend that primes foreign sales of distribution rights. Animated and action features not only draw in young repeat customers, but they offer more opportunities for lucrative merchandise tie-ins and a longer afterlife on DVD and around the world. (There is not a very promising market for Middle Age Man action figures.)

The film industry's attitude toward middle age is captured by a printed notice that occasionally appears on tickets for pre-release film screenings that the invitation does not extend to anyone over 50.

Midlife On-Screen

The privileged status of youth on television and in movies has strongly influenced our conception of middle age. Characters on-screen exert a magnetic force on viewers, simultaneously reflecting and guiding tastes, values, attitudes, and affections. A character can create a fashion trend (Diane Keaton's tie and hat in *Annie Hall*), turn into a cultural touchstone (Snooki in *Jersey Shore*), ignite a generational stance (*Easy Rider*), or coin a catchphrase ("Make my day"). The extraordinary promotional power of being on-screen is what initially turned nameless actors into celebrities and product spokesmen, and is what currently makes movies and TV shows such a valuable adjutant of the Midlife Industrial Complex. Film and television manufacture myths, prototypes, and desires, as well as the gestures, language, and styles to communicate them. They influence both men and women's notions of what sexiness, beauty, patriotism, sincerity, and snobbery look and sound like.

For decades Hollywood has instructed men on how to look cool, how to romance a girl, and how to have a midlife crisis. The hardy trope of leaving your wife, buying a sports car, and running off with a cheerleader at age 40 plotted out in countless films, television episodes, and cartoons has persisted through the years, even making an appearance recently in the Grand Theft Auto video game. (When the aging crime boss buys a sports car, his wife says she can "smell" his midlife crisis.)

In the 1960s and 1970s, films featured middle-aged sellouts exiting the rat race or suffering from existential angst. In *The Arrangement,* Eddie

Anderson (Kirk Douglas) composes ad campaigns for a "clean cigarette" before trying to swerve his Triumph into a tractor trailer, and in *Save the Tiger,* Harry Stoner (Jack Lemmon) careers toward a midlife breakdown as he engages in smarmy attempts to stave off bankruptcy.

In *The Swimmer,* based on John Cheever's short story, Neddy Merrill (Burt Lancaster) realizes one midsummer Sunday while drinking gin at a friend's that a watery route home lies through the backyard pools of his affluent Westchester neighbors. As he progresses on his journey, his whimsical venture turns into a pilgrim's progress in reverse. Films habitually used the successful suburban middle-aged man as a metaphor for social anomie and moral bankruptcy. In 1968, Merrill seemed like a symbol of America in that annus horribilis, when Robert Kennedy was assassinated, riots reverberated through college campuses, and the country seemed to have lost its way in an unpopular war.

Other variations on the theme have waxed and waned. As baby boomers in the 1980s approached middle age, they found fresh inspiration in nostalgia. High jinks, first loves, adolescent insecurities, and post–high school panic were on display in *Ferris Bueller's Day Off, Fast Times at Ridgemont High, Porky's, Pretty in Pink, Risky Business, Sixteen Candles, Say Anything, Weekend at Bernie's, St. Elmo's Fire,* and *The Sure Thing.* John Hughes was the master. The film scholar Robert Sklar called him a "paradigm for the baby boom generation's creative influence on American movies, moving from teen subjects to even younger protagonists as its own prolonged adolescence shifted abruptly toward parenthood."

The more solidly male boomers moved into middle age, the more fun the midlife crisis became. Merry arrested development was the theme of movies from *City Slickers* (1991), where Billy Crystal and his pals go West and play cowboys, to 2010's *Hot Tub Time Machine* (the title says it all). Even in more introspective films like *Sideways* (2004), which follows two disappointed middle-aged souls on a weeklong trip through California wine country, the buddies have a good measure of excellent wine, golf, and sexual antics.

Economic downturns, both in the seventies and now, have produced more sympathetic screen portraits of men thrown into a midlife crisis when they lose their jobs, or are forced to rethink their work and lifestyle, like George Clooney in *Up in the Air* (2010). Male boomers can finally start to relax, however. The angst of midlife crises is being handed off to Generation X, as in *Greenberg* (2010) with Ben Stiller as a former musician whose primary enjoyment at 40 is writing peevish letters of complaint to businesses.

Hollywood has always offered women lessons in sexiness, but it has been more ambivalent about middle-aged women having sex. The response to female lust in midlife has swung between fear and ridicule. In the fifties and sixties, predatory older women were often viewed as deviant, even diabolical. They lured men into ruinous Faustian bargains, like Norma Desmond (Gloria Swanson) in *Sunset Blvd,* Gene Kelly's wealthy patron Milo Roberts (Nina Foch) in *An American in Paris,* and "2-E" or Mrs. Failenson (Patricia Neal) in *Breakfast at Tiffany's*. Science-fiction B-movies in the late fifties fed on these sexual anxieties, serving up *Attack of the 50 Foot Woman,* who cared only about getting revenge on her husband for his affair with a younger woman, and *Wasp Woman,* whose quest for eternal beauty turned her into a murderous insect. The sinister side of midlife sexuality has been a recurring theme on day- and nighttime television soap operas. Sexually driven women were usually mentally unbalanced and mightily punished as in *Fatal Attraction,* when Glenn Close's character is finally killed after wrecking a happy family and boiling a little girl's pet bunny.

Alternately, the lustful middle-aged woman has been mocked as if the combination of sexuality and midlife was by its nature laughable. The libidinous cooking show host Sue Ann Nevins in TV's *The Mary Tyler Moore Show* or the love-starved landlady Mrs. Roper in *Three's Company* were comical characters whose roots reached back to Chaucer's bawdy Wife of Bath. The type is still conspicuous on television sitcoms and in films. They are much more physically appealing, but they can still be dangerous. In the 2011 comedy *Horrible Bosses,* Jennifer Aniston plays a man-eating dentist whose constant sexual harassment of her assistant drives him to contemplate murder. In NBC's *Parks and Recreation,* Tammy (the 58-year-old Megan Mullally) is a voracious sexual piranha who reduces her ex-husband to a beast. Reality shows reinforce a more troubling impression of older women as sexual predators, Mrs. Robinsons pumped up with breast implants and Botox. NBC's *Age of Love* pitted 40-plus women, "cougars," against 20-something "kittens." In 2009, Bravo introduced a variation on the theme, *Cougar,* in which twenty men in their twenties vied for the affections of a perfectly toned 40-year-old blonde.

The emergence of a healthfully sexualized woman in middle age may well be the most dramatic change in a screen character in the past thirty-five years. For a long time, the repressed and joyless middle-aged woman was a stock character as the title of a 1997 study on aging women in popular films illustrates: "Underrepresented, Unattractive, Unfriendly, and Unintelligent." She has pretty much vanished from the screen. In her place, at least on television, is the beautiful, sexually charged woman in midlife bloom. Samantha Jones in *Sex and the City* is the übermodel, but she can be found in some form on nearly every network during prime time. ABC's *Desperate Housewives* has no fewer than four at a time. Unlike the predatory cougar, her carnal appetite is seen as admirable rather than fearsome.

More rare are scripts that tackle the realities of middle-aged sex. The director Nancy Meyers recalled that when she was writing *Something's Gotta Give* (2003), "I showed an early draft to a guy I know who is around 60. . . . There's a joke in the movie where a middle-aged man is making out with a middle-aged woman, and he says, 'What about birth control?' And she replies, 'Menopause.' And this guy said to me: 'Don't mention menopause. Not sexy. Why bring it up?' I said: 'Hey, what do you mean? This woman is 55 years old—I'm not going to write a movie about people this age and have them act like they're 32. It's part of the story.'"

Meyers, known for her privileged, upscale backdrops, is not talking about cinema verité. In *Something's Gotta Give,* Diane Keaton's successful playwright lives in a Hamptons mansion, is whisked to Paris by a handsome young cardiologist (Keanu Reeves), and is followed there by a multimillionaire entrepreneur (Jack Nicholson). The sex scenes allowed only a quick and appealing flash of flesh. It contains nothing of the bracing honesty of *Terms of Endearment* (1983), which had Jack

Nicholson (again an irrepressible aging playboy) and Shirley MacLaine display bulging bellies as they faced each other across a bed for their first sexual encounter. Here middle age could be just as passionate as youth even without a perfect body.

Like the caricatures of middle-aged women as depressed and stodgy, Stepford perfection can reverberate through the culture in a troubling way. The bombardment of images of middle-aged women with long, lustrous hair, smooth faces, and insatiable desire is strong incentive to use Botox, wrinkle cream, and hormone therapy. Absence, the more common fate of middle-aged women in Hollywood, is similarly powerful. When people over 40 are erased from cinematic tales of love, intrigue, excitement, or heroism, the tacit message is that such adventures are for another generation.

Modern screen romances match up men, no matter what their age, with nubile women. In the 2009 film *Crazy Heart,* a well-worn Jeff Bridges, 60, was paired with Maggie Gyllenhaal, 32; in *Lost in Translation* (2003), Bill Murray, then 54, had a deep connection with Scarlett Johansson, 19; and in *Entrapment* (1999), Sean Connery, then 69, teamed up with Catherine Zeta-Jones, 30. Woody Allen has repeatedly cast himself as the object of youthful desire in several of his films.

When actors and actresses are close in age, they are frequently put in different generations. At 36, Anne Bancroft was the predatory Mrs. Robinson in *The Graduate* (1967), although she was a mere six years older than Dustin Hoffman, who played the wet-behind-the-ears college graduate. In the 1962 version of *The Manchurian Candidate,* Angela Lansbury, just three years older than Laurence Harvey, played his mother. More recently, Hope Davis, born in 1964, said that for one movie part, she was asked to be the mother of Johnny Depp, born in 1963. "That tells you something about the absurdity of this industry and the whole age thing," she said. She turned down the role. As one writer suggested, in Hollywood women seem to age in dog years—seven for every one a man experiences.

After retiring, the silent-screen star Lillian Gish recalled: "When I first went into the movies Lionel Barrymore played my grandfather. Later he played my father, and finally he played my husband. If he had lived, I'm sure I would have played his mother. That's the way it is in Hollywood. The men get younger and the women get older."

Today, middle-aged women don't even get to play middle-aged women. In the 2004 film *Alexander,* Angelina Jolie was 28 when she portrayed the mother of Colin Farrell, 27. (Val Kilmer, at 45, was the father.) Men in their 30s are credibly cast as 20-year-olds, whereas women in their 20s are pictured as middle-aged. Hollywood, of course, is in the business of fantasy. Still, a casting formula that excises middle age altogether constricts judgments of style and beauty. American films conform to a different sort of Tayloresque standardization, a uniformity that the novelist Italo Calvino said failed to "teach us to see real women with an eye prepared to discover unfamiliar beauty."

Male stars are also routinely subjected to airbrushing and Botoxing. Hugh Grant, 49, gave an unintentional peek at the contrast between life and Hollywood art when he stood in front of a blown-up publicity shot from the 2010 movie *Did You Hear About the Morgans?* The enlarged picture showed a slimmed-down, line-free face, while that of the flesh-and-blood Grant, still handsome, revealed the realistic signposts of middle age. Even so, men are permitted to age on-screen in a way that women are not. They can play heroes, villains, and everymen as well as romantic leads well into their 60s. ("Sean Connery is 300 years old and he's still a stud," an aging actress tells her plastic surgeon in the 1996 film *The First Wives Club.*) A tiny clutch of privileged actresses like Keaton in *Something's Gotta Give* (2003), Meryl Streep in *Mama Mia!* and *It's Complicated* (2009), and Julia Roberts in *Larry Crowne* (2011) get to play desirable, funny, smart women in their middle years without being reduced to cougars. The available parts are still nowhere near the numbers and range of those available to men. Researchers studying the "double jeopardy" of age and gender bias found that "youth was the most powerful criterion for women who won the Best Actress award, while middle age was the best predictor for male Best Actor winners."

During the ten years it took Helen Hunt to produce *Then She Found Me* (2007), she remembers being bluntly told: "We're not going to make it because it's about a woman who is 40."

Geena Davis, a glamour girl when she entered the business in the late 1970s, found herself in the unaccustomed position of promoting a film, *Accidents Happen,* without a distributor. "I know I've never done any independent film before," the 53-year-old actress said in 2009, "but there aren't that many other scripts out there with great parts for women my age."

When she started in Hollywood, Davis said, "I thought, this is a new era, and I won't have to worry" about parts disappearing for middle-aged women. "It will all be fixed by the time I'm 40! And of course, it wasn't. All of us female actors think we can just keep going and going. . . . You wake up one day and you're flabbergasted to find out . . . so, this has happened to me."

Hollywood had typically been more cruel than kind to women in their middle years.

14

The Arrival of the Alpha Boomer

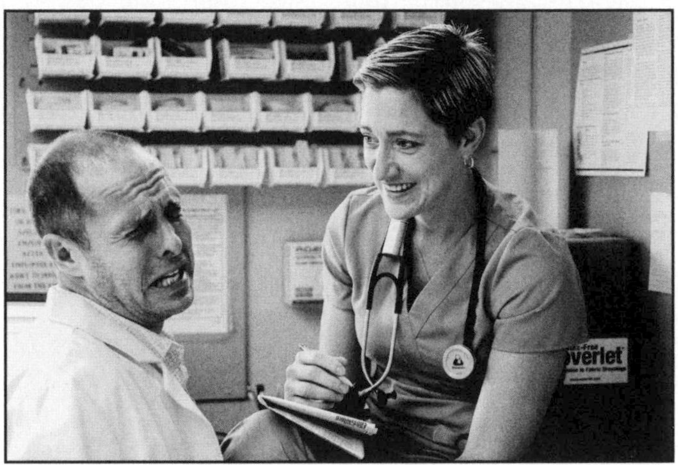

Paul Schulze as Eddie and Edie Falco as Jackie Peyton in *Nurse Jackie*

Middle age is a wonderful country, all the things you thought would never happen are happening.

—John Updike, *Rabbit at Rest* (1981)

The Midlife Industrial Complex is a formidable force in our culture, a vast network of interests intent on reinforcing deep-grained associations of middle age with insecurity and disappointment. Combating them is difficult. Midlife drags around a weight of past insults, expectations, and discrimination. The very words are bathed in negative connotations. Nonetheless, there are encouraging signs that more positive messages about midlife are penetrating the culture. Even within the fortress of the Midlife Industrial Complex, an expanded conception of midlife is gaining traction on television, in advertising, and among businesses.

Meet the Alpha Boomer

NBC Universal had a new character to introduce to reporters, advertisers, and ad buyers who attended a breakfast in December 2010: the alpha boomer, a member of the 55- to 64-year-old demographic, who number 35 million and spend more than $1.8 trillion annually. Clicking through slides filled with pie charts, graphs, and survey data, NBC executives explained that contrary to conventional wisdom, this slice of the population had the second-highest median income (after the beta boomers, those between 45 and 54 years old), frequently switched brands, and was annoyed that advertisers were ignoring them. They spent more on luxury cars, travel, dining, home furnishings and improvements, large appliances, cosmetics and beauty products compared with those between 18 and 49. They also owned more second homes. They adapted to technology like DVRs, broadband, high definition, and the Internet at the same rate as 18- to 34-year-olds, the delicious candy center of television demographics. And in the previous three months, they had spent thirty percent more on electronics and forty-nine percent more on online purchases than a typical Generation Y (born in the early 1980s through 2001) consumer. Like Rip Van Winkle waking from a twenty-year sleep, NBC had discovered that the alpha boomer was in fact the alpha consumer.

NBC's epiphany had come earlier in the year when Nielsen reported that CNBC, the cable news channel, suffered a precipitous drop in ratings. Viewers had not suddenly tuned out. Rather, three of the people in Nielsen's focus group turned 55 and simply disappeared off the ratings radar screen. "Every seven seconds someone turns 55, and once they do, they are eliminated from the highest-end Nielsen demographic measurement," Alan Wurtzel, president of research and media development at NBC Universal, explained.

NBC, which had for years derided CBS's arguments about middle-aged viewers, suddenly got religion, and was pushing Nielsen to track the TV habits of the 55- to 64-year-old group.

Many ad buyers considered NBC's strategy evidence of desperation; when the network introduced the alpha boomer, only one of its shows was on the list of twenty-five highest-rated programs. NBC was failing, yet it was also true that ad buyers had consistently ignored any information that contradicted the 18-to-49 gospel. When research showed that people in midlife switched brands more frequently than younger people and were more avid consumers, television advertisers and buyers altered their rationale instead of their strategy. They stopped citing brand loyalty and spending patterns and declared that young viewers were more valuable because they were so difficult to reach. Baby boomers are a dime a dozen, they argued; they watch television and read magazines and newspapers in large numbers. Young people divide their attention among so many different media that it is hard to capture a sizable audience in one place. Thus, advertisers felt justified in spending two to three times as much to reach scarce viewers in the 18- to 34-year-old age group compared with those over age 35.

Nielsen's own research presented an alternate perspective. Working with Hallmark Channels, a unit of Hallmark Cards, Nielsen discovered in a 2009 survey that middle-agers accounted for the majority of buyers for products generally thought to appeal to younger people, such as beer, soda, and candy. (Junk food and alcohol, it seems, transcend the generations.) The problem derives from misperceptions by people under 25. More than half of the postwar generation describe themselves as "open to new ideas," yet only twelve percent of young adults *think* their elders feel that way. Surveys show that the young imagine much more memory loss, serious illness, infrequent sex, depression, and poverty than people actually experience as they age. In truth, the more years people accumulate, the younger they feel. When the Pew Research Center asked Americans how old they felt, most respondents in midlife said up to ten years younger than their current age, and those over 65 said between ten and twenty years. Callow media buyers have a distorted view of anyone over 35, due, in part, to the way that age group is portrayed in the mass media. It's a self-defeating cycle: young buyers fall victim to the very misconceptions they help to perpetuate.

The deference to youth seems Pavlovian. The average age of a television viewer is 51. Ad buyers keep salivating though the consumers have stopped showing up.

Boomers are also the biggest spenders. Forty-seven used to be the age of maximum consumption, when people spent most of their income; in 2009, it was 54. This generation "has assets, not allowances," said Henry Schleiff, president and chief executive at Hallmark Channels. The trend has held up through the recession. In 2011, Joe Stagaman, a senior vice president at Nielsen, said: "The misconception is that spending drops for people in this age group." But those 55 and up switch brands and buy nearly as much as the 25-to-54 segment.

The determination to defy midlife stereotypes has rendered obsolete the traditional models based on age. "What advertisers are recognizing is that even though youth are still important, you can't look at these big, broad demographic age groups" in a vacuum, said CBS's David Poltrack, for many years the lone voice championing midlife audiences. "There are just too many sub-segments." CBS, the only network to establish a permanent site, in Las Vegas, to test audience reactions to its shows, has poured money into market research. The findings have encouraged the network to move away from broad generational labels altogether. Instead, it has created a bouquet of new psychographic categories, organizing its audience according to affinities and attitudes, like "sports extremists" and "surfers and streamers."

The approach is one that Bernice Neugarten predicted more than twenty years ago: "Perhaps the most constructive ways of adapting to an aging society will emerge by focusing not on age at all but on the more relevant dimensions of human needs, human capacities, and human diversity." Matt Thornhill, president and founder of the Boomer Project, a research and marketing consulting firm in Richmond, Virginia, currently offers his clients similar advice, telling them to bypass appeals based on age and focus on lifestyle. Two other consulting firms that specialize in marketing to consumers over 40 have conjured up their own taxonomies. These categories are not necessarily any more meaningful than previous ones, but they have the virtue of not using age as the sole measure of tastes. Age Wave, a California-based firm, divides middle-aged adults into four groups according to how they envision their retirement: Age-less Explorers (youthful, empowered, and optimistic); the Comfortably Content; the Live for Today (like the ageless explorers but without the bank accounts); the Sick and Tireds (about one-third of adults, who are generally disappointed and more pessimistic about life). Focalyst, a joint venture of AARP and the consulting firm WPP, sliced the pie into narrower pieces. The firm surveyed thirty thousand respondents between the ages of 42 and 87, dividing them into six segments: Prime Time (active and successful); Going in Style (fortunate and ready); Healthy Outlook (positive and responsible); The Business of Me (regular folk); Negative Zone (overwhelmed and unfortunate); and Shutting Down (alone and ill). The four categories with a positive outlook made up seventy-three percent of the respondents; the rest fell into the two largely negative groups.

This doesn't mean that Madison Avenue has been cured of what one consultant calls Chronic Youth Syndrome. In 2011, thirty seconds of ad time on CBS's *The Good Wife,* where sixty percent of the fans are over 55, cost about $25 per thousand viewers, compared with the $47 that Fox's *Glee* is able to charge for a thousand of its younger viewers. Even so, the wall of resistance Poltrack has encountered for decades is cracking.

Television's New Golden Age

Advertising's adjustment to demographic realities is affecting programming. While grown-up films occasionally interrupt the stream of cartoon and action movies Hollywood produces, the small screen is where middle age is most prominently emerging from the trite and the clichéd. TV Land, home to television nostalgia, was launched by Viacom in 1995 to attract a middle-aged audience. The network's viewers have a median age of 55 and, according to Larry Jones, TV Land's 40-something president, they could not be happier about it. "We believe there is this huge market opportunity that Madison Avenue and a lot of marketers haven't really woken up to, haven't embraced in a big way and, quite frankly, the American culture hasn't embraced in a big way," Jones said. In 2010, the station solicited series that other networks rejected because they thought the casts were too old. "We want our audience to feel like they're part of the club," Mr. Jones said.

Other cable networks have greater ambitions, experimenting with new, higher-quality shows featuring off-beat, full-bodied middle-aged characters, often played by well-known stars. Showtime's *Nurse Jackie,* which premiered in 2009 and stars Edie Falco, is a case in point. Jackie, the head nurse in a big-city hospital, is strong, smart, not particularly glamorous, and unapologetically middle-aged, with closely cropped hair and a 40-something waistline. With a weakness for Percocet and lies, she is a mix of noble sentiments and grave flaws, compassion and common sense. Jackie manages to be sexual without being a predatory cougar. By contrast, the series' handsome young doctor is more a figure of scorn than lust, and his romantic entanglements are played for laughs.

Showtime's other midlife series include *Weeds,* with Mary Louise Parker as a suburban mom who becomes a major drug dealer; *The United States of Tara,* with Toni Collete as the owner of at least four different personalities; *The Big C,* with Laura Linney as a teacher and mother who discovers she has terminal cancer; David Duchovny as a middle-aged novelist trying to get back on track in *Californication*; and *Shameless,* with William Macy as the irredeemable, alcoholic father of a large clan. HBO has put middle-aged men at the center of *Curb Your Enthusiasm,* with the misanthropic Larry David; *Hung,* about a broke and divorced middle-aged high school basketball coach who moonlights as a male prostitute; *Good Dog,* about a middle-aged producer; and *40,* with Ed Burns, about four middle-aged men in New York City after the financial crisis.

Ironically, the increasing fragmentation of the national audience has ushered in another Golden Age of television that is every bit as innovative, rich, and sophisticated as the one that shone in the 1950s. Pay-for-view cable companies, such as Showtime and HBO, depend completely on subscribers, which means they do not have to worry about advertisers. "I think the wider the audience, the less special the show, because if you want to appeal to the most people, you have to round off the edges," said Bob Greenblatt, the former executive director of Showtime and the man responsible for presenting series built around talented middle-aged actresses like Falco and Linney. "That's why cable is such a haven."

Greenblatt told me there was no particular mission behind the spate of new programs starring middle-aged female actresses. "I just thought over the last few years, there was a dearth of great female characters on television," he explained. "It's not like it became a goal of ours, it wasn't a big strategy. It's just that there are so many great actresses who you just never see." In November 2010, a few weeks before NBC unveiled the alpha boomer, Bob Greenblatt was named president of NBC Entertainment.

Commercial cable networks aside from TV Land have turned their attention to the flourishing middle age market as well. On TNT, Kyra Sedgwick portrays a Los Angeles deputy police chief in *The Closer*; and Ray Romano, Andre Braugher, and Scott Bakula appeared in the short-lived comedy *Men of a Certain Age*. Lifetime and AMC have also successfully mined the landscape of middle age.

Comcast's purchase of a controlling interest in NBC Universal in 2011 illustrated a shifting balance of power. When the cable company announced the sale, it stressed to its shareholders that its primary interest was NBC's cable channels. The broadcast network, in last place and losing money, was mentioned as if it were an afterthought. The tail has started to wag the dog.

This transformation is shaking up the way television treats middle-aged experiences, characters, and viewers. CBS, long derided for its older *Murder, She Wrote* audience, was the most-watched network in 2009, 2010, and early 2011. Competitors envied the 13.6 million viewers (sixty-five percent of them women) that CBS has attracted for its drama *The Good Wife,* a series that not only stars a complex middle-aged woman but features single, childless women over 40 who do not conform to central casting's standard-issue heartless female careerist.

Even Fox, which has bragged about its younger audiences (the average age is 46), has backed series with middle-aged stars, including the popular *House,* with Hugh Laurie as a misanthropic medical whiz. The magical spell cast by the 18-to-49 demographic has finally been broken. Patricia McDonough, a senior vice president at Nielsen, gave the eulogy: "35 to 64 is becoming a relatively common target now."

The increasing fragmentation of the American public has troubling downsides, including competing versions of the news and the lack of a shared history and sense of civic responsibility. Yet it also shows that America is vast and diverse enough for every midlifer to find a circle that shares his or her tastes and preferences. You can essentially create a tailor-made psychographic group—a tribe based on your own interests or personality traits (at least in the digital world, if not in the real one)—where you can ridicule frozen foreheads, cougars, aging hipsters, accountants on Harleys, sagging butts, or pruney faces to your heart's content.

Marketing to Middle Age

Businesses catering to the middle age market are learning that they can profitably tell other tales besides those that glorify youth and deride midlife. The financial-planning company Freedom 55 reversed the familiar trope of tearful parents dropping off their children at college in its ads, and instead featured Mom and Dad leaving for a backpacking adventure as their college-age kids remind them to keep in touch. Other financial companies, like Bank of America and Merrill Lynch, have offered new services labeled "Second Acts" directed at alpha boomers. Mohegan Sun Casino and Resort is looking to entice middle-aged patrons. "Twenty years ago I was backstage with the band," the ad's middle-aged spokesman says. "Now I'm an actuary driving an eco-friendly car and doing Pilates, but I'm back rockin'."

The hearing aid, an emblem of faltering senescence, is being rebranded as a "hearing device," offered in colors like Crème Brûlée, Pinot Noir, Pure Passion, and Green with Envy, and compared with other devices for the ear, like a Bluetooth or headphones. Targeting middle-aged consumers, Miracle-Ear ran a print ad that featured a sixties-era teenager next to a photo of the same person, some thirty years later: "Back then you chose not to listen. Make today the day you choose to hear better." Chris Toal, senior vice president for Amplifon USA, which manufactures Miracle-Ear, said the company had not gone after an audience this young before.

Entrepreneurs have delved into unexplored areas of the midlife market. Not Your Daughter's Jeans was created in 2003 by Lisa Rudes Sandel, who, at 38, could no longer fit into her old pants. By 2010, it was the largest domestic manufacturer of jeans under $100. One ad pictured a nicely curved behind with the slogan "Bottoms Up!" PixelOptics, a lens technology company based in Roanoke, Virginia, has spent a decade developing electronic eyeglasses that can instantly autofocus, hoping to replace the bifocals and progressive lenses that the middle-aged are compelled to use for nearsightedness. Kellogg's, Sketchers, 5-Hour Energy Drink, Jeep, and other companies and products that have ignored the middle-aged have indicated that they, too, plan to address these consumers.

The shift in narratives can be detected in some corners of the beauty industry. Dayle Haddon, a model who regularly appeared in cosmetics ads in the 1980s, said that when she hit 40, "the industry just said I would never work again." At 57, she was hired by L'Oréal to represent Age Perfect creams, designed for women over 50. Lauren Hutton, fired by Revlon in 1983 when she turned 40, reappeared in cosmetics advertisements in the 1990s. She now has her own line of cosmetics and in 2005, at age 61, appeared in unretouched nude photographs in an issue of *Big* magazine. "I want them [women] not to be ashamed of who they are when they're in bed," Hutton said at the time. "Society has told us to be ashamed." Models and actresses in their 50s and 60s, including Diane Keaton, Susan Sarandon, Catherine Deneuve, Ellen DeGeneres, and Andie MacDowell, are stalwarts of cosmetics advertisements. Marketers discovered that middle-aged women were turned off by products pitched by women half their age.

Dove, a Unilever company, has benefited from its "pro-age" approach for the 50-plus set. Over the face of a 95-year-old woman, one 2006 ad asked: "Wrinkled? Wonderful? Will society ever accept old can be beautiful?" Another showed a gray-haired 45-year-old: "Gray? Gorgeous? Why aren't women glad to be gray?" We've come a long way from Clairol's 1940s-era ads warning that gray hair caused you to be "UNPOPULAR" and "PITIED."

Dove's "Real Women Have Curves" campaign caused a sensation by featuring women of various shapes and sizes in their underwear, probably creating as much free exposure in news coverage and commentary as the company got from its paid ads. In 2006, Dove launched "Beauty Comes of Age" and hired Nancy Etcoff of Harvard Medical School and Susie Orbach, a psychoanalyst and the author of *Fat Is a Feminist Issue,* to survey women between 50 and 65. Nine out of ten of those polled commented that realistic images of women over 50 were rare in advertising and other media.

Dove launched the second phase of its "Pro Age" campaign in February 2007. Its ad agency, Ogilvy, hired Annie Leibovitz to photograph nude but modestly posed women over 50. In New York, forty-foot-high, black-and-white full-body shots of these models stared out from Times Square's billboards. "We are not saying turn back the hands of time, or stop aging, or look ten years younger," said Kathy O'Brien, a marketing director at Dove. "We are saying embrace the age that you are and make the best of it."

Dove was not revealing anything new about young anorexic models. Activists, pundits, scholars, government officials, and parents have criticized the purveyors of this body image for decades. But the source of the message—marketers—was surprising. Questioning the skinny ideal "really hit a nerve," Philippe Harousseau, a marketing executive at Dove, said. "Women were ready to hear this."

The federal government was not. In 2007, when Dove tried to air television ads using these same images, the Federal Communications Commission banned them as obscene after receiving complaints from the American Family Association, a conservative Christian nonprofit based in Tupelo, Mississippi. The group charged that Dove was "focusing on outward beauty and using nudity to do so," and said that showing fully clothed women was a better way to demonstrate respect for them. The FCC maintained that totally naked women were not permitted on television, even if the modest poses ensured that no intimate parts could be seen.

Dove said it was impossible to edit the commercials in a way that would satisfy the FCC. The campaign, Dove explained, is "celebrating women 50-plus and widening the definition of beauty to show that real beauty has no age limit. The advertising campaign is certainly not about nudity, but rather about honesty. We didn't want to cover these women or enhance their appearances, because they are beautiful just as they are."

Dove's campaign for realism seemed to have impressed a few other brands. In 2008, Tylenol ads included elegantly shot black-and-white photographs of various body parts—a hand, foot, shoulder, or back—some smooth, others wrinkled. And Nike introduced an ad campaign for exercise gear that more realistically pictured body parts about which women are most sensitive. "I have thunder thighs," one ad exclaimed next to a photograph of muscular thighs. Another was accompanied by the text:

> *MY BUTT IS BIG*
> And that is just fine
> And those who might scorn it
> Are invited to Kiss it.

The Economy

Before the recession cut deep into the economy in 2008, the conversation about middle age and work had a wonderfully liberating flavor. For many people in their middle years, the prospect of having a series of careers, each more meaningful or enjoyable than the last, seemed possible. People in their 50s considered using their financial cushion to downshift into a different sort of life. Newspapers and magazines ran stories on midlife reawakenings—the middle-aged broker who gave up Wall Street to design gardens or the management consultant who became a comic.

With the financial downturn, those sunny futurescapes were replaced by dark anxieties about losing one's home, job, and emotional moorings. A severe economic recession makes it difficult for anyone to be positive—young, middle-aged, or old. Heartbreaking tales and ominous trends are in abundant supply across the generations. Nonetheless, there are reasons for optimism among the middle-aged even in this unfavorable climate.

Discrimination has been a common theme in every economic downturn since Taylorized factory production gave young men new opportunities and encouraged managers to push out those over 40. In the early decades of the twentieth century, laborers felt the bias most keenly because of the physical demands of many industrial jobs. As youth progressively became more associated with innovation, vitality, and modernity during the twenties, age discrimination further infiltrated the white-collar world, particularly in certain industries like entertainment, advertising, and the media. In 1939, during the Depression's grim years, President Roosevelt reminded employers that a blue-ribbon panel of business, labor, and experts found "no good reasons" to support the continuing prejudice, as he issued a national appeal to hire middle-aged workers.

In 1967, Congress passed the first antidiscrimination legislation making it illegal to discriminate against anyone over 40 because of age. The following year, the psychiatrist Robert Butler coined the term "ageism," explaining that it "allows the younger generations to see older people as different than themselves; thus they subtly cease to identify with their elders as human beings."

Middle-aged workers benefited from cradle-to-grave employment policies in the fifties, sixties, and seventies that rewarded staff who stayed with a company through the decades. The clear ladder of increasing pay and benefits encouraged young people to work their way up, and the rules governing seniority, promotions, and salaries discouraged discrimination. In the 1980s, though, as the economy's foundation shifted from manufacturing to service and technology, many of these employment practices altered. The Reagan administration's sustained battles with organized labor, beginning with the firing of air-traffic controllers who went on strike in 1981, further eroded protections for more senior employees. As globalization took root, white-collar workers in their 40s and 50s were jolted by blanket layoffs and a drop in wages already familiar to blue-collar workers. The aftershocks of the 1982 recession reverberated through the decade. In 1988, the *Los Angeles Times* noted, "Thousands of Americans with years of service at their companies are experiencing the vicissitudes of MAAD—Middle Aged and Downward." The familiar career track for middle-aged workers had derailed. "We are finding that the standard pattern for educated labor, where wages rise with age, is not so true anymore," Frank Levy, an economist at MIT, said in 1994.

The dot-com revolution brought a generation of young technologically savvy college graduates into the labor market, with knowledge and abilities their older colleagues simply did not possess. In the last two decades, economists have observed that jobs at the highest and lowest end of the skills range increased. Positions in the middle—stock clerks, inspectors, telemarketers, payroll workers, sales agents, and software programmers—were more likely to be automated or exported to countries with cheap labor, forcing an unaccustomed number of people over 45 into low-skilled jobs.

The recession has accelerated this "hollowing out" of the job market. Workers over 50 tend to hold on to their jobs longer than younger workers, but when they are displaced they spend much more time unemployed. Chances are their next job will have lower pay, fewer benefits, and less responsibility. Those in midlife who were laid off in 2009, the heart of the recession, saw their wages fall by more than a fifth; a quarter lost their health insurance. At the same time, the financial crisis left a wreckage of their assets; twenty to forty percent of the wealth they worked to build over the years was gone in an instant.

Although the American labor force is for the first time fairly evenly split between men and women, male-dominated industries like manufacturing and construction suffered some of the worst job losses in 2008 and 2009. The education and health-care fields, which are dominated by women and tend to have lower pay and benefits, were initially more insulated. The severe slashes that city, state, and federal officials pushed through in 2011, however, reverberated through those ranks as well.

As the second decade of the twenty-first century began, age discrimination against workers over 40 seemed pervasive despite federal age-discrimination legislation.

Clearly, few can feel secure until the economy recovers more broadly. Yet despite the havoc the economic slump is wreaking, the long-term outlook for workers in their middle decades is brighter because the total size of the American labor force is shrinking dramatically. As life span theory reminds us, the historical moment matters. Generation X has nearly 30 million fewer members than the 78 million strong baby boom generation. Even though many from this group will work past age 65, there will still be fewer employees overall. The Bureau of Labor Statistics projects that within the next ten years the number of workers between 45 and 54 will fall by five percent, while those between 35 and 44 will increase by just one percent. That imbalance will cause other economic stresses as the burdens of a large aging society fall on a smaller number of workers and Social Security is stressed beyond its ability to pay.

But as David DeLong, a research fellow at the MIT AgeLab, argues, the bulk of technical and organizational knowledge that has exploded in the past thirty to forty years primarily resides in these middle-aged brains. The combination of skills and midlife expertise is going to be a particularly desirable commodity because of difficult-to-replace technical knowledge that these employees—whether a utility lineman, a manager, or an engineer—have accumulated over the years.

"Things look bleak for a lot of people today," DeLong said, "but I truly believe that, given the demographics, things are going to get better for older workers in the next decade. The demographics are immutable."

15

In Our Prime

Health & Fitness

The New York Times

New Study Finds Middle Age Is Prime of Life

The *New York Times* headline that greeted the first MacArthur report on midlife, 1999

Youth is the period in which a man can be hopeless. The end of every episode is the end of the world. But the power of hoping through everything, the knowledge that the soul survives its adventures, that great inspiration comes to the middle-aged.

—G. K. Chesterton, *Charles Dickens* (1906)

The standardized sequence of life stages that Frederick Taylor helped inaugurate and that encouraged previous generations to move out, marry, and start families on schedule has lost much of its force. The loud tick of the social clock has been drowned out by a raucous concert of individual timepieces. In the early sixties, forgoing marriage was rare, having a baby out of wedlock was scandalous, and remaining childless in middle age was tragic. Today, all of these are commonplace.

The statistics tell the story. In 1960, sixty-eight percent of adults in their 20s were married and five percent of births were to unwed mothers. Now, only one in four 20-somethings has exchanged vows and single moms give birth to forty-one percent of infants. It is no longer shocking for middle-aged women to skip parenthood (twenty percent of those in their 40s were childless in 2010) or, thanks to fertility treatments, to become pregnant (more than fourteen percent of births were to women over 35).

Women match men's numbers in the workplace and exceed them on college campuses. At the same time, economic shifts have eroded the high-paying industrial jobs that once enabled men in their late teens or early twenties, particularly those without a college degree, to earn enough money to support themselves, let alone a family. Careers are less permanent and more varied. Willingly or not, young men are increasingly postponing the leap to independence. To look at just one segment, 25-year-old white men: a quarter of them lived at home in 2007—before the recession—compared with less than one-eighth in 1970.

Despite the disdain of contemporary life span researchers for stage theories, these changes have prompted some social scientists to argue that the period between 20 and 34 should be reclassified as "emerging adulthood." If you do not marry until your late 20s, do not have children until your 30s, and do not settle into a career until nearly 40, middle age feels less like a midpoint than a starting point. Thomas Cole's portrait of "Youth" stretching through the mid-30s and "Manhood" encompassing the late 30s, 40s, and 50s suddenly seems modern.

On the far side of midlife, another group of academics and consultants have singled out the years between 55 and 75 as a distinct category since with longer life spans so many people are healthy and capable of working past the traditional 65-year-old retirement deadline. Calling this group the "encore generation," "the third age," "midcourse," or "the new old age," advocates have revived the concept of the "young-old" category Bernice Neugarten suggested four decades ago.

Neugarten would, no doubt, be dismayed by the continuing obsession with age-based stages, but the scientific instinct to categorize and classify continues to impel men and women to more precisely situate themselves on that line between birth and death. Invariably, the first question everyone asked me upon learning I was writing about middle age was "When is it?"

Even now, long after I began thinking about this book on that sandy beach several summers ago, I am at a loss to give a simple answer. I take comfort in the fact that after $35 million and twenty years of intensive research, MIDUS has not produced a clear definition either. Survey responses from men and women, office and blue-collar workers, East Coasters and Midwesterners don't result in a typical American; they produce an imaginary one. The particular combination of physical, psychological, social, and spiritual elements that contribute to one's entry into midlife varies from person to person. Not even Justice Potter Stewart's remarkably adaptable definition of obscenity—"you know it when you see it"—seems to apply. Many people who ask me when midlife begins don't seem to know if they've reached it or left it.

The answers MIDUS III will elicit over the coming decade are bound to look different from those gathered during the first phase of research in the mid-nineties. Already we know that middle-aged boomers are more willing to divorce than their parents were. A 2011 report found that the risk of divorce among 50- to 64-year-olds has doubled during the past two decades. "Every fresh generation is a new people," Alexis de Tocqueville wrote in *Democracy in America*. In his work on the Great Depression, Glen Elder discovered just how much a different historical context could affect two contiguous generations. Future visitors to the tableland of middle age are likely to diverge in both their views and experience from today's inhabitants. Members of the baby boom were uniquely shaped by their times. They came of age during an unusual period of extended affluence, social upheaval, civil rights breakthroughs, and an unpopular war. Born before the 1965 immigration law ushered in millions of Africans, Asians, Indians, and Latinos, they are the last band of middle-aged Americans who are so ethnically homogenous. Eighty percent of them are white. As a group, they grew up watching the same television programs and listening to the same records and radio stations. They share an unusually strong generational identity. Their unprecedented numbers have exerted an irresistible gravitational pull on the culture, whether they were watching Bozo the Clown, buying their first home, or helping their own children fill out college applications.

They moved into middle age during an extraordinary transformation of the global economic system, a digital revolution, and a political realignment that shuffled foreign alliances and sharpened domestic partisan politics. They made scads of money, more than any of their predecessors, and spent it with wanton abandon. Girls who saw their mothers burdened by the feminine mystique grabbed at the thrilling surfeit of opportunities when their turn came and delayed marriage and motherhood, sometimes discovering belatedly that they had permanently deferred them. Boys whose fathers hid behind a newspaper have become expert diaper changers and class parents.

The next generation of midlifers will be molded by disparate circumstances. They have grown up in a faster and more connected world, where one in five Americans speaks a foreign language at home, television channels number in the hundreds, and texting is preferred to phoning. Young women who want children are more conscious of their biological clocks and more willing to remain single. College graduates, chastened by the harsh recession, bypass exhortations to "follow your passion," and look for vocational jobs with benefits. Despite enormous medical breakthroughs, if the epidemic of obesity persists, physical problems may make them feel middle-aged sooner even if they live longer. Their midlife is likely to be overshadowed by the seismic growth of the elderly population.

If there is one lesson that the history of middle age offers, it is just how malleable this cultural fiction can be. The definition has been stretched and massaged over the last century and a half, and bears the fingerprints of every generation through which it has passed. Today, longer life spans provide additional opportunities to switch directions and to shape the world our children and parents occupy. The passage of years bestows the experience and skills to ride out unexpected, even crushing setbacks, and to accomplish goals previously considered out of reach. Middle age can bring undiscovered passions, profound satisfactions, and newfound creativity. It is a time of extravagant possibilities.

Acknowledgments

I have many people to thank, but three deserve special mention: my friend Susan Lehman, my agent Scott Moyers, and my husband, Eddie Sutton. Susan helped me come up with the idea for the book and gave advice and assistance all the way through. Scott wrote me a fan letter after reading my work to say I had a book in me, and then he made it happen. He guided and encouraged me, and introduced me to one of the truly great editors. Eddie offered unstinting love, childcare, and ice cream.

I am extraordinarily lucky to work at the *New York Times,* where the reporters and editors inspire and amaze me every day with their dedication and talent. Particular thanks to Jon Landman, Chip McGrath, Scott Heller, Bill Carter, the brilliant lunch table, and the colleagues whose work is frequently cited in these pages. I am forever indebted to Jeff Roth. If it weren't for him, there would be no pictures in this book. Mary Hardiman has frequently lent me her creative gifts. Thanks to Fred Conrad. I am very grateful to friends who offered to read drafts and engage in lengthy discussions, including Jennifer Gordon, Phoebe Hoban, Christina Malle, Michael Massing, Celia McGee, Esther Perel, Tina Rosenberg, David Serlin, Dinitia Smith, and Chuck Sabel, who also doubled as a dedicated researcher.

I am indebted to the people who took time from their own work to help me do mine, particularly Bert Brim, Margie Lachman, Richard Davidson, Nikki Rute, Susan Jensen, Abbe Raven, David Poltrack, and Richie Jackson. I received research help early on from the smart and enthusiastic Natasha Degen.

I have benefited from the intelligence and hard work of many other scholars and authors who have written about aging, culture, and related subjects, including Margaret Morganroth Gullette, Howard Chudacoff, Thomas Cole, W. Andrew Achenbaum, Robert Kanigel, David and Sheila Rothman, Sander Gilman, Roland Marchand, Warren Susman, Glen Elder, and Anne Hollander.

Nan Graham was a demanding and wise editor, and this is a better book because of her. I am grateful to many people at Scribner who worked on my manuscript, including Daniel Burgess, Paul Whitlatch, Katie Hanson, Katie Monaghan, Katie Rizzo, Susan Moldow, Rex Bonomelli, Roz Lippel, and Kara Watson. Mindy Werner helped me work through difficult organizational problems. Andrew Wylie and his wonderful staff thankfully picked up where Scott left off.

The MacDowell Colony was a heaven-sent haven where I got an enormous amount of work done in a very short time. I also love the New York Public Library.

I am fortunate to have a surrogate family, a dear circle of close friends who were understanding when I dropped out of sight for months, and who offer love and support whether or not I am writing a book. I also want to thank my son, Alex, for putting up with my long evenings and weekends at the computer and my absence from so many of his soccer games.

Most of all, I owe an immeasurable debt to my mother and my late father, who always showered me with love and believed I could do anything.

Notes

Chapter 1: The Prime Meridian

4 *"The hero of our 20th century":* Philippe Ariès, *Centuries of Childhood,* trans. by Robert Baldick (New York: Vintage Books, 1962), 30.

4 *Yet if this is the best possible moment:* For example, Daphne Merkin, "Reinventing Middle Age," *New York Times Magazine,* May 6, 2007; William Safire, "The Way We Live Now: Halfway Humanity," *New York Times Magazine,* May 6, 2007; Winifred Gallagher, "Midlife Myths," *Atlantic Monthly,* May 1993, 51.

6 *But only in the last 150 years:* Thomas R. Cole, *The Journey of Life: A Cultural History of Aging in America* (New York: Cambridge University Press, 1993), x, 10–11.

6 *Middle age is a "cultural fiction":* Bradd Shore, "Status Reversed," in *Welcome to Middle Age! (And Other Cultural Fictions),* Richard Shweder, ed. (Chicago: University of Chicago Press, 1998), xiv–xv, 109.

7 *Despite a freighter's worth of books:* Margaret Morganroth Gullette is one of the few scholars who have written about the history of middle age.

8 *The task of improving our midlife:* Alfred Kazin, "The Freudian Revolution Analyzed," *New York Times Magazine,* May 6, 1956.

8 *Forty has long been:* Robert Kastenbaum, ed. *Encyclopedia of Adult Development* (Phoenix: Oryx Press, 1993), 32–34; Stanley Brandes, *Forty: The Age and the Symbol* (Knoxville: University of Tennessee Press, 1987).

9 *Extensive surveys reveal that the:* Subjective Aging, MIDUS newsletter, http://www.midus.wisc.edu/newsletter/ (accessed June 11, 2011).

9 *In 2009, Pew asked:* Pew Research Center staff, *Growing Old in America: Expectations vs. Reality,* Pew Research Center (June 2009), http://pewsocialtrends.org/2009/06/29/growing-old-in-america-expectations-vs-reality/ (accessed June 30, 2009).

9 *The mammoth ongoing study:* Midlife in the United States was originally funded by the MacArthur Foundation and called the MacArthur Foundation Network on Successful Midlife Development. When the federal government took it over in 2002, the name changed.

9 *We are like the tourists:* ID: 122649, published in *New Yorker,* July 10, 2006.

9 *As Bernice Neugarten, a pioneer:* Bernice Neugarten, "The Awareness of Middle Age," in *Middle Age and Aging: A Reader in Social Psychology,* Bernice Neugarten, ed. (Chicago: University of Chicago Press, 1973), 97.

11 *It is a "missing category":* Katherine S. Newman, "Place and Race: Midlife Experience in Harlem," in *Welcome to Middle Age!,* Shweder, ed., 283; Katherine S. Newman, *A Different Shade of Gray: Midlife and Beyond in the Inner City* (New York: New Press, 2003).

12 *Middle age was an unavoidable:* Gail Sheehy, *Passages* (New York: E. P. Dutton, 1976), 17.

12 *As researchers attempted to redefine:* Margie Lachman, "Development in Midlife," *Annual Review of Psychology* 55 (2004): 305–31.

Chapter 2: Now and Then

15 *"Surprisingly little attention has been":* Orville Gilbert Brim, Carol D. Ryff, and Ronald C. Kessler, *How Healthy Are We? A National Study of Well-Being at Midlife* (Chicago: University of Chicago Press, 2004), 1.

19 *"People in midlife raise":* MacArthur Foundation Study of Successful Midlife Development, *ICPSR Bulletin* XX, no. 4 (Summer 2000).

20 *As Brim declared:* Brim et al., *How Healthy Are We?,* 1–2; Orville Gilbert Brim interview with author, June 8, 2008.

21 *"Considering the major studies":* Laurel Lippert, "Women at Midlife: Implications for Theories of Women's Adult Development," *Journal of Counseling & Development* 76, no. 1 (Winter 1997): 16–22.

21 *MacArthur recruited nearly 7,200 men:* Brim et al., *How Healthy Are We?,* 2–22.

21 *Middle age begins:* Margaret Morganroth Gullette, "Midlife Discourses," in *Welcome to Middle Age!,* Shweder, ed., 17.

22 *"Sometimes things that really":* Shirley S. Wang, "Is Happiness Overrated?," *Wall Street Journal,* March 15, 2011.

22 *Are you sad, nervous, restless:* MIDUS website, http://www.midus.wisc.edu/midus1/ (accessed June 11, 2011).

23 *In the early 1990s:* Deborah Carr interview with author, 2008.

23 *All in all, respondents answered:* MIDMAC website, http://midmac.med.harvard.edu/ (accessed June 12, 2011).

23 *The National Institutes of Health:* MIDUS website, http://www.midus.wisc.edu/midus2/ (accessed June 14, 2011); Brim interview with author, 2008.

24 *Midlife was a "watershed period":* Alice S. Rossi, "Social Responsibility to Family and Community," in Brim et al., *How Healthy Are We?,* 556.

24 *Freud rejected patients:* Eda Goldstein, *When the Bubble Bursts: Clinical Perspectives on Midlife Issues* (Hillsdale, NJ: Analytic Press, 2005), 10.

25 *When researchers asked people:* David Almeida and Melanie C. Horn, "Is Daily Life More Stressful During Middle Adulthood?," in Brim et al., *How Healthy Are We?,* 445.

25 *"From many points of view":* Rossi, "Social Responsibility to Family and Community," 581.

25 *In 2010, Carol Ryff and her colleagues:* J. A. Morozink et al., "Socioeconomic and Psychosocial Predictors of Interleukin-6 in the MIDUS National Sample," *Health Psychology* 29, no. 6 (November 2010): 626–35.

26 *you can travel to:* Another version of the series (1842) is at the National Gallery of Art in Washington, D.C.

26 *The young have "vigor and firmness":* Andrew W. Achenbaum, *Old Age in the New Land: The American Experience Since 1790* (Baltimore: Johns Hopkins University Press, 1978), 9.

26 *"It appears, in fact, that":* John Demos, *Past, Present, and Personal: The Family and the Life Course in American History* (New York: Oxford University Press, 1986), 117.

26 *Popular illustrations sold:* Cole, *Journey of Life,* xxix.

27 *In the seventeenth and eighteenth:* David Hackett Fischer, *Growing Old in America* (New York: Oxford University Press, 1978), 86–87.

27 *As the historian Howard Chudacoff:* Howard P. Chudacoff, *How Old Are You? Age Consciousness in American Culture* (Princeton, NJ: Princeton University Press, 1989), 107.

27 *The word "midlife" first appeared:* Lachman, "Development in Midlife."

27 *References to the various:* Ariès, *Centuries of Childhood,* 20–32.

28 *Prior to 1850, age was rarely used to measure status:* Demos, *Past, Present, and Personal,* 98, 127; John Demos, *A Little Commonwealth: Family Life in Plymouth Colony* (New York: Oxford University Press, 1970).

28 *Thomas Cole's eulogist:* William Cullen Bryant, *On the Life of Thomas Cole,* a funeral oration delivered before the National Academy of Design, New York, May 4, 1848, http://www.catskillarchive.com/cole/wcb.htm (accessed June 11, 2011).

28 *The term "happy birthday":* http://ngrams.googlelabs.com/, author search.

28 *The practice of sending cards:* Chudacoff, *How Old Are You?,* 133.

28 *Mothers gave birth:* Fischer, *Growing Old in America*; Carole Haber, *Beyond Sixty-Five: The Dilemma of Old Age in America's Past* (Cambridge, MA: Cambridge University Press, 1983).

28 *A prolapsed uterus was:* Mabel Collins Donnelly, *The American Victorian Woman: The Myth and the Reality* (Westport, CT: Greenwood Press, 1968).

29 *And the soulful encounter:* Fischer, *Growing Old in America,* 53–56; Demos, *Past, Present, and Personal.*

29 *Adults worked nearly eighty hours:* Robert Fogel et al., *The Changing Body: Health, Nutrition, and Human Development in the Western World Since 1700* (Cambridge, MA: Cambridge University Press, 2011).

29 *Sunday church services:* W. B. Irwin, monograph, *George Irwin and His Family (1794–1846),* New York Public Library.

29 *Women outside cities:* Christiane Fischer, *Let Them Speak for Themselves, Women in the American West 1849–1900* (New York: Archon Books, 1977).

30 *Today, a 50-something reader:* Christopher Buckley, *Boomsday: A Novel* (New York: Twelve, 2007).

31 *"Just as they neared the":* Fischer, *Let Them Speak for Themselves,* 85–86.

Chapter 3: The Tick of the Time Clock

32 *"Taylor seems to have":* Robert Kanigel, *The One Best Way: Frederick Winslow Taylor and the Enigma of Efficiency* (New York: Viking, 1997), 12.

32 *At a memorial at the National:* Bryant, *On the Life of Thomas Cole.*

33 *"Thirty is the age of the gods":* Cincinnati, Methodist Episcopal Church, *The Ladies' Repository: A Monthly Periodical, Devoted to Literature, Arts, and Religion* 1, no. 3 (March 1868), 172–75, http://name.umdl.umich.edu/acg2248.3-01.003 (accessed June 12, 2011); "Holidays for Middle-Age," *Scribner's Monthly* 9, no. 2 (December 1874); "Middle Age," *Harper's Bazar,* October 26, 1889.

33 *In 1881, the* New York Times *declared:* "In the Middle Age," *New York Times,* November 6, 1881.

34 *the introduction of new novelistic:* James Wood, *The Art of Fiction* (New York: Picador, 2009), 87: "One of the obvious reasons for the rise of this kind of significantly insignificant detail is that it is needed to evoke the passage of time, and fiction has a new and unique project in literature—the management of temporality."

34 *In 1878, the year Bryant died:* Kanigel, *One Best Way.*

35 *Whether or not Taylor:* Jill Lepore, "Not So Fast," *New Yorker,* October 12, 2009.

35 *In 1913, Ford's workers:* Harold Evans, *The American Century* (New York: Alfred A. Knopf, 2000), 113.

35 *One management scholar judged:* Kanigel, *One Best Way,* 18.

35 *Clocks began adorning walls in the 1830s:* Chudacoff, *How Old Are You?,* 49–50.

36 *Laying out his ideas:* Kanigel, *One Best Way,* 123, 439.

37 *He was born in 1856:* Ibid., 44, 49–51, 104–5; Sudhir Kakar, *Frederick Taylor: A Study in Personality and Innovation* (Cambridge, MA: MIT Press, 1970).

37 *There he witnessed:* Kanigel, *One Best Way,* 215.

38 *Complaints of bad eyesight:* Ibid., 13, 123; Kakar, *Frederick Taylor.*

38 *Robert Kanigel, Taylor's biographer, compares:* Kanigel, *One Best Way,* 13.

38 *Even modernist artists were:* Peter Watson, *The Modern Mind: An Intellectual History of the 20th Century* (New York: HarperCollins, 2001).

38 *Growing government bureaucracies:* Chudacoff, *How Old Are You?,* 65.

39 *Women's clubs became:* Ibid., 105–7.

39 *In 1900, the Swedish writer:* Watson, *Modern Mind,* 77; Ellen Key, *The Century of the Child* (New York: G. P. Putnam's Sons, 1909).

39 *Arguing the aged should:* Louis Bishop, "The Relation of Old Age to Disease with Illustrative Cases," *American Journal of Nursing* (Philadelphia: J. B. Lippincott Co., 1904), 679.

40 *Five years later:* Chudacoff, *How Old Are You?,* 53, 114; A. M. Clarfield, "Dr. Ignatz Nascher and the Birth of Geriatrics," *CMAJ: Canadian Medical Association Journal* 143, no. 9 (November 1, 1990): 944–48.

40 *Hall defined the stage:* G. Stanley Hall, *Adolescence: Its Psychology and Its Relations to Physiology, Anthropology, Sociology, Sex, Crime, Religion, and Education* (New York: D. Appleton & Co., 1904); Chudacoff, *How Old Are You?,* 67; Cole, *Journey of Life,* 195.

40 *A look at early life expectancy charts can:* Fischer, *Growing Old in America,* 107; Haber, *Beyond Sixty-Five*; "Table 12: Estimated Life Expectancy at Birth in Years, by Race and Sex: Death-Registration States, 1900–1928, and United States, 1929–2004—Con.," *National Vital Statistics Reports* 56, no. 9 (December 28, 2007): 35.

41 *With fewer babies and more time and money:* Peter Gay, *Schnitzler's Century: The Making of Middle-Class Culture 1815–1914* (New York: W. W. Norton, 2002), 40.

41 *who counseled families on the logistics of:* Ibid., 53–54.

41 *The invention of vulcanized:* H. Youssef, "The History of the Condom," *Journal of the Royal Society of Medicine* 84, no. 4 (April 1993): 226–28, PMCID: PMC1293956.

41 *By 1900, the typical mother:* Fischer, *Growing Old in America,* 144–45.

42 *As historians note, societies are governed by:* Peter Gay, *Modernism: The Lure of Heresy* (New York: W. W. Norton, 2010), 27.

42 *The number of urban residents:* U.S. Census, http://www.census.gov/population/censusdata/urpop0090.txt (accessed June 11, 2011).

42 *Divisions were not as:* Chudacoff, *How Old Are You?*; Fischer, *Growing Old in America.*

42 *Age consciousness was most:* Watson, *Modern Mind,* 50.

42 *Dire economic conditions:* Arthur Herman, *The Idea of Decline in Western Civilization* (New York: Free Press, 1997), 166.

42 *In 1900, fewer than a fifth:* Claude Fischer, *Made in America: A Social History of American Culture and Character* (Chicago: University of Chicago Press, 2011), 48.

43 *The cable lines and periodicals:* Richard D. Brown, *Knowledge Is Power: The Diffusion of Information in Early America, 1700–1865* (Oxford, UK: Oxford University Press, 1989); Evans, *American Century,* xx; Robert S. Lynd and Helen Merrell Lynd, *Middletown: A Study in Modern American Culture* (New York: Harcourt, Brace and Co., 1929), 479, 491.

43 *Residents from coast to coast:* Anne Hollander, *Seeing Through Clothes* (New York: Viking Press, 1978), 349–50; Warren I. Susman, *Culture as History: The Transformation of American Society in the Twentieth Century* (Washington, D.C.: Smithsonian Institution Press, 2003).

43 *By the end of the century:* "Old Ladies' Fashions," *Los Angeles Times,* February 24, 1895, 22.

43 *Mrs. Wilson Woodrow:* Mrs. Wilson Woodrow, "The Woman of Fifty," *Cosmopolitan: A Monthly Illustrated Magazine,* March 1903, 344, 5, APS Online, 505–12; *Harper's Bazar,* October 26, 1889.

43 *"The New Styles That":* "The New Styles That Are Designed for the Young, Old and Middle Aged Men," *San Francisco Call,* June 5, 1904.

44 *James Foster Scott, a:* Chudacoff, *How Old Are You?,* 54.

44 *According to John Henry Kellogg:* Lois W. Banner, *In Full Flower: Aging Women, Power, and Sexuality* (New York: Alfred A. Knopf, 1992), 278.

44 *"The haste and impetuosity":* Chudacoff, *How Old Are You?,* 59.

44 *Failure to conform to these:* http://ngram.googlelabs.com chart, author search; Lynd and Lynd, *Middletown,* 478–95.

44 *As assorted experts displaced religious authorities:* Not that the two are necessarily contradictory.

45 *In the health field:* John Harvey Kellogg, *The Battle Creek Sanitarium System* (Battle Creek, MI: Gage Printing Co., 1908), 1.

45 *Also in the domestic arena:* Barbara Ehrenreich and Deirdre English, *For Her Own Good: Two Centuries of the Experts' Advice to Women* (New York: Anchor Books, 2005), 161–62.

45 *The following year, Christine Frederick:* Ibid., 163; Christine Frederick, "The New Housekeeping: Efficiency Studies in Home Management," *Ladies'*

Home Journal, September–December 1912, excerpted by the National Humanities Center, Research Triangle Park, NC, 2005, http://hearth.library.cornell.edu/; http://lcweb2.loc.gov:8081/ammem/amrlhtml/dtchrist.html (accessed June 12, 2011).

45 *In 1913,* Life *magazine:* Kanigel, *One Best Way,* 514.

46 *After* Principles *appeared, Samuel Gompers:* Ibid., 504.

46 *"Here's the specifications":* Sinclair Lewis, *Babbitt,* Project Gutenberg, http://www.gutenberg.org/catalog/world/readfile?fk_files=1444770 (accessed June 12, 2011).

46 *Pauline Manford, the wealthy modern:* Edith Wharton, *Twilight Sleep* (New York: Scribner, 1997), 98.

47 *Christine Frederick explained the:* Frederick, "The New Housekeeping."

47 *John D. Rockefeller established:* Ehrenreich and English, *For Her Own Good,* 207–8.

47 *If an inhabitant of 1890:* Lynd and Lynd, *Middletown,* 153–78; Norman F. Cantor, *The American Century: Varieties of Culture in Modern Times* (New York: Harper Perennial, 1997).

Chapter 4: The Renaissance of the Middle-Aged

49 *In a 1701 sermon:* Cotton Mather, *A Father's Resolutions,* http://www.spurgeon.org/~phil/mather/resolvd.htm (accessed June 10, 2011).

50 *On this spiritual journey:* Wilbur Hervey, *The Monitor,* vol. 2 (Boston: Cummings, Hilliard and Co., 1824), 174.

50 *G. Stanley Hall claimed youth symbolized purity:* Cole, *Journey of Life,* 214.

51 *"It is a tarnished, travestied youth that":* Randolph Silliman Bourne, *Youth and Life* (Boston: Houghton Mifflin, 1913), 14.

51 *"Middle age has the prestige":* Ibid., 90.

51 *Resources and expertise:* George Miller Beard, *A Practical Treatise on Nervous Exhaustion (Neurasthenia)* (New York: E. B. Treat, 1880), 80.

51 *The revered Harvard psychologist:* Michael Bellesiles, *1877: America's Year of Living Violently* (New York: New Press, 2010), 276.

51 *Beard believed nervous breakdowns:* Edward M. Brown, "An American Treatment for the 'American Nervousness': George Miller Beard and General Electrization," presented to the American Association of the History of Medicine, Boston, 1980.

52 *Middle-class Victorian women were:* Gay, *Schnitzler's Century,* 132–38; Elaine Showalter, *Hystories: Hysterical Epidemics and Modern Media* (New York: Columbia University Press, 1998); "Hysteria or Insanity," *New York Times,* October 13, 1883; Jean Strouse, *Alice James: A Biography* (Cambridge, MA: Harvard University Press, 1999), ix, 103–4, 301–2; Alice James, *The Diary of Alice James* (New York: Penguin, 1964), 206–7.

52 *He investigated how long:* George Beard, *American Nervousness: Its Causes and Consequences* (New York: G. P. Putnam, 1881), 193–230.

53 *This idea of a limited number of constructive:* Anthony Trollope, *The Fixed Period* (London: Penguin 1882, 1993); Cole, *Journey of Life.*

53 *After deciding to leave the:* Sir William Osler, *Aequanimitas, with Other Addresses to Medical Students, Nurses and Practitioners of Medicine* (London: H. K. Lewis, 1906), 391; Cole, *Journey of Life*; G. Stanley Hall, *Senescence: The Last Half of Life* (New York: D. Appleton & Co., 1922), 4.

54 *Reports of Osler's joking references:* Jonathan B. Imber, "Twilight of the Prosthetic Gods: Medical Technology and Trust," *Hedgehog Review* (Fall 2002).

54 *In eighteenth-century America:* Fischer, *Growing Old in America,* 82–86.

54 *A 1904 article in the* New York Times*:* "Youth Crowding Out Even Middle Age," *New York Times,* October 10, 1904.

55 *Oliver Wendell Holmes, who disdained contemporaries:* Louis Menand, *The Metaphysical Club: A Story of Ideas in America* (New York: Farrar, Straus and Giroux, 2002), 338.

55 *In a revealing study of:* Martin U. Martel, "Age-Sex Roles in Magazine Fiction," in *Middle Age and Aging,* Bernice Neugarten, ed. (Chicago: University of Chicago Press, 1973), 56.

55 *In 1905, the same year Osler:* "Middle Aged Folks," *Gainesville Daily Sun,* May 3, 1905, 3.

56 *Those who became active:* Carroll Smith-Rosenberg, *Disorderly Conduct: Visions of Gender in Victorian America* (New York: Alfred A. Knopf, 1985), 87, 173–75.

56 *A number of these reformers:* Banner, *In Full Flower,* 332.

56 *"The needs of the world":* "Middle Age: When the Children Marry," *Harper's Bazar,* October 25, 1889.

57 *Whether they worked in a factory or an office:* Neugarten, *Middle Age and Aging,* 11.

57 *In 1900, about a fifth:* Fact Sheet 2006, Professional Women: Vital Statistics, AFL-CIO, Department for Professional Employees.

57 *As the writer Gertrude Atherton:* Gertrude Atherton, *Adventures of a Novelist* (New York: Liveright Inc., 1932).

57 *A 45-year-old who:* "Middle Age—Freedom of Movement," *Harper's Bazar,* August 8, 1899, 32, 37.

57 *Martin Martel, the sociologist:* Martel, "Age-Sex Roles in Magazine Fiction," 56.

57 *Between 1890 and 1920:* Banner, *In Full Flower,* 276.

57 *Those thirty years:* A.M.B., Letters to the Editor, "The Woman of Middle Age," *New York Times,* October 11, 1922.

58 *In 1906, a British writer:* Mary Mortimer-Maxwell, "An Englishwoman in New York: The Bachelor Girl," *New York Times,* May 20, 1906.

58 *The* Gainesville Daily Sun*:* "Middle Aged Folks," *Gainesville Daily Sun.*

58 *Whether or not mammas were thrown:* Smith-Rosenberg, *Disorderly Conduct,* 176.

58 *"Today the most influential":* Mrs. Wilson Woodrow, "Youth Crowding Out Even Middle Age," *Cosmopolitan,* October 10, 1904.

58 *Edith Wharton, after suffering through a sexless:* Kennedy Fraser, *Ornament and Silence: Essays on Women's Live from Edith Wharton to Germaine Greer* (New York: Vintage Books, 1998), 77.

58 *She pronounced menopause:* Banner, *In Full Flower,* 274.

58 *Successive generations of New:* Smith-Rosenberg, *Disorderly Conduct,* 34.

Chapter 5: The Middle-Aged Body

60 *"The building up":* Bernarr Macfadden, *Vitality Supreme,* Project Gutenberg ebook, 12, http://www.gutenberg.org/catalog/world/readfile?fk_files=1515612 (accessed June 11, 2011).

61 *Health reformers spoke:* Cole, *Journey of Life,* 93–101.

61 *During one of* Physical Culture*'s:* http://www.bernarrmacfadden.com/macfadden2.html (accessed June 14, 2011).

61 *success depended on "developing the":* Macfadden, *Vitality Supreme,* 14.

61 *Physical fitness could work:* Mark Adams, *Mr. America: How Muscular Millionaire Bernarr Macfadden Transformed the Nation Through Sex, Salad, and the Ultimate Starvation Diet* (New York: HarperCollins, 2009), 98–99.

61 *Even Randolph Bourne, whose body:* Bourne, *Youth and Life,* 14.

62 *The use of the word "hygiene":* http://ngram.googlelabs.com, author search of "hygiene."

62 *Science had transformed the body:* Herbert Tucker, ed., *A Companion to Literature & Culture* (Malden, MA: Blackwell Publishing, 1999), 105.

62 *John Henry Kellogg wrote:* Kellogg, *Battle Creek Sanitarium System,* 1.

62 *McFadden also ran a sanitarium:* http://www.bernarrmacfadden.com/macfadden2.html (accessed June 14, 2011).

62 *A healthy body was seen as:* Cole, *Journey of Life,* 173–74.

62 *Cesare Lombroso, the Italian doctor:* Herman, *Idea of Decline in Western Civilization,* 109–30.

63 *Elie Metchnikoff, who won the Nobel Prize:* Clarfield, "Dr. Ignatz Nascher and the Birth of Geriatrics."

63 *The flush of spending and display:* Thorstein Veblen, *Theory of the Leisure Class* (New York: New American Library, 1953), 60.

64 *"All, with hardly an exception":* Hall, *Sensescence,* 101.

64 *America had turned into what the poet:* Vachel Lindsay, *The Art of the Moving Picture,* http://www.fullbooks.com/The-Art-Of-The-Moving-Picture1.html, 37 (accessed June 12, 2011).

64 *D. W. Griffith invented the close-up*: Gay, *Modernism,* 369.

64 *"Is Your Skin Younger or Older Than You Are?":* Ad*Access, Duke University Libraries, http://library.duke.edu/digitalcollections/images/eaa/P/P01/P0160/P0160-lrg.jpeg (accessed June 10, 2011).

65 *Films reinforced expectations about:* Hollander, *Seeing Through Clothes,* 344–47.

65 *Gibson Girl drawings, created:* Ibid., 23.

65 *"When it came to age":* Ad*Access, Duke University Libraries, http://library.duke.edu/digitalcollections/images/eaa/P/P01/P0160/P0160-lrg.jpeg (accessed June 10, 2011).

65 *On occasion, customers even:* William Ewing, "The Shock of Photography," in *100,000 Years of Beauty: Modernity/Globalisation,* Elizabeth Azoulay, ed. (Paris: Gallimard, 2009), 22–28.

66 *This heightened degree of:* Kirk Curnutt, *Cambridge Introduction to F. Scott Fitzgerald,* http://www.scribd.com/doc/25371235/F-Scott-Fitzgerald, 31 (accessed June 10, 2011).

66 *As photographs and film images:* Hollander, *Seeing Through Clothes.*

66 *At the turn of the century:* "Forty and Still Fair," *Chicago Daily Tribune,* November 14, 1886, 17; Banner, *In Full Flower,* 281.

66 *"Until this century, and until the movies":* Anne Hollander, *Sex and Suits: The Evolution of Modern Dress* (New York: Alfred A. Knopf, 1994), 137; Fischer, *Growing Old in America,* 223.

66 *Mrs. Woodrow explained the:* Wilson, "Youth Crowding Out Even Middle Age."

66 Harper's Bazar *noted in 1912:* "Old Women's Gowns," *Harper's Bazar,* April 1912, 46, 4, APS online, 192.

67 *By 1925, the 20-year-old:* Hollander, *Sex and Suits,* 137–38.

67 *Abstract graphic design incorporating:* Hollander, *Seeing Through Clothes.*

67 *For the first time, young:* Ibid., 329–44.

67 *A 1927 ad for Ivory Soap:* Ad*Access, Duke University Libraries, http://library.duke.edu/digitalcollections/adaccess.BH0800/pg.1/ (accessed June 10, 2011).

67 *In Edith Wharton's* Twilight Sleep*:* Wharton, *Twilight Sleep,* 231.

68 *Thomas Edison was described:* Jackson Lears, *Fables of Abundance: A Cultural History of Advertising in America* (New York: Basic Books, 1994), 193.

68 *Revolutionary-era physicians:* Cole, *Journey of Life,* 101.

68 *"There seemed to be a more":* Hall, *Senescence,* xv.

68 *Fevered talk of "an elixir of youth":* Rebecca Skloot, *The Immortal Life of Henrietta Lacks* (New York: Broadway, 2011), 61.

68 *In 1918, Leo L. Stanley:* Carole Haber, "Anti-Aging Medicine: The History," *Journals of Gerontology Series A: Biological Sciences and Medical Sciences* 59 (2004): B515–B522.

69 *During a visit to the:* "Voronoff Hooted by French Doctors," *New York Times,* October 6, 1922, 21; Floyd Gibbons, "Monkey Gland Men on Exhibit," *Chicago Daily Tribune,* October 5, 1922.

69 *In October 1922, the French Academy:* Floyd Gibbons, "Crowds Attend Voronoff Story of Renewed Men," *Chicago Daily Tribune,* October 6, 1922, 5.

69 *The French press threw:* "Voronoff's New Tests Gain Press Support," *New York Times,* October 9, 1922, 4.

69 *Popular sentiment may have accounted:* "Paris Doctors Life Ban on Voronoff," *New York Times,* January 11, 1923, 44.

70 *"Dr. Voronoff's triumph was":* Henry Wales, "Voronoff Wins Paris Cynics to Monkey Glands," *Chicago Daily Tribune,* October 13, 1923.

70 *By 1926, an article in the:* Van Buren Thorne, "Voronoff's Dramatic Experiments in Rejuvenation," *New York Times,* May 30, 1926.

70 *Voronoff kept at it:* "Famous Surgeon Arrives to See the World's Fair," *New York Times,* May 16, 1939, 11.

70 *World War I's heedless:* Pope Brock, *Charlatan: America's Most Dangerous Huckster, the Man Who Pursued Him, and the Age of Flimflam* (New York: Crown, 2008), 32; Gay, *Schnitzler's Century,* 150, mentions views of "seminal liquor."

70 *In his 1920 tract,* Life*:* Gay, *Schnitzler's Century,* 38.

70 *Celebrated physicians with impressive:* Brock, *Charlatan,* 20–21.

71 *Medical diploma mills and fraud:* Ibid., 88.

71 *As David and Sheila Rothman:* Sheila M. Rothman and David J. Rothman, *The Pursuit of Perfection: The Promise and Perils of Medical Enhancement* (New York: Pantheon Books, 2003), 139.

71 *The book tells the story:* Gertrude Atherton, *Black Oxen* (New York: A. L. Burt Company, 1923).

71 *Atherton—an arresting beauty with:* Emily Wortis Leider, *California's Daughter: Gertrude Atherton and Her Time* (Stanford, CA: Stanford University Press, 1991), 14, 28, 43, 102, 298; Atherton, *Adventures of a Novelist.*

72 *Like Brown-Séquard before him:* Rothman and Rothman, *Pursuit of Perfection,* 138.

72 *In the 1950s, he counseled:* Jan Morris, *Conundrum* (New York: NYRB Classics, 2006), 49.

73 *Some of Steinach's critics:* Hall, *Senescence,* 302.

73 *After examining a handful:* "Gland Operation to Retard Senility," *New York Times,* November 20, 1921.

73 *As soon as Atherton read it:* Atherton, *Adventures of a Novelist,* 14.

73 *"Poor Dr. Benjamin! I nearly ruined him":* Ibid., 560, 562.

73 *Here, two scientists discover:* Susan Merrill Squier, *Liminal Lives: Imagining the Human at the Frontier of Biomedicine* (Durham, NC: Duke University Press, 2004), 159–60.

74 *Steinach believed his treatments:* Rothman and Rothman, *Pursuit of Perfection,* 140.

74 *Hormone therapy could claim:* Ibid.

75 *Reviewing the history of:* Sander L. Gilman, *Making the Body Beautiful: A Cultural History of Aesthetic Surgery* (Princeton, NJ: Princeton University Press, 1999), 16–21.

75 *After Darwin, the nineteenth-century:* David Serlin, *Replaceable You: Engineering the Body in Postwar America* (Chicago: University of Chicago Press, 2004), 12–13.

75 *Lombroso, who treated crime:* Herman, *Idea of Decline in Western Civilization*; Bellesiles, *1877,* 211–12.

75 *Later Alexis Carrel, who gained fame:* Skloot, *Immortal Life of Henrietta Lacks.*

75 *In Nathaniel Hawthorne's 1846 story:* Gilman, *Making the Body Beautiful,* 45–46.

76 *"Keep in mind the great":* Harvey Newcomb, *How to Be a Lady: A Book for Girls, Containing Useful Hints on the Formation of Character* (Boston: Gould, Kendall, and Lincoln, 1850), 15, http://name.umdl.umich.edu/AJF2301.0001.001 (accessed June 16, 2011).

76 *William Mathews, an English professor:* William Mathews, *Getting On in the World: Or, Hints on Success in Life* (Chicago: University of Chicago Press, 1878), 187.

76 *Orison Swett Marden, an unflagging:* Orison Swett Marden, *Character: The Grandest Thing in the World,* http://orisonswettmarden.wwwhubs.com/ctgtitw.html (accessed June 10, 2011).

76 *Hundreds of self-help books:* Susman, *Culture as History,* 275–76, 280.

77 *Later social scientists like Erving Goffman:* Erving Goffman, *The Presentation of Self in Everyday Life* (New York: Anchor Books, 1959); David Riesman with Nathan Glazer and Reuel Denney, *The Lonely Crowd* (New Haven, CT: Yale University Press, 1969), 46–47; Christopher Lasch, *The Culture of Narcissism: American Life in an Age of Diminishing Expectations* (New York: W. W. Norton, 1991).

77 *That is why in the early years of the twentieth century:* Gilman, *Making the Body Beautiful,* 104.

77 *The first plastic surgery specifically:* Elizabeth Haiken, *Venus Envy: A History of Cosmetic Surgery* (Baltimore: Johns Hopkins University Press, 1997); Rothman and Rothman, *Pursuit of Perfection,* xi; Gilman, *Making the Body Beautiful,* 104.

78 *Jonathan Edwards, the New England:* Edward Dolnick, *The Clockwork Universe: Isaac Newton, the Royal Society, and the Birth of the Modern World* (New York: HarperCollins, 2011), 11.

78 *What makes aesthetic surgery:* Sander Gilman, "Operation Happiness," in *100,000 Years of Beauty,* Azoulay, ed., 68.

78 *The analyst serves as the mostly silent:* Peter Gay makes this observation about the analyst in *Schnitzler's Century,* 277.

79 *In 1924, the* New York Daily Mirror*:* Haiken, *Venus Envy,* 98.

79 *Many surgeons considered the:* Gilman, *Making the Body Beautiful,* 295–319.

Chapter 6: Middle Age Enters the Modern Age

80 *"The large national advertisers fix":* Sinclair Lewis, *Babbitt* (New York: bartleby.com, 1997), chapter 7, section 3, paragraph 32.

81 *He poured his reflections:* Hall, *Senescence,* vii; Cole, *Journey of Life,* 212–26.

81 *A few years later:* Lynd and Lynd, *Middletown,* 30–35.

82 *"Even in the professions such":* Ibid., 35–36.

82 *Periodicals more broadly echoed:* Chudacoff, *How Old Are You?*

82 *It was widely believed, said Stanley Burnshaw:* Roland Marchand, *Advertising the American Dream: Making Way for Modernity, 1920–1940* (Berkeley: University of California Press, 1985), 46.

82 *Elmer Rice's 1923 play:* Gullette, "Midlife Discourses," in *Welcome to Middle Age!,* Shweder, ed., 23.

83 *In* Senescence, *Hall:* Hall, *Senescence,* 2.

83 *This fever, which can strike:* In Cole, *Journey of Life,* 220. Cole argues it is the first academic discussion of this phenomenon.

83 *In Hall's view, passing as:* Cole, *Journey of Life,* 217, 220.

83 *The venerable psychologist turned:* Hall, *Senescence,* 29.

84 *Writing from the front:* Jon Savage, *Teenage: The Creation of Youth Culture* (New York: Viking, 2007), 199.

84 *"Young students try to":* F. Scott Fitzgerald, *This Side of Paradise,* 200.

84 *In 1924, the critic Edmund:* A. Scott Berg, *Max Perkins: Editor of Genius* (New York: Riverhead Books, 1997).

84 *Modernism reversed the baleful eighteenth century:* Gay, *Modernism,* 2.

85 *Novelists of all stripes:* Gullette, "Midlife Discourses," in *Welcome to Middle Age!,* Shweder, ed., 20.

85 *They "proudly proclaimed":* Marchand, *Advertising the American Dream,* xxi.

85 *Born in 1886, he grew up:* Richard M. Fried, *The Man Everybody Knew: Bruce Barton and the Making of Modern America* (Chicago: Ivan R. Dee, 2005); Susman, *History as Culture.*

86 *"Two out of three parlors":* Lewis, *Babbitt,* chapter 7, section 1, paragraph 5.

86 *In 1900, approximately:* Ellen Mazur Thomson, *The Origins of Graphic Design in America* (New Haven, CT: Yale University Press, 1997), 27.

86 *Purchasing a car that was:* Marchand, *Advertising and the American Dream,* 158–59.

87 *"The American citizen's first":* Lynd and Lynd, *Middletown,* 87.

87 *Throughout the twenties:* Hollander, *Seeing Through Clothes,* 20.

87 *When American Telephone and Telegraph:* Marchand, *Advertising and the American Dream,* 117–18, 156–58.

87 *Jesus "picked up twelve men from the bottom":* Fried, *The Man Everybody Knew,* 4, 66; Bruce Barton, *The Man Nobody Knows: The Discovery of the Real Jesus* (Chicago: I. R. Dee, 2000), 37–40.

88 *In "Creed of the Advertising Man":* Marchand, *Advertising and the American Dream,* 8–9, 128.

88 *Calvin Coolidge offered:* Susman, *Culture as History,* xxvi; Marchand, *Advertising and the American Dream,* 158–59.

88 *"All fixed, fast-frozen relations, with":* Karl Marx and Friedrick Engels, *The Communist Manifesto,* chapter 1, http://www.marxists.org/archive/marx/works/1848/communist-manifesto/ch01.htm (accessed June 16, 2011).

89 *After World War II, mass:* Lizbeth Cohen, *A Consumers' Republic: The Politics of Mass Consumption in Postwar America* (New York: Alfred A. Knopf, 2003).

89 *President George W. Bush, in:* http://www.americanrhetoric.com/speeches/gwbush911addresstothenation.htm (accessed June 11, 2011).

89 *A month later, New York mayor:* Guy Trebay, "For a Shopping Spree, the Closet's the Place," *New York Times,* November 20, 2001.

89 *Then as now, young people:* Susman, *Culture as History,* 39.

89 *Helen Woodward, a consumer:* Stuart Ewen, *Captains of Consciousness: Advertising and the Social Roots of the Consumer Culture* (New York: McGraw-Hill, 1976), 147.

90 *In 1928, Paul Nystrom, a marketing:* Stanley C. Hollander, *Was There a Pepsi Generation Before Pepsi Discovered It? Youth-Based Segmentation in Marketing* (Chicago: American Marketing Association, 1992), 24.

90 *Roland Marchand summed up the:* Marchand, *Advertising and the American Dream,* 191.

90 *William Esty, an account representative:* Ibid., 13; Susman, *Culture as History*; Lears, *Fables of Abundance.*

90 *The Laundry Owners Association inflamed:* Marchand, *Advertising and the American Dream,* 194.

91 *A 1920s ad for Gillette blue blades:* Marchand, *Advertising and the American Dream,* 216, 354.

91 *Alfred Adler's term even:* Susman, *Culture as History,* 200.

91 *In the teens and twenties, she:* Hollander, *Was There a Pepsi Generation Before Pepsi Discovered It?,* 73.

91 *An internal newsletter circulated in 1924:* Ad*Access, Duke University Libraries, http://library.duke.edu/digitalcollections/adaccess/ (accessed on June 12, 2011).

91 *Pollsters soon joined the cadres:* Susman, *Culture as History,* 212–13.

91 *Replacing God and Nature, the:* Sarah Igo, *The Averaged American: Surveys, Citizens, and the Making of a Mass Public* (Cambridge, MA: Harvard University Press, 2007), 124, 287–88.

92 *Nicky and his fiancée, Bunty:* Savage, *Teenage,* 234.

92 *By consistently using the body:* Hall, *Senescence,* viii.

92 *"In Europe, a woman at forty":* Sinclair Lewis, *Dodsworth.*

92 *In 1932, a letter writer to:* Edward C. Rybicki, "Letters to the Editor: Problems of Middle Age," *New York Times,* November 21, 1932.

93 *"How little even our brightest":* Walter B. Pitkin, *Life Begins at Forty* (New York: Blue Ribbon Books, 1934), 20.

93 *In 1939, the Social Science Research:* "Jobs Few in Middle Age," *New York Times,* January 16, 1939.

93 *Four months after the report appeared:* Felix Belair Jr., "Roosevelt Scores Ban on Middle Age," *New York Times,* April 28, 1939.

94 *"It is glorious to be middle-aged":* "Sees Glory in Middle Age," *New York Times,* December 11, 1939.

94 *Fears of middle-aged superfluity:* Conard Miller Gilbert, *We Over Forty:*

America's Human Scrap Pile (Philadelphia: Westbrook Publishing Co., 1948), 12–13; Brandes, *Forty,* 44.

94 *After carefully analyzing the differing narratives:* Martel, "Age-Sex Roles in Magazine Fiction," in *Middle Age and Aging,* Neugarten, ed., 55–56.

Chapter 7: The Sixties and Seventies: The Era of Middle Age

99 *"We cannot live the afternoon":* Deirdre Bair, *Jung: A Biography* (Boston: Little, Brown, 2003).

100 *"Middle age is certainly the":* Thomas C. Desmond, "America's Unknown Middle-Agers," *New York Times,* July 29, 1956.

100 *As for psychologists, when it:* Richard M. Lerner, *Concepts and Theories of Human Development* (Mahwah, NJ: Lawrence Erlbaum Associates, Publishers, 2002), 71.

100 *Freud thought middle-aged patients:* Eda G. Goldstein, *When the Bubble Bursts: Clinical Perspectives on Midlife Issues* (Hillsdale, NJ: Analytic Press, 2005), 10.

100 *In his eighth decade G. Stanley Hall:* Hall, *Senescence,* 100.

101 *In 1913, his bitter falling-out:* Bair, *Jung,* 242, 254, 288–89.

101 *The more mature man has had:* Ibid., 394; C. G. Jung, *The Essential Jung,* revised ed. (Princeton, NJ: Princeton University Press, 1999), 24.

101 *Bernice L. Neugarten, a groundbreaking:* Dail Ann Neugarten, ed., *The Meanings of Age: Selected Papers of Bernice L. Neugarten* (Chicago: University of Chicago Press, 1996), 5–9.

102 *"No one earlier had seemed":* "Growing as Long as We Live: An Interview with Bernice L. Neugarten," *Second Opinion,* November 1, 1990.

102 *He arrived in the United States:* Lawrence Jacob Friedman, *Identity's Architect: A Biography of Erik H. Erikson* (New York: Scribner, 1999), 19–20, 104, 147.

102 *Shocked and bewildered, Erikson immediately:* Ibid., 163.

103 *Both Friedman and Erikson's daughter:* Sue Erikson Bloland, *In the Shadow of Fame: A Memoir by the Daughter of Erik H. Erikson* (New York: Viking, 2005); Friedman, *Identity's Architect,* 218–19.

103 *"My life cycle theory":* Daniel Goleman, "Erikson, in His Own Old Age, Expands His View of Life," *New York Times,* June 14, 1988.

103 *Like her husband, Joan was skeptical:* Erik H. Erikson, *The Life Cycle Completed: Extended Edition* (New York: W. W. Norton & Co., 1997), 1–3.

104 *As he summarized in a lecture:* Erik H. Erikson, ed., *Adulthood* (New York: W. W. Norton, 1978), 124. It was the Jefferson Lectures, 1973.

105 *In the Eriksons' typology, called:* Erik Erikson, *Childhood and Society* (New York: W. W. Norton, 1985).

105 *Nearly a century earlier, John:* John Stuart Mill, *The Autobiography of John Stuart Mill* (Sioux Falls, SD: NuVisions Publications, 2007), 73.

105 *"Human personality in principle":* Erikson, *Childhood and Society.*

106 *It spurred psychologists to revise:* Neugarten, "The Awareness of Middle Age," in *Middle Age and Aging,* Neugarten, ed., vii.

106 *"Eriksonian became almost a":* Friedman, *Identity's Architect,* 241.

106 *His daughter, Sue, remembers eating:* Bloland, *In the Shadow of Fame,* 2.

107 *Born in 1916 in the small town:* Neugarten, *Meanings of Age.*

108 *"Many people talk about":* "Growing as Long as We Live," *Second Opinion.*

109 *Listing White House occupants:* "Demography: The Command Generation," *Time,* July 29, 1966.

109 *In 1967, Neugarten wrote up her findings from:* Neugarten and Moore, "The Changing Age-Status System," in *Middle Age and Aging,* Neugarten, ed., 11.

109 *"Most of the women interviewed":* Neugarten, "The Awareness of Middle Age," in *Middle Age and Aging,* Neugarten, ed., 96.

110 *In a 1982 study:* Miriam Bernard, Judith Phillips, Linda Machin, and Val Harding Davies, eds., *Women Ageing: Changing Identities, Challenging Myths* (New York: Routledge, 2000).

110 *Aging is both a biological and a:* Simone de Beauvoir, *The Coming of Age,* first American edition 1972, French edition 1970 (New York: W. W. Norton, 1996), 9, 13.

111 *As one woman wrote in a 1973 column:* Cynthia Bell, "Why Middle Age Isn't the End," *New York Times,* July 29, 1973.

111 *He assembled a supposedly random sample:* Elliott Jaques, "Death and the Midlife Crisis," *International Journal of Psychoanalysis* 46 (1965): 502–14.

112 *G. Stanley Hall, too, had presented:* Hall, *Senescence,* 21.

113 *"Ordinarily we cling to our past":* Azoulay, ed., *100,000 Years of Beauty.* Jung and Huxley's *Brave New World* were juxtaposed in Azoulay.

113 *Jung's description of this perverse:* Aldous Huxley, *Brave New World* (London: Vintage Books, 1994).

114 *Poorly adjusted individuals, he maintained:* Jaques, "Death and the Midlife Crisis."

114 *Freud had a particularly:* Banner, *In Full Flower,* 297.

114 *Psychoanalytic interpretations assumed fertility:* Margaret Lock, "Deconstructing the Change," in *Welcome to Middle Age!,* Shweder, ed., 50.

115 *a term, he later said:* Leslie Bennetts, "Now It's Daniel Levinson's Turn," *New York Times,* April 2, 1978.

115 *Transition points are critical in determining:* Daniel Levinson, *The Seasons of a Man's Life* (New York: Alfred A. Knopf, 1978), 272.

116 *Sheehy adopted Erikson's central:* Gail Sheehy, *Passages: Predictable Crises of Adult Life* (New York: Ballantine Books/E. P. Dutton, 1976).

116 *She labeled the years between 35 and 45:* Ibid., 242–43.

116 *"Changing one's personality":* Tom Wolfe, "The 'Me' Decade and the Third Great Awakening," *New York,* August 23, 1976.

116 *In 1973, an article about popular psychologist:* Nadine Brozan, *New York Times,* March 29, 1973.

117 *"It was a very exciting time":* George Vaillant, *Adaptation to Life* (Boston: Little, Brown, 1977)

117 *The very existence of these novel:* Neugarten, ed., *Middle Age and Aging,* vii.

118 *Vaillant declared that the Boston:* Vaillant, *Adaptation to Life,* 80.

118 *"Our self-assurance, our tendency":* Ibid., 284–85.

118 *"If such events occur during the dangerous":* Ibid., 223.

119 *Looking back, Vaillant's Harvard:* Ibid., 226.

119 *"Lives are lived in specific historical times and places":* Glen H. Elder Jr., *The Life Course in Time and Place,* presented at the International Symposium on Institutions, Interrelations, Sequences: The Bremen Life-Course Approach, Bremen, Germany, September 26–28, 2001, http://www.unc.edu/~elder/presentations/Life_course_in_time.html (accessed June 11, 2011).

119 *The Oakland children who were young teenagers:* Glen H. Elder Jr., *The Life Course and Aging: Some Accomplishments, Unfinished Tasks, and New Directions*, Prepared for Distinguished Scholar Lecture Section on Aging, ASA, August 10, 1999, http://www.unc.edu/~elder/pdf/asa-99talk.pdf (accessed June 11, 2011).

120 *Elder realized some of these problems as early as:* Ibid.

121 *"If historical times and places change":* Elder, *Life Course in Time and Place,* 2001.

121 *In 1974, the same year that* Children of the Great Depression*:* B. L. Neugarten, "Age Groups in American Society and the Rise of the Young-Old," *Annals of the American Academy of Political and Social Science* 415, no. 1 (January 1974): 187–98.

121 *"The psychological themes and preoccupations":* Neugarten, *Meanings of Age,* 369–70; Orville Gilbert Brim Jr., *Ambition: How We Manage Success and Failure Throughout Our Lives* (New York: Basic Books, 1992), 91.

Chapter 8: Middle Age Under the Microscope

123 *"Stage theories are a little like horoscopes":* Anne Rosenfeld, Elizabeth Stark, and Richard Cohen, "The Prime of Our Lives," *Psychology Today* 21 (May 1987): 62 (9).

124 *Seated at his dining room table:* Brim interview with author, 2008.

125 *Over a lifetime, shifts:* Glen H. Elder Jr., *The Life Course and Aging: Some Accomplishments, Unfinished Tasks, and New Directions,* presented at the annual meeting of the Gerontological Society of America, Boston, Massachusetts, November 11, 2002.

125 *In 1998, the psychologist Anne Colby:* Ibid.

125 *Brim remembered the reaction to:* Orville G. Brim and Jerome Kagan, *Constancy and Change in Human Development* (Cambridge, MA: Harvard University Press, 1980), 1.

125 *When Brim and Kagan presented their:* Brim interview with author, 2008.

126 *Nineteenth-, twentieth-, and twenty-first-century:* Lerner, *Concepts and Theories of Human Development,* 71.

126 *finite supply of the vital "male principle":* Rothman and Rothman, *Pursuit of Perfection,* 132–33.

126 *or that a human being was physiologically*: Siddhartha Mukherjee, *The Emperor of All Maladies: A Biography of Cancer* (New York: Scribner, 2010), 496.

126 *At a 1997 White House conference:* Malcolm Gladwell, "Baby Steps," *New Yorker,* January 10, 2000, http://www.gladwell.com/2000/2000_01_10_a_baby.htm (accessed June 12, 2011).

127 *As the eighties progressed, middle age:* "Life Course Perspectives: Report for 1983–1984," Social Science Research Council, 82.

127 *During those years, Brim and Baltes:* Brim interview with author, June 14, 2011.

127 *"It's obvious," Brim recalled:* Brim interview with author, 2008; *SRCD Oral History Interview of Orville Gilbert Brim,* January 17, 2009, in Vero Beach, Florida, conducted by David L. Featherman, professor of sociology and psychology, University of Michigan, 51, 67.

128 *They gathered a large random:* Brim et al., *How Healthy Are We?,* 7–8.

128 *Political parties in the nineteenth century:* U.S. Department of Health, Education & Welfare, Children's Bureau, *The Story of the White House Conferences on Children and Youth,* 1967, 3–4.

128 *By 1944, both political parties:* Neugarten, "The Changing Age Status System," in *Middle Age and Aging,* 19–20. In 1950, the name of the White House Conference expanded to include "Children and Youth."

128 *"That really did put middle":* Brim interview with author, June 2009.

128 *"this enterprise established":* Featherman, *SRCD Oral History Interview of Orville Gilbert Brim,* 55–56.

129 *"Midlife is more flexible than":* Brim et al., *How Healthy Are We?*

129 *middle age wasn't so bad:* Erica Goode, "New Study Finds Middle Age Is Prime of Life," *New York Times,* February 16, 1999; Ronald Kotulak, "Study Finds Midlife 'Best Time, Best Place to Be,'" *Chicago Tribune,* February 16, 1999; "Midlife Without the Crisis," *Washington Post,* February 16, 1999.

129 *The research debunked a number of popular:* Brim et al., *How Healthy Are We?,* 161, 445, 603.

129 *Divorce in midlife was relatively rare:* Larry Bumpass interview with author, May 10, 2010.

130 *Nearly sixty-two percent said*: Alice S. Rossi, "Menopausal Transition" in Brim et al., *How Healthy Are We?,* 170.

130 *So while middle-aged women might have: ICPSR Bulletin* XX, no. 4 (Summer 2000): 4.

130 *Although many people made it:* Lachman, "Development in Midlife," 325.

130 *Less than ten percent of those:* Brim et al., *How Healthy Are We?,* 611.

131 *Brim told me he believes that people:* Brim interview with author; Brim, *Ambition.*

131 *Alice S. Rossi, a sociologist and MacArthur investigator, suggested:* Rossi, "Social Responsibility to Family and Community," in Brim et al., *How Healthy Are We?,* 581; Alice S. Rossi, "Life-Span Theories and Women's Lives," *Signs* 6, no. 1 (Autumn 1980), 4–32.

132 *"Shortcomings that date from earlier years":* Hall, *Senescence,* ix.

132 *So David Foster Wallace, a deeply insightful:* D. T. Max, "The Unfinished," *New Yorker,* March 9, 2009.

132 *Lars von Trier:* Dennis Lim, "Danish Director Barred from Film Festival After Making Hitler Jokes," *New York Times,* May 19, 2011.

132 *As David Almeida, a psychologist at:* Sue Marquette Poremba, *Probing Question: Is the Midlife Crisis a Myth?,* Research Penn State, http://www.rps.psu.edu/probing/midlifecrisis.html (accessed June 11, 2011).

132 *"One spends a lifetime reconstructing":* Brim, *Ambition,* 85.

133 *"For investigators trying to sort":* Lachman, "Development in Midlife."

133 *When it came to describing:* Brim et al., *How Healthy Are We?,* 617–35.

134 *Educational divisions revealed other unexpected:* Ibid., 306–15.

134 *A similar class divide showed up:* Rossi, "Social Responsibility to Family and Community," in Brim et al., *How Healthy Are We?,* 364.

135 *From their early 30s through:* "Marital Status," MIDUS newsletter, http://www.midus.wisc.edu/newsletter/ (accessed June 12, 2011).

136 *The MacArthur project attempted to probe more deeply:* Brim et al., *How Healthy Are We?,* 21, 374, 390, 418; MIDMAC website, http://midmac.med.harvard.edu/research.html (accessed June 12, 2011).

137 *"When you get to be 40," said Geoffrey Powers:* Katherine Newman, *A Different Shade of Gray: Midlife and Beyond in the Inner City* (New York: New Press, 2006), 99.

137 *Katherine Newman, a sociologist at Princeton University, oversaw:* Newman, *Different Shade of Gray,* 16–17, 51–52, 96, 114–15, 122, 221; Katherine Newman, "Place and Race," in *Welcome to Middle Age!,* Shweder, ed., 283, 290.

Chapter 9: The Middle-Aged Brain

140 *In 2004, ten years after Bert Brim's:* Midlife in the United States website, http://www.midus.wisc.edu/midus2/ (accessed June 12, 2011).

142 *Despite claims that emerged in the 1990s:* Richard Davidson interview with author, 2008 and 2009; Elkhonon Goldberg, *The Wisdom Paradox: How Your Mind Can Grow Stronger as Your Brain Grows Older* (New York: Gotham Books, 2005), 41–42.

143 *"That's been a spectacular strategy":* Davidson interview with author, 2008.

143 *Davidson and his colleagues plan to follow:* Davidson interview with author, 2008 and 2009.

144 *He had kept this passion:* Dirk Johnson, "Dalai Lama Donates to Center in Wisconsin," *New York Times,* September 26, 2010; excerpts from Dr. Richard Davidson's keynote address on contemplative neuroscience at the Center for Mindfulness 7th Annual International Conference in Worcester, Massachusetts, in March 2009, http://www.youtube.com/watch?v=PAGu1LeE-SE (accessed June 12, 2011).

145 *"This I (that is to say, my soul by which":* Nicholas Bunnin, ed., *The Blackwell Companion to Philosophy* (Oxford, UK: Blackwell, 1995), 509–21.

145 *"I was interested in emotion":* Davidson interview with author, 2008.

145 *impact of the telescope:* Goldberg, *Wisdom Paradox,* 238.

146 *"Spinoza prefigured in a remarkable way":* Harcourt Brace interview with author, *Interview with Antonio Damasio,* 2003, transcript available at http://www.harcourtbooks.com/authorinterviews/bookinterview_damasio.asp (accessed May 20, 2011).

147 *In one study, monks who had spent:* Davidson interview with author; Benedict Carey, "Scientists Bridle at Lecture Plan for Dalai Lama," *New York Times,* October 19, 2005.

147 *One possibility, Davidson hypothesizes:* Lutz, A., H. A. Slagter, J. Dunne, and R. J. Davidson, "Attention Regulation and Monitoring in Meditation," *Trends in Cognitive Sciences* 12, no. 4 (2008): 163–69, NIHMS no. 82882.

147 *Stephen Kosslyn, a Harvard psychologist:* Stephen Hall, "Is Buddhism Good for Your Health?," *New York Times Magazine,* September 15, 2003; http://www.positscience.com/human-brain/brain-plasticity/brain-plasticity-luminaries/Richard-Frackowiak (accessed June 12, 2011).

148 *Neuroplasticity—the ability of the brain to change:* Richard Davidson, "Transform Your Mind, Change Your Brain," Google Tech Talk, September 23, 2009, http://www.youtube.com/watch?v=7tRdDqXgsJ0&feature=related (accessed June 15, 2011).

148 *An experiment published in 2009:* Robert Schneider, Sanford Nidich, Jane Morley Kotchen, Theodore Kotchen, Clarence Grim, Maxwell Rainforth, Carolyn Gaylord King, John Salerno, "Reducing Negative Emotions, Promoting Health and Improving Quality of Life; Abstract 1177: Effects of Stress Reduction on Clinical Events in African Americans with Coronary

Heart Disease: A Randomized Controlled Trial," *Circulation* 120 (2009): S461.

148 *In 2011, a group of scientists at Massachusetts General Hospital reported:* "Mindfulness Practice Leads to Increases in Regional Brain Gray Matter Density," *Behavioral Medicine Report,* January 21, 2011, http://www.bmedreport.com/archives/22292 (accessed May 20, 2011); Britta K. Hölzel, James Carmody, Mark Vangel, Christina Congleton, Sita M. Yerramsetti, Tim Gard, Sara W. Lazar, "Mindfulness Practice Leads to Increases in Regional Brain Gray Matter Density," *Psychiatry Research: Neuroimaging* 191, no. 1 (January 30, 2011): 36–43, DOI: 10.1016/j.pscychresns.2010.08.006) (accessed June 12, 2011).

149 *Myelin itself can deteriorate:* Barbara Strauch, *The Secret Life of the Grown-Up Brain: The Surprising Talents of the Middle-Aged Mind* (New York: Viking, 2010), 86.

149 *Scientists began questioning assumptions:* Sharan Merriam, *Learning in Adulthood: A Comprehensive Guide* (San Francisco: Jossey-Bass, 2007), 366; "Tests of Ability to Learn Earn Praise of Middle Age," *New York Times,* April 22, 1928.

150 *In the 1970s:* Stephen Hall, "The Older and Wiser Hypothesis," *New York Times Magazine,* May 6, 2007, 58.

150 *Some differences in test results:* Daniel Goleman, "The Aging Mind Proves Capable of Long-Term Growth," *New York Times,* February 21, 1984.

151 *Most people do not naturally:* James Flynn, *What Is Intelligence? Beyond the Flynn Effect* (Cambridge, UK: Cambridge University Press, 2007); "The IQ Conundrum," *Cato Unbound,* November 2007 (accessed August 13, 2011).

151 *Paul Baltes, one of the originators of life span theory:* Stephen Hall, "The Older and Wiser Hypothesis," *New York Times Magazine,* May 6, 2007; Henry Alford on http://incharacter.org/pro-con/is-there-really-such-a-thing-as-wisdom-part-1/ (accessed June 12, 2011).

152 *Sternberg, a former president of the American:* Robert Sternberg, *A Handbook of Wisdom: Psychological Perspectives* (Cambridge, UK: Cambridge University Press, 2005); Hall, "The Older and Wiser Hypothesis."

152 *The influential Harvard psychologist Howard Gardner:* Howard Gardner, *Frames of Mind: The Theory of Multiple Intelligences* (New York: Basic Books, 1985), xi.

152 *"While the theme of youth is flexibility":* Merriam, *Learning in Adulthood,* 347.

153 *His in-laws, both in their 70s:* Gene Cohen, *The Mature Mind: The Positive Power of the Aging Brain* (New York: Basic Books, 2006), 2.

154 *About a thousand miles east:* Margie Lachman interview with author, May 11, 2011.

154 *A trained interviewer initiated each:* Patricia A. Tun and Margie E. Lachman, "Age Differences in Reaction Time and Attention in a National Telephone Sample of Adults: Education, Sex, and Task Complexity Matter," *Developmental Psychology* 44, no. 5 (September 2008): 1421–429; description of Lachman and Tun's study, http://www.midus.wisc.edu/midus2/project3/ (accessed May 21, 2011).

155 *The preliminary results:* Strauch, *Secret Life of the Grown-Up Brain,* 14, 20–21.

156 *The discrepancy with MIDUS's:* Lachman interview with author, May 11, 2011.

157 *So far, the professors have found:* Tun and Lachman, "Age Differences in Reaction Time and Attention in a National Telephone Sample of Adults."

157 *Most encouraging was evidence that:* M. E. Lachman, S. Agrigoroaei, C. Murphy, and P. Tun, "Frequent Cognitive Activity Compensates for Education Differences in Episodic Memory," *American Journal of Geriatric Psychiatry* 18, no. 1 (January 2010): 4–10.

157 *Using a computer:* Margie Lachman, "The Association Between Computer Use and Cognition Across Adulthood: Use It So You Won't Lose It?" *Psychology and Aging* 25, no. 3 (2010): 560–68; Lachman interview with author, May 25, 2011.

158 *Lachman found the same phenomenon:* M. E. Lachman and S. Agrigoroaei, "Promoting Functional Health in Midlife and Old Age: Long-Term Protective Effects of Control Beliefs, Social Support, and Physical Exercise," *PLoS ONE* 5, no. 10 (2010): e13297, doi:10.1371/journal.pone.0013297 (accessed June 9, 2011); Margie E. Lachman and Kimberly M. Prenda Firth, "The Adaptive Value of Feeling in Control During Midlife," in Brim et al., *How Healthy Are We?,* 320–40; Lachman interview with author, April 25, 2011.

Chapter 10: Consuming Desire

163 *"Middle age doesn't exist":* Walter Tevis, *The Color of Money* (New York: Thunder's Mouth Press, 2003).

164 *As* GQ *noted when it:* Mark Kirby, "Lordy, Lordy, This Woman Is Forty," *GQ,* January 2009.

164 *By comparison, the media-produced:* Ira Levin, *The Stepford Wives* (New York: Harper Torch, 2004).

165 *"She looks old enough":* Marchand, *Advertising the American Dream,* 14.

165 *The poor Lysol-less woman:* Lois Banner and Nancy Etcoff make similar points in their books. Banner, *In Full Flower*; Nancy Etcoff, *Survival of the Prettiest: The Science of Beauty* (New York: Anchor Books, 2000).

166 *Pauline Manford in Edith Wharton's:* Wharton, *Twilight Sleep,* 98.

166 *"We have become so":* Natasha Singer, "Is Looking Your Age Now Taboo?," *New York Times,* March 1, 2007; Daphne Merkin, "FACE; Houston, We Have Face-Lift," *New York Times Magazine,* February 28, 2010.

166 *In some affluent circles: Real Housewives of Orange County,* Bravo, May 2011.

166 *A 2005 Harris survey found:* Harris survey, 2005.

166 *One Virginia clinic located:* Associated Press, "Job Hunters Get Out the Wrinkles," June 5, 2009.

167 *"Looking hip is not just about vanity":* Natasha Singer, "Nice Résumé. Have You Considered Botox?," *New York Times,* January 24, 2008; Karsten Witte, "Introduction to Siegried Kracauer's 'The Mass Ornament,'" *New German Critique,* no. 5 (Spring 1975): 59–66.

167 *During the health-care debate:* Judith Warner, "Bo-Tax Backlash," *New York Times* online, December 3, 2009, http://tiny.cc/jcqi7 (accessed May 21, 2011).

168 *Passing can also be seen:* Charles Taylor, *The Ethics of Authenticity* (Cambridge, MA: Harvard University Press, 1992); Brooke Kroeger, *Passing: When People Can't Be Who They Are* (New York: PublicAffairs, 2003), 134–48, 212.

168 *Recent studies have found:* Ewing, "The Shock of Photography," in *100,000 Years of Beauty,* Azoulay, ed., 24.

169 *"No devices to give a deceitful":* Robert Tomes, *Bazar Book of Decorum: The Care of the Person, Manners, Etiquette, and Ceremonials* (New York:

Harper & Bros., 1873), http://quod.lib.umich.edu/m/moa/AJF2367.0001.001?view=toc (accessed June 12, 2011).

169 *Recall that Gertrude Atherton:* Atherton, *Adventures of a Novelist,* 62.

169 *"Nice women do color their hair":* http://library.duke.edu/digitalcollections/adaccess_BH0310/ (accessed May 21, 2011).

169 *"Because of her prematurely":* Ad*Access, Duke University Libraries, http://library.duke.edu/digitalcollections/adaccess/?keyword=pitied (accessed May 21, 2011).

169 *In 1956, when Clairol came:* Malcolm Gladwell, "True Colors: Hair Dye and the Hidden History of Postwar America," *New Yorker,* March 22, 1999.

170 *"This is an age of mass production":* Edward Bernays, "Manipulating Public Opinion: The Why and the How," *American Journal of Sociology* 33, no. 6 (May 1928): 958–71.

170 *The new class of:* Savage, *Teenage,* 219.

171 *In his book* Propaganda*:* Edward Bernays, *Propaganda* (New York: Ig Publishing, 1928).

171 *As one trade press:* Marchand, *Advertising the American Dream,* 131.

171 *When George Washington Hill:* Neal Gabler, "The Lives They Lived: Edward L. Bernays and Henry C. Rogers; The Fathers of P.R.," *New York Times,* December 31, 1995, http://www.nytimes.com/books/98/08/16/specials/bernays-father.html (accessed May 21, 2001).

172 *The consultant Paco Underhill describes:* Paco Underhill, *Why We Buy: The Science of Shopping* (New York: Simon & Schuster Paperbacks, 1999, 2008), 126.

172 *In his classic 1979 critique:* Lasch, *Culture of Narcisissm,* 72. The cultural critic Kennedy Fraser makes a similar point. Observing how the Me Decade's therapeutic self-help infused consumption with even greater significance, she said: "Americans, acting under the combined influence of rampant acquisitiveness and psychoanalytical self-absorption, seem particularly inclined to mesh possessions with their sense of self-esteem, and to view them as social signposts and emotional milestones." Kennedy Fraser, *The Fashionable Mind: Reflections on Fashion, 1970–1982* (New York: Alfred A. Knopf, 1981), 53.

172 *"Bourgeois Bohemians" flaunted:* David Brooks, *Bobos in Paradise: The New Upper Class and How They Got There* (New York: Simon & Schuster Paperbacks, 2004).

173 *One Beverly Hills:* Natasha Singer, "Who Is the Real Face of Plastic Surgery?," *New York Times,* August 16, 2007; Natasha Singer, "Defy Another Day," *New York Times, T: Style Magazine,* April 17, 2007.

173 *The overwhelming majority of American:* Gullette, *Agewise,* 106.

173 *Four out of five:* Quoted in Susan J. Douglas, *Enlightened Sexism* (New York: Times Books, 2010), 225–26.

174 *Newer nonsurgical treatments:* American Society for Aesthetic Plastic Surgery news release, "Demand for Plastic Surgery Rebounds by Almost 9%," April 4, 2011, http://www.surgery.org/media/news (accessed May 21, 2011).

174 *High-end sports clubs:* Alex Wichtel, "Where Jaded Muscles Exercise Their Options," *New York Times,* June 9, 2006.

174 *More troubling is a 2011 study:* Pamela Paul, "With Botox, Looking Good and Feeling Less," *New York Times,* June 17, 2011.

174 *Since then, purchases:* Allergan Inc. website, "Sales Outlook for 2011," http://agn.client.shareholder.com/releasedetail.cfm?ReleaseID=547064 (accessed May 21, 2011).

175 *"Forty is the sweet spot":* Caroline Van Hove interview with author, 2008.

175 *"The project's goal," copywriters wrote:* Juvéderm press conference, August 31, 2008.

176 *At an annual meeting of the:* Singer, "Defy Another Day."

176 *At a press conference for the:* Juvéderm press conference, August 31, 2008.

176 *"I am a proponent of healthy aging":* Ibid.

177 *"I'm celebrating the 'big 4-0' this year":* http://multivu.prnewswire.com/mnr/allergan/41442/ (accessed March 16, 2010).

177 *"In 1985, I saw a tape":* Singer, "Nice Résumé. Have You Considered Botox?"

178 *In the summer of 2011, Indiana:* Mark Bennett, "Will Revised Indiana Alcohol ID Law Cause Hoosier Run on Botox?," *Tribune-Star,* June 2, 2011.

178 *Margaret Morganroth Gullette, who has written:* Gullette, *Agewise,* 5–6.

178 *A headline in the* New York Times*:* Jennifer 8. Lee, "Big Tobacco's Spin on Women's Liberation," *New York Times,* October 10, 2008.

Chapter 11: Middle Age Medicine

181 *As the political philosopher Harvey Wheeler:* Harvey Wheeler, "The Rise of the Elders," *Saturday Review,* December 5, 1970.

181 *"We believe that there can be an end":* Robert Klatz, http://www.worldhealth.net/.

182 *The official sounding "academy":* Duff Wilson, "Aging—Disease or Business Opportunity?," *New York Times,* April 15, 2007; American Academy of Anti-Aging Medicine website, "About the A4M," http://worldhealth.net/about-a4m/ (accessed on September 15, 2011).

183 *The makers of Ion Magnum:* "Ion Magnum, High-Speed Muscle Building," Pacemaker Technology booklet, 2008.

184 *Although the medical establishment rejects:* Andrew Pollack, "Forget Botox. Anti-Aging Pills May Be Next," *New York Times,* September 21, 2003; L. F. Cherkas et al., "The Effects of Social Status on Biological Aging as Measured by White-Blood-Cell Telomere Length," *Aging Cell* 5, no. 5 (October 2006): 361–65.

184 *"Wrinkled, sagging skin is not:* Alex Wichtel, "Perriconology," *New York Times,* February 6, 2005.

184 *"Under no circumstances is the reader":* Ronald Klatz and Robert Goldman remarks, A4M conference, Chicago, 2004.

185 *Growth hormones gained notice:* Wilson, "Aging—Disease or Business Opportunity?"

185 *Cells start dying off while we are:* Natalie Angier, *Woman: An Intimate Geography* (New York: Anchor Books, 2000), 3–4; Skloot, *Immortal Life of Henrietta Lacks.*

186 *The academy was not charged:* Gina Kolata, "Chasing Youth, Many Gamble on Hormones," *New York Times,* November 22, 2002, A1.

186 *"Simply put, the death cult of":* Robert Klatz, *Grow Young with HGH: The Amazing Medically Proven Plan to Reverse Aging* (New York: Harper Paperbacks, 1998).

187 *"Antiaging" today is like "antiwar" in the 1960s:* Singer, "Defy Another Day."

188 *At 68, he arrived:* Joseph Maroon and Nicholas DiNubile interviews with author, 2008 and 2009.

189 *"Boomers are the first generation":* Bill Pennington, "Baby Boomers Stay Active, and So Do Their Doctors," *New York Times,* April 16, 2006.

189 *"When I first started practicing":* DiNubile interview with author, December 2008.

190 *To DiNubile, the medical establishment still lags:* Ibid.

190 *"This is a highly motivated group":* Pennington, "Baby Boomers Stay Active, and So Do Their Doctors."

Chapter 12: Middle Age Sex

193 *the* American Mercury, *the monthly magazine:* L. M. Hussey, "The Pother about Glands," *American Mercury Magazine,* January 1924, 93.

193 *Yet, in 1936, at age 56:* Brock, *Charlatan,* 207.

193 *Oreton, a drug manufactured by the Schering:* Rothman and Rothman, *Pursuit of Perfection.*

193 *In 1939, the prestigious:* Arlene Weintraub, *Selling the Fountain of Youth: How the Anti-Aging Industry Made a Disease Out of Getting Old, and Made Billions* (New York: Basic Books, 2010), 136–37.

194 *An issue of the science-fiction magazine:* Serlin, *Replaceable You,* 113–37.

194 *In 2002, the Commission of the European Communities:* EMAS website, http://www.emas.man.ac.uk/main.asp (accessed May 15, 2011).

194 *In June 2010, the* New England Journal of Medicine*:* Sora Song, "Examining Male Menopause: Myth or Malady?," *Time,* June 16, 2010.

194 *In 2011, scientists discovered that fatherly activities:* Pam Belluck, "In Study, Fatherhood Leads to Drop in Testosterone," *New York Times,* September 12, 2011.

195 *As one critic put it:* Weintraub, *Selling the Fountain of Youth,* 139–40. Innovaro report, "Pipeline and Commercial Insight: Testosterone Replacement Therapy—Topical Formulations Drive Market Growth," September 2010, http://reports.innovaro.com/reports/pipeline-and-commercial-insight-testosterone-replacement-therapy-topical-formulations-drive-market-growth (accessed June 3, 2011).

195 *Promotors in Las Vegas:* Wilson, "Aging—Disease or Business Opportunity?"

195 *The National Institute on Aging undertook:* National Institute on Aging news release, "NIH-Supported Trial to Study Testosterone Therapy in Older Men," http://www.nia.nih.gov/NewsAndEvents/PressReleases/PR20091102-Testosterone.htm (accessed May 21, 2011).

195 *Gynecologists and psychoanalysts frequently:* Shweder, ed., *Welcome to Middle Age!,* 52–53; Banner, *In Full Flower,* 256.

196 *A range of female hormonal therapies:* Rothman and Rothman, *Pursuit of Perfection,* 35–46.

196 *photographs of kicking showgirls:* Ibid., 56–57.

196 Charm, *a magazine for working women:* Serlin, *Replaceable You,* 131.

197 *In the 1950s, William Masters:* Rothman and Rothman, *Pursuit of Perfection,* 23, 35–36, 67–69.

197 *Psychotropic drugs were similarly marketed:* Sandra Coney, *The Menopause Industry: How the Medical Establishment Exploits Women* (New York: Hunter House, 1994), 68–69.

197 *"It's not just about branding the drug":* Katharine Greider, *The Big Fix: How the Pharmaceutical Industry Rips Off American Consumers* (New York: PublicAffairs, 2003), 118.

198 *Simone de Beauvoir observed:* Beauvoir, *Second Sex,* 575.

198 *It is "probably the least glamorous":* Margaret Morganroth Gullette, *Declining to Decline: Cultural Combat and the Politics of the Midlife* (Charlottesville: University of Virginia Press, 1997).

198 *The gynecologist Sherwin Kaufman:* Rothman and Rothman, *Pursuit of Perfection,* 73–74.

199 *Throughout the sixties and seventies:* Weintraub, *Selling the Fountain of Youth,* 76–80, 83.

199 *Only after his death did documents:* Ehrenreich and English, *For Her Own Good,* 348–50; Gina Kolata, "Hormone Replacement Study a Shock to the Medical System," *New York Times,* June 10, 2002.

199 *The elitist bias that infused:* Serlin, *Replaceable You,* 152.

199 *His animosity is reminiscent of:* Susan Squier, "Incubabies and Rejuvenates," in *Figuring Age: Women, Bodies, Generation,* Kathleen Woodward, ed. (Bloomington: Indiana University Press, 1999).

199 *In 1975, doctors wrote:* Rothman and Rothman, *Pursuit of Perfection,* 73–93; Brandes, *Forty,* 117–23.

200 *Then, in December of that year:* Harry K. Ziel and William D. Finkle, "Increased Risk of Endometrial Carcinomas Among Users of Conjugated Estrogens," *New England Journal of Medicine* 293, no. 23 (1975): 1167–170; D. C. Smith et al., "Association of Exogenous Estrogen and

Endometrial Carcinoma," *New England Journal of Medicine* 293, no. 23 (1975): 1164–167.

200 *A few weeks later, the Food:* "Letter on a Drug Assailed by FDA," *New York Times,* January 9, 1976, 28.

200 *By the end of the 1970s:* Rothman and Rothman, *Pursuit of Perfection,* 73–93.

200 *"More than 30 million women in the":* Linda Roach Monroe, "Menopause: Baby Boomers' Next Step," *Los Angeles Times,* December 5, 1989.

201 *For most women, menopause was not:* Alice S. Rossi, "Menopausal Transitions in Midlife," *MIDMAC Bulletin,* no. 1 (1993), http://midmac.med.harvard.edu/bltnidx.html (accessed May 21, 2011).

201 *MIDUS researchers found that women most:* Alice S. Rossi, "The Menopausal Transition and Aging Processes," in Brim et al., *How Healthy Are We?,* 191.

201 *In April 2011, the Women's Health:* Tara Parker-Pope, "Estrogen Lowers Risk of Heart Attack and Breast Cancer in Some," *New York Times,* April 5, 2011, http://well.blogs.nytimes.com/2011/04/05/estrogen-lowers-risk-of-heart-attack-and-breast-cancer-in-some/?scp=7&sq=hormones%20tara?20april&st=cse (accessed May 31, 2011).

202 *Fifteen, twenty, or thirty years:* William Kennedy, *Billy Phelan's Greatest Game* (New York: Penguin, 1978).

202 *In 1998, when the Food and Drug Administration:* Natasha Singer, "Sure It's Treatable, But Is It a Disorder?," *New York Times,* December 13, 2009.

202 *The effort to find a pharmacological answer:* Barry James, "Drug Firms Accused of Devising Female Malady," *New York Times,* January 4, 2003.

203 *Writing in the* British Medical Journal*:* Naomi Kresge, "Desire Drug May Really Prove Sex Is All in Her Head," Bloomberg.com, November 13, 2009.

203 *More recent surveys have estimated:* Daniel Bergner, "Women Who Want to Want," *New York Times,* November 29, 2009.

204 *As a Harvard Medical School newsletter:* "What Is Female Sexual Dysfuntion," http://www.health.harvard.edu/newsweek/What_is_female_sexual_dysfunction.htm (accessed May 21, 2011).

204 *The level of female desire*: Carol Groneman, *Nymphomania: A History* (New York: W. W. Norton, 2000), http://www.nytimes.com/books/first/g/groneman-nymphomania.html (accessed June 2, 2011).

204 *Female sexual dysfunction was:* Janice Irvine, *Disorders of Desire* (Philadelphia: Temple University Press, 2005), 160, 172. See also: http://www

.healthyplace.com/sex/female-sexual-dysfunction/classification-of-female-sexual-disorders/menu-id-66/.

205 *pressure to have "sex":* Leonore Tiefer, *Sex Is Not a Natural Act and Other Essays* (New York: Westview Press, 2004), 245.

205 *Some plastic surgeons:* Mireya Navarro, "The Most Private of Makeovers," *New York Times,* November 28, 2004.

205 *Lori Brotto, a psychologist who is overseeing:* Daniel Bergner, "Women Who Want to Want."

205 *In 2010, researchers who:* S. T. Lindau and N. Gavrilova, "Sex, Health, and Years of Sexually Active Life Gained Due to Good Health: Evidence from Two U.S. Population Based Cross Sectional Surveys of Ageing," *British Medical Journal* 340, c810 (2010).

205 *Tiefer believes the push for a "female Viagra":* Leonore Tiefer interview with author, 2010.

205 *Pfizer initially undertook testing:* Duff Wilson, "Push to Market Pill Stirs Debate on Sexual Desire," *New York Times,* June 16, 2010.

206 *The German pharmaceutical company:* Catherine Elton, "Female Sexual Dysfunction: Myth or Malady?," *Time,* November 18, 2009.

206 *None existed, so the FDA:* Caroline Von Hove interview with author, 2009.

206 *The American Society of Plastic and Reconstructive Surgeons:* Nicholas Regush, "Toxic Breasts," *Mother Jones,* January–February 1992, 26.

207 *As the 2010 date:* Wilson, "Push to Market Pill Stirs Debate on Sexual Desire"; Duff Wilson, "Maker Plays Up Sexual Disorder, with a Pill in Waiting," *New York Times,* June 16, 2010; Cory Silverberg blog: http://sexuality.about.com/b/2009/11/17/meet-your-new-experimental-sex-drug-flibanserin.htm; http://www.drpetra.co.uk/blog/new-trials-of-female-sexual-dysfunction-drug-flibanserin-will-be-reported-this-week/ (accessed June 17, 2010).

207 *Michael Sand, director of clinical:* Elton, "Female Sexual Dysfunction: Myth or Malady?"

207 *A Kinsey Institute survey:* Harvard Medical Newsletter, http://www.health.harvard.edu/newsweek/What_is_female_sexual_dysfunction.htm (accessed May 21, 2011).

207 *In June 2010, the FDA recommended:* Duff Wilson, "F.D.A. Panel Opposes Sexual Desire Drug for Women," *New York Times,* June 18, 2010, http://

www.nytimes.com/2010/06/19/business/19sexpill.html?scp=3&sq=flibanserin&st=cse (accessed June 10, 2011).

208 *In the 1920s, Williams Shaving Cream:* Ewen, *Captains of Consciousness,* 155.

208 *Refusal to partake in consumerist:* Lois Banner in *In Full Flower* and *American Beauty* and Nancy Etcoff in *Survival of the Prettiest* make similar points.

209 *As George Carlin joked:* Micki McGee, *Self-Help, Inc.: Makeover Culture in American Life* (New York: Oxford University Press, 2005).

209 *Anorexia, bulimia, and other:* Randy Hutter Epstein, "When Eating Disorders Strike in Midlife," *New York Times,* July 13, 2009.

209 *"In our culture, remaining cute":* Janice Gaston, "Old Problem, New Victims: More Middle-Aged Women Suffering from Eating Disorders as They Strive for an Image," *Wall Street Journal,* May 26, 2009; John Naish, "Broken Bones, Depression and Lung Disease: Why Being Skinny Is Bad for You," *Daily Mail,* July 5, 2011.

209 *Jean Kilbourne, the creator of the 1995:* Tanya Wenman Steel, "Boomers Hit a Bump: Wrinkles," *New York Times,* August 25, 1996, 49.

Chapter 13: Complex Accomplices

211 *Publications that had virtually ignored:* Kathy Peiss, *Hope in a Jar: The Making of America's Beauty Culture* (New York: Metropolitan Books, 1998), 123–24.

212 *A* Vogue *cover promises advice: Vogue,* December 2008.

212 O, The Oprah Magazine *seemed to:* Debra Ollivier, "Age-Defying Oprah: Denial, Delusion or Dermabrasion?," HuffPost Media, May 19, 2011, http://www.huffingtonpost.com/debra-ollivier/oprah-aging_b_852107.html (accessed May 19, 2011).

213 *The June 2010 issue of* Esquire*: Esquire,* June 2010.

213 *"Change Your Life Television" programming:* Douglas, *Enlightened Sexism,* 148–50.

213 *One trade paper:* Mary McNamara, "Dr. Raven's Prescription for Youth," *Multichannel News,* September 4, 2006.

214 *Attracting younger viewers became the:* Abbe Raven interview with author, 2009; "A&E Posts Best Year in Network History," December 18, 2008, http://newsgroups.derkeiler.com/Archive/Rec/rec.arts.tv/2008-12/msg02494.html; Stuart Elliot, "The Older Audience Is Looking Better Than Ever," *New York Times,* April 19, 2009.

214 *The fledgling networks wanted to:* David Poltrack interview with author, April 24, 2008.

215 *Born in 1911, Smith grew:* John S. Wright, "Leaders in Marketing: Wendell Smith," *Journal of Marketing* 30, no. 4 (October 1966): 64–65.

216 *In the thirties, department stores:* Juliet Schor, *Born to Be Big: The Commercialized Child and the New Consumer Culture* (New York: Scribner, 2005), 43.

216 *He argued that the strategy of selling the same item:* Wendell Smith, "Product Differentiation and Market Segmentation and Marketing as Alternative Marketing Strategies," *Journal of Marketing* 21, no. 1 (July 1956): 3–8.

216 *As early as 1940:* Sarah Igo, *The Averaged American: Surveys, Citizens, and the Making of a Mass Public* (Cambridge, MA: Harvard University Press, 2007), 114, 118.

217 *As the business historian:* Richard S. Tedlow, *New and Improved: The Story of Mass Marketing in America* (Boston: Harvard Business School Press, 1996).

217 *The spirit of youthful nonconformity:* Thomas Frank, *The Conquest of Cool: Business Culture, Counterculture and the Rise of Hip Consumerism* (Chicago: University of Chicago Press, 1997).

217 *"The old fragmentation was based":* Tedlow, *New and Improved.*

218 *"I went to Hollywood":* Jeremy Gerard, "TV Mirrors a New Generation," *New York Times,* October 30, 1988; Frank, *Conquest of Cool,* 1.

218 *The prime-time cable audience:* Susan Faludi, *Backlash: The Undeclared War Against American Women* (New York: Anchor Books, 1992), 147.

218 *"The worse TV nets perform":* Neal Gabler, "The Tyranny of 18 to 49: American Culture Held Hostage," Norman Lear Center, University of Southern California, April 9, 2003, at http://www.learcenter.org/images/event_uploads/Gabler18to49.pdf (accessed May 21, 2011).

219 *Throughout the 1990s and early 2000s:* Marc Gunther, "Turnaround Time for CBS Star-Driven Shows for Aging Boomers Should Get the Ailing Network Back on Track," *Fortune,* August 19, 1996, http://money.cnn.com/magazines/fortune/fortune_archive/1996/08/19/215603/index.htm (accessed June 12, 2011). Also see: Horst Stipp, "Why Youth Rules: A Network Response," *American Demographics,* May 1995, 30; David Lieberman and Melanie Wells, "Off Target," *USA Today,* December 8, 1997; Christine Larsen, "Forever Young—Television Network Targeting

of Viewers by Age Group," *Brandweek,* May 10, 1999; Jonathan Dee, "The Myth of '18 to 24,'" *New York Times Magazine,* October 13, 2002; Dan Ackman, "CBS Finds New Way to Slice Audience," *Forbes,* July 22, 2003; Frank Ahrens, "Networks Debate Age Groups' Value to Advertisers," *Washington Post,* May 21, 2004; Diane Holloway, "Networks Woo Older Viewers," Cox News Service, September 12, 2006; Laura Blum and Steve McClellan, "Aging Baby Boomers Defy Easy Classification," *Adweek,* September 8, 2006; "Baby Boomers Upset That TV Isn't All About Them," AP on MSNBC, November 28, 2006, http://www.msnbc.msn.com/id/15806591/from/ET/ (accessed May 14, 2009).

219 *The preference showed up in ad prices:* Elizabeth White, "This Sweeps, CBS Bets Older Is Better," *Media Life,* April 27, 2001.

219 *The head of sales for Fox at the time:* Gunther, "Turnaround Time for CBS," *Fortune.*

219 *In 1993–94 the median age of prime-time:* Michael Schneider, "TV Viewers Average Age Hits 50," *Variety,* June 29, 2008.

219 *A&E's Raven thinks the 20-somethings:* Abbe Raven interview with author, May 2009.

219 *No one knows that better than:* David Poltrack interview with author, April 24, 2008.

220 *The neglect of middle age in the movies:* Richard Maltby, *Hollywood Cinema* (New York: Wiley-Blackwell, 2003), 21–30; Robert Sklar, *Movie-Made America: A Cultural History of American Movies* (New York: Vintage, 1994), 304–5.

220 *Forty percent of frequent:* "Theatrical Market Statistics," Motion Picture Association of America, 2008.

222 *The film scholar Robert Sklar:* Sklar, *Movie-Made America,* 348.

222 *Merry arrested development was the theme:* Barbara Ellen, "Wine, Women, Motorbikes, Bonding . . . Who Says Middle Age Is a Crisis for Men?," *Observer,* April 15, 2007.

224 *For a long time:* Doris G. Bazzini et al., "The Aging Woman in Popular Film: Underrepresented, Unattractive, Unfriendly, and Unintelligent," *Sex Roles* 36, no. 7/8 (1997).

224 *The director Nancy Meyers recalled:* Nancy Griffin, "Diane Keaton Meets Both Her Matches," *New York Times,* December 14, 2003.

225 *More recently, Hope Davis, born in 1964:* Precious Williams, "Hope Davis, the Star Unrecognized by Millions," *Times of London,* March 2, 2006.

225 *As one writer suggested:* Hadley Freeman, "Oh, Mother," *Guardian,* March 24, 2009.

225 *"When I first went into":* Official Web Site of Lillian Gish, http://www.lilliangish.com/about/quotes.html (accessed June 12, 2011).

226 *the novelist Italo Calvino said:* Jerome Charyn, *Movieland: Hollywood and the Great American Dream Culture* (New York: New York University Press, 1996), 23.

226 *A tiny clutch of privileged actresses:* Mimi Swartz, "Sunset Strip," *Slate,* January 5, 2004, http://www.slate.com/id/2093444/ (access June 12, 2011).

226 *The available parts are still:* Nancy Signorielli, "Aging on Television: Messages Relating to Gender, Race, and Occupation in Prime Time," *Journal of Broadcasting & Electronic Media* 48, no. 2 (June 2004): 23; Martha M. Lauzen, *The Celluloid Ceiling: Behind-the-Scenes Employment of Women on the Top 250 Films of 2008,* 2009; Anne E. Lincoln and Michael Patrick, "Double Jeopardy in Hollywood: Age and Gender in the Careers of Film Actors, 1926–1999," *Sociological Forum* 19, no. 4 (December 2004): 628; Martha Lauzen and D. M. Dozier, "Maintaining the Double Standard: Portrayals of Age and Gender in Popular Films," *Sex Roles* 52 (2005): 437–46; Margie Rochlin, "What She Really Wants to Do Is . . . ," *New York Times,* April 13, 2008; Neil Genzlinger, "An Actress of a Certain Age Eyes the Beauty Cult," *New York Times,* January 20, 2004; Screen Actors Guild Casting Data Report, "A Different America on Screen," *Screen Actor* (Winter 2007): 55; Bosley Cruthers, "Romantic Middle-Aged Men and Women," *New York Times,* September 12, 1963; Mary F. Pols, "They're Women, Directors and Few," *Contra Costa Times,* July 8, 2007; Michelle Goldberg, "Where Are the Female Directors?," *Salon,* August 27, 2002, http://www.salon.com/ent/movies/feature/2002/08/27/women_directors/print.html; Dave McNary, "Little Diversity Progress Among Writers," *Variety,* November 17, 2009; David Robb, "Over-40 Actresses Are Losing Out," *BackStage,* April 30, 1999.

226 *During the ten years it:* Rochlin, "What She Really Wants to Do Is."

226 *Geena Davis, a glamour girl:* Rachel Syme, "Still in a League of Her Own," *Daily Beast,* April 27, 2009, http://www.thedailybeast.com/blogs

-and-stories/2009-04-27/still-in-a-league-of-her-own/?cid=tag:all (accessed April 27, 2009).

Chapter 14: The Arrival of the Alpha Boomer

228 *"Middle age is a wonderful country":* John Updike, *Rabbit at Rest* (New York: Fawcett Columbine, 1996).

229 *Clicking through slides filled with pie charts, graphs:* Slide show, "Alphaboomer," NBC presentation, December 2010.

229 *"Every seven seconds someone":* Sheila Shayon, "NBCU to Marketers: Respect Your Elders," *Brandchannel,* November 5, 2010, http://www.brandchannel.com/home/post/2010/11/05/NBCU-Touts-Alpha-Boomers.aspx (accessed November 5, 2010).

230 *ad buyers have consistently ignored any information:* Lorne Manly, "The New Middle Ages: TV's Silver Age," *New York Times Magazine,* May 6, 2007; Diane Holloway, "TV Goes Gray," *Austin American-Statesman,* June 28, 2007; Michael Schneider, "TV Viewers' Average Age Hits 50," *Variety,* June 29, 2008; Bill Carter, "Young Viewers Flocking to CBS in a Season of Disappointments," *New York Times,* November 2, 2008; Bill Carter, "New on the Networks: Safe Formulas from the Past," *New York Times,* January 25, 2009.

230 *They stopped citing brand loyalty:* Dee, "The Myth of '18 to 24.' "

230 *Working with Hallmark Channels:* Elliot, "The Older Audience Is Looking Better Than Ever."

230 *More than half of the postwar generation:* Pew Research Center staff, "Growing Old in America."

230 *Surveys show that the young:* Pew Research Center staff, *Growing Old in America: Expectations vs. Reality,* June 29, 2009, http://pewsocialtrends.org/2009/06/29/growing-old-in-america-expectations-vs-reality/ (accessed June 12, 2011): "Among 18- to 29-year-olds, about half say they feel their age, while about a quarter say they feel older than their age and another quarter say they feel younger. By contrast, among adults 65 and older, fully 60 percent say they feel younger than their age, compared with 32 percent who say they feel exactly their age and just 3 percent who say they feel older than their age. The gap in years between actual age and 'felt

age' widens as people grow older. Nearly half of all survey respondents ages 50 and older say they feel at least 10 years younger than their chronological age. Among respondents ages 65 to 74, a third say they feel 10 to 19 years younger than their age, and one-in-six say they feel at least 20 years younger than their actual age." The inability of one generation to understand another goes much further back and is the theme of a short story by Edward Bellamy, "The Old Folks' Party," *Scribner's Monthly,* 0011, no. 5 (March 1876): 660–69.

231 *Forty-seven used to be the age:* "Talkin' 'Bout My Generation: The Economic Impact of Aging US Boomers," McKinsey Global Institute, June 2008; David Welch, "Baby Boomers Curb Free-Spending Habit," *Bloomberg Businessweek,* July 27, 2009, http://www.msnbc.msn.com/id/32126775/ns/business-personal_finance/ (accessed May 30, 2010).

231 *This generation "has assets":* Elliot, "The Older Audience Is Looking Better Than Ever."

231 *"What advertisers are recognizing":* Blum and McClellan, "Aging Baby Boomers Defy Easy Classification," *Adweek;* Brian Steinberg, "Nielsen: This Isn't Your Grandfather's Baby Boomer," *Ad Age,* July 19, 2010.

231 *"Perhaps the most constructive ways":* Steven Weiland, "Berniece L. Neugarten," Jewish Women's Archive, A Comprehensive Historical Encyclopedia, http://jwa.org/encyclopedia/article/neugarten-bernice-l.

231 *Two other consulting firms that specialize:* Focalyst View Survey, *The Focalyst View,* 2006; Age Wave website, http://www.agewave.com/research/landmark_revisioningRetirement.php (accessed June 12, 2011).

232 *This doesn't mean that Madison:* Jim Gilmartin, "The Crisis of Faulty Marketing Paradigms," MediaPost Blogs, March 7, 2011, http://www.mediapost.com/publications/?fa=Articles.showArticle&art_aid=145689 (accessed June 12, 2011).

232 *"We believe there is this":* Manly, "The New Middle Ages: TV's Silver Age."

232 *In 2010, the station solicited series that:* Amy Chozick, "Television's Senior Moment," *Wall Street Journal,* March 29, 2011, http://online.wsj.com/article/SB10001424052748703559604576174983272665032.html (accessed June 12, 2011).

233 *"I think the wider the":* Bob Greenblatt interview with author, 2010.

234 *This transformation is shaking*: Bill Carter and Tim Arango, "An Unsteady Future for Broadcast," *New York Times,* November 22, 2009; Bill Carter, "New on the Networks: Safe Formulas from the Past," *New York Times,* January 25, 2009; Carter, "Young Viewers Flocking to CBS in a Season of Disappointments"; Wilson, "Aging—Disease or Business Opportunity?"; Gilmartin, "The Crisis of Faulty Marketing Paradigms"; Jan Hoffman, "'The Good Wife' and Its Women," *New York Times,* April 29, 2011.

234 *Patricia McDonough, a senior vice president:* Bill Carter and Tanzina Vega, "TV Industry Takes Second Look at Older Viewers," *New York Times,* May 13, 2011.

235 *The hearing aid, an emblem of:* Elizabeth Simpson, "Marketers Work to Make Hearing Aids a Fashion Must-Have," *Virginian-Pilot,* August 4, 2008; Nicole Garrison Sprenger, "Ad Digest," *Minneapolis St. Paul Business Journal,* June 2, 2006.

236 *Kellogg's, Sketchers, 5-Hour Energy Drink:* Carter and Vega, "TV Industry Takes Second Look at Older Viewers."

236 *Dayle Haddon, a model who regularly:* Valli Herman, "Cosmetics Firsts Try a New Wrinkle in Ads," *Los Angeles Times,* June 26, 2006.

236 *She now has her own line:* "Lauren Hutton Poses Nude, at 61," ABC News, October 21, 2005, http://abcnews.go.com/GMA/BeautySecrets/story?id=1236581&page=1 (accessed June 5, 2011).

236 *Dove's "Real Women Have Curves":* Dove global study: http://www.campaignforrealbeauty.com/flat4.asp?id=7137; http://www.campaignforrealbeauty.com (accessed March 8, 2009).

237 *"We are not saying turn back":* Natasha Singer, "Skin Deep: Is Looking Your Age Now Taboo?," *New York Times,* March 1, 2007.

237 *Questioning the skinny ideal:* Rob Walker, "Consumed: Social Lubricant," *New York Times Magazine,* September 5, 2005.

237 *In 2007, when Dove tried to air:* "Dove's New Pro-Age Campaign for Real Beauty, Banned Because of Nudity," Adland.tv, March 7, 2007, http://adland.tv/content/doves-new-pro-age-campaign-real-beauty-banned-because-nudity (accessed June 12, 2011); Gudrun Schultz, "Boycott of Dove Products Urged as Nude Ads Air Prime Time," LifeSiteNews.com, March 5, 2007, http://www.lifesitenews.com/news/archive/ldn/2007/mar/07030501 (accessed June 12, 2011); Larry Jaffee, "Dove TV Ad Rejected

for Its 'Implied Nudity,'" Promo, March 23, 2007, http://promomagazine.com/news/pma_fcc_nixed_dove_tv_spot_022307/ (accessed June 12, 2011).

239 *during the Depression's grim years:* Felix Belair, *New York Times,* 1939.

239 *In 1967, Congress passed the first antidiscrimination:* David Stout, "Supreme Court Eases Age Bias Suits for Workers," *New York Times,* June 20, 2008.

239 *Middle-aged workers benefited:* Steven Greenhouse, *The Big Squeeze: Tough Times for the American Worker* (New York: Alfred A. Knopf, 2008); Louis Uchitelle, *The Disposable American: Layoffs and Their Consequences* (New York: Alfred A. Knopf, 2006).

239 *The aftershocks of the 1982 recession:* Gullette, *Declining to Decline,* 16; David Lamb, "Downwardly Mobile: Many Find Gold Year Tarnished," *Los Angeles Times,* June 18, 1988.

239 *"We are finding that the standard":* Louis Uchitelle, "Male, Educated and Falling Behind," *New York Times,* February 11, 1994.

240 *Workers over 50 tend to:* Michael Luo, "Longer Unemployment for Those 45 and Older," *New York Times,* April 12, 2009.

240 *Although the American labor force is for the:* Catherine Rampell, "As Layoffs Surge, Women May Surpass Men in Job Force," *New York Times,* February 5, 2009; Floyd Norris, "In This Recession, More Men Are Losing Jobs," *New York Times,* March 13, 2009.

240 *That imbalance will cause other economic:* "Social Security Board of Trustees: Projected Trust Fund Exhaustion One Year Sooner," Social Security Administration news release, May 13, 2011.

241 *David DeLong, a research fellow:* "Over 50 and Out of Work," http://www.overfiftyandoutofwork.com/experts/david-delong/ (accessed June 12, 2011).

Chapter 15: In Our Prime

242 *Youth is the period in which a man:* G. K. Chesterton, *Charles Dickens,* 190, http://www.lang.nagoya-u.ac.jp/~matsuoka/CD-Chesterton-CD-1.html#II (accessed May 30, 2011).

242 *In 1960, sixty-eight percent of adults in:* Gretchen Livingston and D'Vera Cohn, "The New Demography of American Motherhood," Pew Research Center, May 6, 2010. These average figures mask a racial, ethnic, and class

divide: college-educated men and women are much more likely to marry than those who stopped their formal education after high school; and seventy-two percent of black women giving birth were single compared with fifty-three percent of Hispanic women and twenty-nine percent of white women.

243 *Women match men's numbers in the workplace:* Patricia Cohen, "The Long Road to Adulthood," *New York Times,* June 12, 2010; Richard Settersten and Barbara E. Ray, *Not Quite Adults: Why 20-Somethings Are Choosing a Slower Path to Adulthood, and Why It's Good for Everyone* (New York: Bantam, 2010); Roni Caryn Rabin, "Grown-Up, But Still Irresponsible," *New York Times,* October 9, 2010; Robin Marantz Henig, "What Is It About 20-Somethings?," *New York Times Magazine,* August 18, 2010.

244 *Already, middle-aged boomers over 50:* "Divorce in Middle and Later Life: Estimates from the 2008 American Community Survey," Susan L. Brown and I-Fen Lin, presented at Population Association of America 2011 annual meeting in Washington, D.C.

244 *"Every fresh generation is a new people":* Alexis de Tocqueville, *Democracy in America,* http://www.gutenberg.org/files/815/815-h/815-h.htm (accessed June 12, 2011).

Selected Bibliography

Achenbaum, Andrew W. *Old Age in the New Land: The American Experience Since 1790.* Baltimore: Johns Hopkins University Press, 1978.

Adams, Mark. *Mr. America: How Muscular Millionaire Bernarr Macfadden Transformed the Nation Through Sex, Salad, and the Ultimate Starvation Diet.* New York: Harper, 2009.

American Nurses' Association, Nurses' Associated Alumnae of the United States, American Society of Superintendents of Training Schools for Nurses, and National League of Nursing Education (U.S.). *The American Journal of Nursing.* J. B. Lippincott Co. for the American Journal of Nursing Co., 1904.

Angel, Jacqueline L. *Handbook of the Sociology of Aging.* New York: Springer, 2011.

Angier, Natalie. *Woman: An Intimate Geography.* New York: Anchor Books, 2000.

Ariès, Philippe. *Centuries of Childhood: A Social History of Family Life.* Translated by Robert Baldick. New York: Vintage Books, 1962.

Atherton, Gertrude. *Adventures of a Novelist.* New York: Liveright, 1932.

———. *Black Oxen.* New York: A. L. Burt Company, 1923.

Atlas, James. *My Life in the Middle Ages: A Survivor's Tale.* New York: HarperCollins, 2005.

Azoulay, Elizabeth, ed. *100,000 Years of Beauty.* Paris, France: Gallimard, 2009.

Bair, Deirdre. *Jung: A Biography.* Boston: Little, Brown, 2003.

Banner, Lois. *In Full Flower: Aging Women, Power, and Sexuality: A History.* New York: Vintage Books, 1993.

Barrett, Anne, and Cheryl Robbins. "The Multiple Sources of Women's Aging Anxiety and Their Relationship with Psychological Distress." *Journal of Aging and Health* (February 2008).

Barton, Bruce. *The Man Nobody Knows.* Chicago: Ivan R. Dee, 2000.

Beard, George Miller. *American Nervousness: Its Causes and Consequences.* New York: G. P. Putnam Son's, 1881.

———. *A Practical Treatise on Nervous Exhaustion.* New York: E. B. Treat, 1880.

Beauvoir, Simone de. *The Coming of Age.* 1st American edition, 1972, French 1970 ed. New York: Norton, 1996.

———. *The Second Sex.* Translated and edited by H. M. Parshley. New York: Vintage Books, 1989.

Berkowitz, Edward D. *Something Happened: A Political and Cultural Overview of the Seventies.* New York: Columbia University Press, 2006.

Bernard, Miriam, Judith Phillips, Linda Machin, and Val Harding Davies, eds. *Women Ageing: Changing Identities, Challenging Myths.* New York: Routledge, 2000.

Bernays, Edward. *Propaganda.* Brooklyn, NY: Ig Publishing, 2005.

———. "Manipulating Public Opinion: The Why and the How." *American Journal of Sociology* 33, no. 6 (May 1928): 958–71.

Blair, Hugh. *Sermons.* London: Baynes and Son, 1824.

Bloland, Sue Erikson. *In the Shadow of Fame: A Memoir by the Daughter of Erik H. Erikson.* New York: Viking, 2005.

Bourne, Randolph. *Youth and Life.* Boston: Houghton Mifflin, 1913.

Brandes, Stanley. *Forty: The Age and the Symbol.* Knoxville: University of Tennessee Press, 1987.

Brice, Carleen, ed. *Middle Age Ain't Nothing but a Number: Black Women Explore Middle Life.* Boston: Beacon Press, 2003.

Brim, Gilbert. *Ambition: How We Manage Success and Failure Throughout Our Lives.* New York: Basic Books, 1992.

———. *Constancy and Change in Human Development.* Cambridge, MA: Harvard University Press, 1980.

———. *How Healthy Are We? A National Study of Well-Being at Midlife.* Chicago: University of Chicago Press, 2004.

Brock, Pope. *Charlatan: America's Most Dangerous Huckster, the Man Who Pursued Him, and the Age of Flimflam.* New York: Crown Publishers, 2008.

Brogan, Hugh. *The Penguin History of the United States of America.* New York: Penguin, 1990.

Brokaw, Tom. *Boom! Voice of the Sixties: Personal Reflections on the '60s and Today.* New York: Random House, 2007.

Brooks, David. *Bobos in Paradise: The New Upper Class and How They Got There.* New York: Simon & Schuster Paperbacks, 2004.

Buckley, Christopher. *Boomsday: A Novel.* New York: Twelve, 2007.

Bunnin, Nicholas, and E. P. Tsui-James, eds. *The Blackwell Companion to Philosophy.* Oxford, UK: Blackwell Publishers, 1995.

Cantor, Norman F. *The American Century: Varieties of Culture in Modern Times.* New York: Harper Perennial, 1997.

Carr, Deborah. "The Fulfillment of Career Dreams at Midlife: Does It Matter for Women's Mental Health?" *Journal of Health and Social Behavior* 38, no. 4 (December 1997): 331–44.

Cato Unbound. "The IQ Conundrum." November 2007. http://cato-unbound .org.

Charyn, Jerome. *Movieland: Hollywood and the Great American Dream Culture.* New York: New York University Press, 1996.

Chudacoff, Howard. *Children at Play: An American History.* New York: New York University Press, 2007.

———. *How Old Are You? Age Consciousness in American Culture.* Princeton, NJ: Princeton University Press, 1989.

Cohen, Gene. *The Mature Mind: The Positive Power of the Aging Brain.* New York: Basic Books, 2006.

Cohen, Lizabeth. *A Consumers' Republic: The Politics of Mass Consumption in Postwar America.* New York: Vintage Books, 2004.

Cole, Thomas. *The Journey of Life: A Cultural History of Aging in America.* New York: Cambridge University Press, 1993.

Comfort, Alex. *The Biology of Senescence.* New York: Rinehart, 1956.

Cook, Daniel Thomas. *The Commodification of Childhood: The Children's Clothing Industry and the Rise of the Child Consumer.* Durham, NC: Duke University Press, 2004.

Costa, Dora L. *National Bureau of Economic Research: The Evolution of Retirement: An American Economic History, 1880–1990.* Chicago: University of Chicago Press, 1998.

Cotter, Kelly A., and Margie E. Lachman. "No Strain, No Gain: Psychosocial Predictors of Physical Activity Across the Adult Lifespan." *Journal of Physical Activity & Health* 7, no. 5 (September 2010): 584–94.

Croly, Herbert. *The Promise of American Life.* New Brunswick, NJ: Transaction Publishers, 1993.

Cross, Gary. *An All-Consuming Century: Why Commercialism Won in Modern America.* New York: Columbia University Press, 2000.

Curnutt, Kirk. *Cambridge Introduction to F. Scott Fitzgerald.* New York: Cambridge University Press, 2007.

Davidson, Richard. "Spirituality and Medicine: Science and Practice." *Annals of Family Medicine* 6, no. 5 (September 2008): 388–89.

———. "Empirical Explorations of Mindfulness: Conceptual and Methodological Conundrums." *Emotion* 10, no. 1 (2010): 8–11.

Demos, John. *A Little Commonwealth: Family Life in Plymouth Colony.* New York: Oxford University Press, 1970.

———. *Past, Present and Personal: The Family and the Life Course in American History.* New York: Oxford University Press, 1986.

Dickstein, Morris. *Dancing in the Dark: A Cultural History of the Great Depression.* New York: W. W. Norton, 2009.

Di Renzo, Anthony, ed. *If I Were Boss: The Early Business Stories of Sinclair Lewis.* Carbondale: Southern Illinois University Press, 1997.

Dolnick, Edward. *The Clockwork Universe: Isaac Newton, the Royal Society, and the Birth of the Modern World.* New York: HarperCollins, 2011.

Donnelly, Mabel Collins. *The American Victorian Woman: The Myth and the Reality.* Westport, CT: Greenwood Press, 1968.

Douglas, Susan J. *Dimensions of Human Behaviour: The Changing Life Course.* 4th ed. London: Sage, 2010.

———. *Enlightened Sexism: The Seductive Message That Feminism's Work Is Done.* New York: Times Books, 2010.

———. *Where the Girls Are: Growing Up Female with the Mass Media.* New York: Three Rivers Press, 1995.

Ehrenreich, Barbara. *For Her Own Good: Two Centuries of the Experts' Advice to Women.* New York: Anchor Books, 2005.

Elder, Glen H., Jr. *Children of the Great Depression,* 25th Anniversary Edition. Boulder, CO: Westview Press, 1998.

Ellis, Alan L. *Gay Men at Midlife: Age Before Beauty.* Binghamton, NY: Harrington Park Press, 2001.

Ephron, Nora. *I Feel Bad About My Neck: And Other Thoughts on Being a Woman.* New York: Alfred A. Knopf, 2006.

Erikson, Erik H. *Adulthood.* New York: W. W. Norton, 1978.

———. *Childhood and Society.* New York: W. W. Norton, 1985.

———. *Dimensions of a New Identity: Jefferson Lectures 1973.* New York: W. W. Norton, 1974.

———. *Identity and the Life Cycle.* New York: W. W. Norton, 1980, reissued 1994.

———. *The Life Cycle Completed: Extended Version.* New York: W. W. Norton, 1997.

Essig, Mark. *Edison & the Electric Chair: A Story of Light and Death.* New York: Walker & Co., 2005.

Etcoff, Nancy. *Survival of the Prettiest: The Science of Beauty.* New York: Anchor Books, 2000.

Evans, Harold. *The American Century.* New York: Alfred A. Knopf, 2000.

Ewen, Stuart. *Captains of Consciousness: Advertising and the Social Roots of the Consumer Culture.* New York: McGraw-Hill, 1976.

Faludi, Susan. *Backlash: The Undeclared War Against American Women.* New York: Anchor Books, 1992.

Featherman, Drew. *SRCD Oral History Interview of Orville Gilbert Brim.* January 17, 2009.

Fischer, Christiane, ed. *Let Them Speak for Themselves: Women in the American West, 1849–1900.* New Haven, CT: Archon Books, 1977.

Fischer, Claude. *Made in America: A Social History of American Culture and Character.* Chicago: University of Chicago Press, 2010.

Fischer, David. *Growing Old in America.* New York: Oxford University Press, 1978.

Flynn, James. *What Is Intelligence? Beyond the Flynn Effect.* New York: Cambridge University Press, 2007.

Fox, Richard Wightman, and T. J. Jackson Lears, eds. *The Culture of Consumption: Critical Essays in American History, 1880–1980.* New York: Pantheon, 1983.

Frank, Thomas. *The Conquest of Cool: Business Culture, Counterculture, and the Rise of Hip Consumerism.* Chicago: University of Chicago Press, 1997.

Fraser, Kennedy. *The Fashionable Mind.* New York: Alfred A. Knopf, 1981.

———. *Ornament and Silence: Essays on Women's Lives from Edith Wharton to Germaine Greer.* New York: Vintage Books, 1998.

Freedman, Marc. *The Big Shift: Navigating the New Stage Beyond Midlife.* New York: PublicAffairs, 2011.

Fried, Richard M. *The Man Everybody Knew: Bruce Barton and the Making of Modern America.* Chicago: Ivan R. Dee, 2005.

Friedan, Betty. *The Feminine Mystique.* New York: W. W. Norton, 1997.

———. *The Second Sex.* New York: Summit Books, 1981.

Friedman, Howard S., and Leslie R. Martin. *The Longevity Project.* New York: Hudson Street Press, 2011.

Friedman, Lawrence Jacob. *Identity's Architect: A Biography of Erik H. Erikson.* New York: Scribner, 1999.

Gardner, Howard. *Frames of Mind: The Theory of Multiple Intelligences.* New York: Basic Books, 1985.

Gaustad, Edwin, and Leigh Schmidt. *The Religious History of America: The Heart of the American Story from Colonial Times to Today.* San Francisco: Harper, 2002.

Gay, Peter. *Modernism: The Lure of Heresy: From Baudelaire to Beckett and Beyond.* New York: W. W. Norton, 2010.

———. *Schnitzler's Century: The Making of Middle-Class Culture, 1815–1914.* New York: W. W. Norton, 2002.

Gillick, Muriel R. *The Denial of Aging: Perpetual Youth, Eternal Life, and Other Dangerous Fantasies.* Cambridge, MA: Harvard University Press, 2006.

Gilman, Sander L. *Making the Body Beautiful: A Cultural History of Aesthetic Surgery.* Princeton, NJ: Princeton University Press, 1999.

Goffman, Erving. *The Presentation of Self in Everyday Life.* New York: Anchor Books, 1959.

Goldberg, Elkhonon. *The Wisdom Paradox: How Your Mind Can Grow Stronger as Your Brain Grows Older.* New York: Gotham Books, 2005.

Goldstein, Eda G. *When the Bubble Bursts: Clinical Perspectives on Midlife Issues.* Hillsdale, NJ: Analytic Press, 2005.

Gomez, Jewelle. "In the Heat of Shadow." In *Age Ain't Nothing but a Number*, ed. Carleen Brice. Boston: Beacon Press, 2003.

Gray, John. *The Immortalization Commission: Science and the Strange Quest to Cheat Death.* New York: Farrar, Straus and Giroux, 2011.

Greenfield, E. A. "Felt Obligation to Help Others as a Protective Factor Against Losses in Psychological Well-Being Following Functional Decline in Middle and Later Life." *Journals of Gerontology Series B: Psychological Sciences and Social Sciences* 64B, no. 6 (October 2009): 723–32.

Greenhouse, Steven. *The Big Squeeze.* New York: Alfred A. Knopf, 2008.

Greider, Katharine. *The Big Fix: How the Pharmaceutical Industry Rips Off American Consumers.* New York: PublicAffairs, 2003.

Gullette, Margaret. *Agewise: Fighting the New Ageism in America.* Chicago: University of Chicago Press, 2011.

———. *Declining to Decline: Cultural Combat and the Politics of the Midlife.* Charlottesville: University of Virginia Press, 1997.

———. *Safe at Last in the Middle Years: The Invention of the Midlife Progress Novel: Saul Bellow, Margaret Drabble, Anne Tyler, John Updike.* Berkeley: University of California Press, 1988.

Haber, Carole. *Beyond Sixty-Five: The Dilemma of Old Age in America's Past.* Cambridge, MA: Cambridge University Press, 1983.

Haiken, Elizabeth. *Venus Envy: A History of Cosmetic Surgery.* Baltimore: Johns Hopkins University Press, 1997.

Hall, G. Stanley. *Adolescence: Its Psychology and Its Relations to Physiology, Anthropology, Sociology, Sex, Crime, Religion, and Education.* New York: D. Appleton & Co., 1904.

———. *Senescence.* New York: D. Appleton & Co., 1922.

Haskell, Molly. *Holding My Own in No Man's Land.* New York: Oxford University Press, 1997.

Herman, Arthur. *The Idea of Decline in Western History.* New York: Free Press, 1997.

Hollander, Anne. *Seeing Through Clothes.* New York: Viking Press, 1978.

———. *Sex and Suits: The Evolution of Modern Dress.* New York: Alfred A. Knopf, 1994.

Hollander, Stanley C. *Was There a Pepsi Generation Before Pepsi Discovered It? Youth-Based Segmentation in Marketing.* Chicago: American Marketing Association, 1992.

Hölzel, Britta K., James Carmody, Mark Vangel, Christina Congleton, Sita M. Yerramsetti, Tim Gard, and Sara W. Lazar. "Mindfulness Practice Leads to Increases in Regional Brain Gray Matter Density." *Psychiatry Research: Neuroimaging* 191, no. 1 (January 2011): 36–43.

Igo, Sarah Elizabeth. *The Averaged American: Surveys, Citizens, and the Making of a Mass Public.* Cambridge, MA: Harvard University Press, 2007.

Irwin, W. B. *George Irwin and His Family (1794–1846).* New York Public Library.

James, Alice. *The Diary of Alice James.* New York: Penguin, 1964.

James, Henry. *Shorter Masterpieces, Volume 1.* Sussex, NJ: Harvester Press, Barnes & Noble Books, 1984.

Jaques, Elliott. "Death and the Mid-Life Crisis." *International Journal of Psychoanalysis* 46 (1965): 502–14.

Jones, Landon. *Great Expectations: America and the Baby Boom Generation.* New York: Coward McCann & Geoghegan, 1980.

Jung, C. G. *The Development of Personality: Papers on Child Psychology, Education and Related Subjects.* Translated by R. F. C. Hull. Princeton, NJ: Princeton University Press, 1981.

———. *The Essential Jung: Selected Writings.* Introduced by Anthony Storr. Princeton, NJ: Princeton University Press, 1999.

Kakar, Sudhir. *Frederick Taylor: A Study in Personality and Innovation.* Cambridge, MA: MIT Press, 1970.

Kanigel, Robert. *The One Best Way: Frederick Winslow Taylor and the Enigma of Efficiency.* New York: Viking Press, 1997.

Kastenbaum, Robert. *Encyclopedia of Adult Development.* Phoenix, AZ: Oryx Press, 1993.

Kellogg, John Henry. *Battle Creek Sanitarium System.* Battle Creek, MI: Gage Printing Co., 1908.

Kemp, Giles, and Edward Claflin. *Dale Carnegie: The Man Who Influenced Millions.* New York: St. Martin's Press, 1989.

Kennedy, William. *Billy Phelan's Greatest Game.* New York: Penguin Books, 1983.

Kerr, Catherine, Stephanie R. Jones, Qian Wan, Dominique L. Pritchett, Rachel H. Wasserman, Anna Wexler, Joel J. Villanueva, Jessica R. Shaw, Sara W. Lazar, Ted J. Kaptchuk, Ronnie Littenberg, Matti S. Hämäläinen, Christopher I. Moore. "Effects of Mindfulness Meditation Training on Anticipatory Alpha Modulation in Primary Somatosensory Cortex." *Brain Research Bulletin* 85, nos. 3–4, 30 (May 2011): 96–103.

Key, Ellen. *The Century of the Child.* New York: G. P. Putnam's Sons, 1909.

Keyes, Corey. "Feeling Good and Functioning Well." *Journal of Positive Psychology* 3, no. 5 (May 2009).

———. "The Black-White Paradox in Health: Flourishing in the Face of Social Inequality and Discrimination." *Journal of Personality* 77, no. 6 (December 2009).

Kroeger, Brooke. *Passing: When People Can't Be Who They Are.* New York: PublicAffairs, 2003.

Lachman, Margie. "Development in Midlife." *Annual Review of Psychology* 55 (2004): 305–31.

Lachman, Margie E., and Stefan Agrigoroaei. "Promoting Functional Health in Midlife and Old Age: Long-Term Protective Effects of Control Beliefs, Social Support, and Physical Exercise." Edited by Bernhard T. Baune. *PLoS ONE* 5, no. 10 (October 2010): e13297.

Lachman, Margie, Stefan Agrigoroaei, Chandra Murphy, and Patricia A Tun. "Frequent Cognitive Activity Compensates for Education Differences in Episodic Memory." *American Journal of Geriatric Psychiatry* 18, no. 1 (2010): 4–10, 10.1097/JGP.0b013c3181ab8b62.

Lasch, Christopher. *The Culture of Narcisissm.* New York: W. W. Norton, 1979, 1991.

Lauzen, Martha M. *The Celluloid Ceiling: Behind-the-Scenes Employment of Women on the Top 250 Films of 2008.* 2009.

Lauzen, Martha M., and D. M. Dozier. "Maintaining the Double Standard: Portrayals of Age and Gender in Popular Films." *Sex Roles* 52 (2005).

Lears, T. *Fables of Abundance: A Cultural History of Advertising in America.* New York: Basic Books, 1994.

———. *No Place of Grace: Anti-Modernism and the Transformation of American Culture, 1880–1920.* New York: Pantheon Books, 1981.

Lee, Hermione. *Edith Wharton.* New York: Alfred A. Knopf, 2007.

Leider, Emily Wortis. *California's Daughter: Gertrude Atherton and Her Times.* Stanford, CA: Stanford University Press, 1991.

Lerner, Richard. *Concepts and Theories of Human Development.* Mahwah, NJ: L. Erlbaum Associates, 2002.

Levin, Ira. *The Stepford Wives.* New York: Harper Torch, 2004.

Levinson, Daniel. *The Seasons of a Man's Life.* New York: Alfred A. Knopf, 1978.

Lewis, Sinclair, Babbitt. Bartleby.com, 1999.

———. *Main Street.* New York: Signet Classics, 1998.

Lincoln, Anne E., and Michael Patrick. "Double Jeopardy in Hollywood: Age and Gender in the Careers of Film Actors, 1926–1999." *Sociological Forum* 19, no. 4 (December 2004).

Lindsay, Vachel. *The Art of the Moving Picture.* Charleston, SC: BiblioBazaar, 2007.

Lippert, Laurel. "Women at Midlife: Implications for Theories of Women's Adult Development." *Journal of Counseling & Development* 76, no. 1 (Winter 1997): 16–22.

Lynd, Robert S., and Helen Merrell Lynd. *Middletown: A Study in Modern American Culture.* New York: Harcourt, Brace & Co., 1929.

———. *Middletown in Transition: A Study in Cultural Conflicts.* New York: Harcourt, Brace & Co., 1937.

Macfadden, Bernarr. *Vitality Supreme.* New York: Physical Culture Publishing Co., 1915.

Maltby, Richard. *Hollywood Cinema.* Malden, MA: Wiley-Blackwell, 2003.

Marchand, Roland. *Advertising the American Dream: Making Way for Modernity, 1920–1940.* Berkeley: University of California Press, 1985.

McGee, Micki. *Self-Help, Inc.: Makeover Culture in American Life.* New York: Oxford University Press, 2005.

Menand, Louis. *The Metaphysical Club: A Story of Ideas in America.* New York: Farrar, Straus & Giroux, 2002.

Merriam, Sharan. *Learning in Adulthood: A Comprehensive Guide.* San Francisco: Jossey-Bass, 2007.

Midlife in the United States website. http://midus.wisc.edu.

MIDMAC: Research Network on Successful Midlife Development website. http://midmac.med.harvard.edu.

Morozink, Jennifer A., Elliot M. Friedman, Christopher L. Coe, and Carol D. Ryff. "Socioeconomic and Psychosocial Predictors of Interleukin-6 in the MIDUS National Sample." *Health Psychology: Official Journal of the Division of Health Psychology, American Psychological Association* 29, no. 6 (November 2010): 626–35.

Mortimer, Jeylan T., and Michael J. Shanahan, eds. *Handbook of the Life Course.* New York: Springer, 2006.

Mukherjee, Siddhartha. *The Emperor of All Maladies: A Biography of Cancer.* New York: Scribner, 2010.

Neugarten, Bernice, ed. *Middle Age and Aging: A Reader in Social Psychology.* Chicago: University of Chicago Press, 1973.

Neugarten, Bernice Levin, and Dail Ann Neugarten. *The Meanings of Age: Selected Papers of Bernice L. Neugarten.* Chicago: University of Chicago Press, 1996.

Newman, Katherine S. *A Different Shade of Gray: Midlife and Beyond in the Inner City.* New York: New Press, 2003.

Orbach, Susie. *Bodies.* New York: Picador, 2008.

Peiss, Kathy. *Cheap Amusements: Working Women and Leisure in Turn-of-the-Century New York.* Philadelphia: Temple University Press, 1986.

———. *Hope in a Jar: The Making of America's Beauty Culture.* New York: Metropolitan Books, 1998.

Pitkin, Walter B. *Life Begins at 40.* New York: Blue Ribbon Books, 1934.

Postman, Neil. *The Disappearance of Childhood.* New York: Vintage, 1994.

Ricks, Christopher. *Essays in Appreciation.* New York: Oxford University Press, 1998.

Riesman, David, with Nathan Glazer and Reuel Denney. *The Lonely Crowd.* New Haven, CT: Yale University Press, 1969.

Rossi, Alice S. *Caring and Doing for Others: Social Responsibility in the Domains of Family, Work and Community.* Chicago: University of Chicago Press, 2001.

———. "Life-Span Theories and Women's Lives"; "Women: Sex and Sexuality, Part 2." *Signs* 6, no.1 (Autumn 1980): 4–32.

Rothman, Sheila, and David Rothman. *The Pursuit of Perfection: The Promise and Perils of Medical Enhancement.* New York: Pantheon Books, 2003.

Savage, Jon. *Teenage: The Creation of Youth Culture.* New York: Viking Press, 2007.

Schor, Juliet B. *Born to Buy: The Commercialized Child and the New Consumer Culture.* New York: Scribner, 2005.

Schulman, Bruce J. *The Seventies: The Great Shift in American Culture, Society, and Politics.* New York: Free Press, 2001.

Seaman, Barbara. *The Greatest Experiment Ever Performed on Women: Exploding the Estrogen Myth.* New York: Hyperion. 2004.

Serlin, David. *Replaceable You: Engineering the Body in Postwar America.* Chicago: University of Chicago Press, 2004.

Settersten, Richard. *Not Quite Adults: Why 20-Somethings Are Choosing a Slower Path to Adulthood, and Why It's Good for Everyone*. New York: Bantam Books Trade Paperbacks, 2010.

———. *On the Frontier of Adulthood: Theory, Research, and Public Policy*. Chicago: University of Chicago Press, 2005.

Sheehy, Gail. *New Passages: Mapping Your Life Across Time*. New York: Random House, 1995.

———. *Passages: Predictable Crises of Adult Life*. New York: Ballantine Books, 2006.

Showalter, Elaine. *Hystories: Hysterical Epidemics and Modern Media*. New York: Columbia University Press, 1998.

Shweder, Richard, ed. *Welcome to Middle Age! (And Other Cultural Fictions)*. Chicago: University of Chicago Press, 1998.

Signorielli, Nancy. "Aging on Television: Messages Relating to Gender, Race, and Occupation in Prime Time." *Journal of Broadcasting & Electronic Media* 48, no. 2 (June 2004): 279.

———. "Aging on Television: The Picture in the Nineties." *Generations* 25, no. 3 (Fall 2001): 34–38.

Sklar, Robert. *Movie-Made America: A Cultural History of American Movies*. New York: Vintage Books, 1994.

Skloot, Rebecca. *The Immortal Life of Henrietta Lacks*. New York: Broadway, 2011.

Smith, Wendell. "Product Differentiation and Market Segmentation as Alternative Marketing Strategies." *Journal of Marketing* 21, no. 2 (July 1956).

Smith-Rosenberg, Carroll. *Disorderly Conduct: Visions of Gender in Victorian America*. New York: Alfred A. Knopf, 1985.

Squier, Susan Merrill. *Liminal Lives: Imagining the Human at the Frontier of Biomedicine*. Durham, NC: Duke University Press, 2004.

Sternberg, Robert. *A Handbook of Wisdom: Psychological Perspectives*. Cambridge, UK: Cambridge University Press, 2005.

Strauch, Barbara. *The Secret Life of the Grown-Up Brain: The Surprising Talents of the Middle-Aged Mind*. New York: Viking Press, 2010.

Strouse, Jean. *Alice James: A Biography*. Cambridge, MA: Harvard University Press, 1999.

Susman, Warren I. *Culture as History: The Transformation of American Society in the Twentieth Century*. Washington, D.C.: Smithsonian Institution Press, 2003.

Taylor, Charles. *The Ethics of Authenticity*. Cambridge, MA: Harvard University Press, 1992.

Tedlow, Richard. *New and Improved: The Story of Mass Marketing in America*. Boston, MA: Harvard Business School Press, 1996.

Tevis, Walter. *The Color of Money*. New York: Thunder's Mouth Press, 2003.

Thomson, Ellen Mazur. *The Origins of Graphic Design in America*. New Haven, CT: Yale University Press, 1997.

Tiefer, Leonore. *Sex Is Not a Natural Act and Other Essays*. New York: Westview Press, 2004.

Tomes, Robert. *The Bazar Book of Decorum: The Care of the Person, Manners, Etiquette, and Ceremonials*. 2005. http://name.umdl.umich.edu/AJF2367.0001.001.

Trollope, Anthony. *The Fixed Period*. London: Penguin, 1882, 1993.

Tucker, Herbert F., ed. *A Companion to Victorian Literature & Culture*. Oxford: B. Blackwell, 1999.

Tun, Patricia A., and Margie Lachman. "The Association Between Computer Use and Cognition Across Adulthood: Use It So You Won't Lose It?" *Psychology and Aging* 25, no. 3 (2010): 560–68.

Uchitelle, Louis. *The Disposable American: Layoffs and Their Consequences*. New York: Alfred A. Knopf, 2006.

Underhill, Paco. *Why We Buy: The Science of Shopping*. New York: Touchstone, 1999.

Updike, John. *Rabbit at Rest*. New York: Fawcett Columbine, 1996.

U.S. Department of Health, Education & Welfare, Children's Bureau. *The Story of the White House Conferences on Children and Youth*. Washington, D.C., 1967.

Vaillant, George. *Adaptation to Life*. Cambridge, MA: Harvard University Press, 1995.

———. *Aging Well: Surprising Guideposts to a Happier Life from the Landmark Harvard Study of Adult Development*. New York: Little, Brown, 2002.

Veblen, Thorstein. *The Theory of the Leisure Class*. New York: New American Library, 1953.

Watson, Peter. *The Modern Mind: An Intellectual History of the 20th Century*. New York: HarperCollins, 2001.

Weintraub, Arlene. *Selling the Fountain of Youth: How the Anti-Aging Industry*

Made a Disease Out of Getting Old, and Made Billions. New York: Basic Books, 2010.

Wheeler, Helen. *Women & Aging: A Guide to the Literature*. Boulder, CO: Lynne Rienner Publishers, 1997.

Wilbur, Hervey. *The Monitor: Designed to Improve the Taste, the Understanding, and the Heart*, volume 2. Boston: Cummings, Hilliard & Co., 1824.

Willis, Garry. *John Wayne's America: The Politics of Celebrity*. New York: Simon & Schuster, 1997.

Witte, Karsten. "Introduction to Siegried Kracauer's 'The Mass Ornament.'" *New German Critique*, no. 5 (Spring 1975): 59–66.

Wood, James. *How Fiction Works*. New York: Picador, 2009.

Woodward, Kathleen, ed. *Figuring Age: Women, Bodies, Generations*. Bloomington: Indiana University Press, 1999.

Wright, John S. "Wendell R. Smith." *Journal of Marketing* 30, no. 4 (October 1966): 64–65.

Wuthnow, Robert. *After the Baby Boomers: How Twenty- and Thirty-Somethings Are Shaping the Future of American Religion*. Princeton, NJ: Princeton University Press, 2007.

Youssef, H. "The History of the Condom." *Journal of the Royal Society of Medicine* 86, no. 4 (April 1993): 226–28.